CLINICAL CHAOS

CLINICAL CHAOS:
A Therapist's Guide to Nonlinear Dynamics and Therapeutic Change

Edited by
Linda Chamberlain and
Michael R. Bütz

BRUNNER/MAZEL
Taylor & Francis Group

USA	Publishing Office:	BRUNNER/MAZEL *A member of the Taylor & Francis Group* 325 Chestnut Street Philadelphia, PA 19106 Tel: (215) 625-8900 Fax: (215) 625-2940
	Distribution Center:	BRUNNER/MAZEL *A member of the Taylor & Francis Group* 47 Runway Road Levittown, PA 19057 Tel: (215) 629-0400 Fax: (215) 629-0363
UK		BRUNNER/MAZEL *A member of the Taylor & Francis Group* 1 Gunpowder Square London EC4A 3DE Tel: +44 171 583 0490 Fax: +44 171 583 0581

CLINICAL CHAOS: A Therapist's Guide to Nonlinear Dynamics and Therapeutic Change

1   2   3   4   5   6   7   8   9   0

Printed by Braun-Brumfield, Ann Arbor, MI, 1998.

A CIP catalog record for this book is available from the British Library.
⊗ The paper in this publication meets the requirements of the ANSI Standard Z39.48-1984 (Permanence of Paper).

Library of Congress Cataloging-in-Publication Data
Clinical chaos: a therapist's guide to nonlinear dynamics and therapeutic change / edited by Michael Bütz and Linda Chamberlain.
        p.   cm.
Includes bibliographical references and index.
ISBN 0-87630-925-2 (case: alk. paper). – ISBN (invalid) 0-87630-925-0 (pbk.: alk. paper)
1. Psychology–Philosophy. 2. Chaotic behavior in systems. 3. Psychology–Philosophy. I. Bütz, Michael R. II. Chamberlain, Linda L.
RC437.5.C57 1998   98-25958
616.89'14'01–dc21   CIP

ISBN 0–87630–925–2 (case: alk. paper)
ISBN 0–87630–926–0 (pbk.: alk. paper)

Contents

Preface

Linda Chamberlain

My introduction to chaos theory began rather innocently. A supervisor was helping me explore the dynamics of a family I had been working with when he off-handedly suggested that I might find it helpful to read a book that had just been released, James Gleick's *Chaos* (1987). By the end of the Prologue, I was enthralled. It seemed as if the world had become re-enchanted. Again, there was the possibility of surprise, wonder, spontaneity, and unpredictable growth that had always been important concepts for me to hold in mind when trying to assist others in sorting through human dilemmas.

For more than a decade, I had been experiencing mounting dissatisfaction and despair at the course that the social sciences were pursuing. The "physics envy" that propelled psychology into the realm of empiricism seemed more often to limit an understanding of human behavior rather than enhance it. Breaking human beings down into tiny, out-of-context, unrelated bits of activity somehow robbed psychology of much of the relevance and richness that one would expect the science of human behavior to provide. The model of people as biological machines or, more recently, as conscious computers, never captured the inherent individuality and diversity of human nature.

More that 100 years of scientific pursuit had left us with only isolated fragments of an understanding of human behavior. Still, for lack of a model that guided our curiosity, social scientists did what most people do when they get stuck; we applied the model with even more determination; one might say, deterministic determination. Increasingly rigorous, reductionistic rules were applied for determining what could be studied (and published!). During behaviorism's heyday, human experiences such as devotion, prejudice, intuition, and joy were forced into claustrophobic stimulus-response patterns. Linearity, with it's dedication to cause and effect, was the law under which we proceeded. We clung to the promise of logical positivism that if we could compile enough data following empiricist formulas for gathering scientific evidence, then human behavior would be predictable and controllable. The certainty that there are basic "codes," structures, rules and replicable patterns to account for all human behavior still drives much of the research in psychology, particularly in the area of neuropsychology. Surely, we can be understood through the interactions of our neurotransmitters once we become sufficiently sophisticated in our understanding of neurochemistry. Maybe . . . maybe not.

Many of our colleagues, particularly those practicing psychotherapy, simply became mavericks. We assumed the mantle of "hard" science when required to produce publishable research, but followed a more undefined, amorphous, intuitive understanding when dealing with real human behavior and dilemmas. We all secretly knew that regardless of how carefully we followed the empirical rules, there was something inherently too complex about humans and their interactions to ever make them predictable or controllable. The constriction of empiricism meant that we couldn't prove what we knew.

Only recently has it become apparent that what we needed most was a new model. This is true not only in the social sciences, but in the earth sciences, physics, and other applied sciences like engineering and medicine. Despite the marvelous successes in technology that empirical science has achieved, the world is not always made better, safer, saner, or healthier by our scientific accomplishments. In fact, some of the problems inherent in traditional science have contributed tremendously to the global challenges we now face. Empiricism led us to believe that we could manipulate "subjects" without being affected ourselves. The idea of objectivity led us to feel invulnerable to the effects of our experiments, manipulations, and technologies.

Chaos theory, and its newest permutation, complexity theory, offers a new, exciting, and potentially revolutionary leap forward in the evolution of scientific thought. These theories challenge the assumption that traditional scientific reductionism is the only way of systematically and logically understanding complex phenomena. In fact, traditional science has steered away from complex systems largely because the methodology didn't fit the dynamics. Especially at the human level, behavior and the variables at work even in simple situations are just too complicated to be accounted for or controlled. As Heinz von Foerster (1972) once noted, "the 'hard sciences' are successful because they deal with 'soft problems'; 'soft sciences' have to struggle, since they are dealing with 'hard problems' (p. 17)."

The implications of this new science of chaos and complexity can be startling and somewhat disorienting when those of us trained in empirical methodology first encounter some aspects of the theory. I remember feeling as if I were wearing a pair of inverted-prism glasses when I first tried to "see" clinical phenomena using paradigms from the theory. Chaos and complexity challenge the laws of order and predictability. This new paradigm in science rejects many of the assumptions underlying traditional scientific methodology. At last, science can again encompass surprise, transformation, unpredictability, and pattern. The quest for empirical validity that has been such a strong motivating force in psychology and other social sciences is not likely to change without a period of significant disruption. Nor is empiricism something to be abolished in our field. Important information and research will continue to be generated using the established experimental, linear model. Chaos science simply offers a means of looking beyond the confines of empiricism.

This book is intended to introduce social scientists to chaos through paths that are already familiar. It is our hope that by pairing some of the tenets of chaos theory with various orientations and specialty areas in clinical work, we will provide mental health practitioners a safe starting point for further exploration. Also, linking chaos theory with existing psychological theories and established areas of clinical pursuit is a way to emphasize the relevance of this new science in providing a more flexible, useful model for describing and understanding human behavior.

Some of the concepts that you will be asked to suspend (at least temporarily) as you venture into chaos are:

1. behavior is predictable (if we get enough data)
2. behavior is replicable
3. behavior changes slowly
4. it takes a lot of input to get a lot of output
5. events or behaviors can be understood in isolation
6. chaos is destructive, aberrant, avoidable, and unproductive
7. observation can be objective

The book is divided into four main parts. In Part I (Chapters 1 and 2), the basics of chaos theory and non-linear dynamics will be described as an introduction to several concepts that will resurface throughout the book. An overview of the implications that chaos theory has for clinicians will also be outlined. In Part II (Chapters 3 through 7), we begin to weave together the familiar territory of various clinical orientations with paradigms from chaos and complexity. Depending on the reader's theoretical foundation, we hope that at least one of the chapters in this section will provide the starting point for a closer examination of the application of non-linear dynamics to an understanding of human behavior. Part III (Chapters 8 through 14) focuses on specific applications of chaos theory in clinical research and practice. Issues including substance abuse, family systems, stress management, and psychopharmacology will be explored. Finally, in Part IV (Chapters 15 through 17), special issues including multiculturalism, research methods, and the future of psychotherapy will be considered.

The goal of this book is to guide clinicians and others in the behavioral sciences through some of the landscape of chaos. Be prepared for encounters with butterflies, strange attractors, phase space, autopoesis, fractals, and other creatures that inhabit this new paradigm. If you are a novice, chaos offers a new map for exploring a once familiar landscape. If you are already acquainted with chaos and complexity, I hope this book will add more color, definition, and detail to your map. As you read through these chapters, it is possible that some disruption of your view of the world could occur. I hope that if the focus changes as you see through a "chaos lens," you will find your vision enhanced, enriched, and enchanted. Enjoy your journey.

REFERENCES

Gleick, J. (1987). *Chaos: Making a new science*. New York: Viking.

von Foerster, H. (1972). The responsibilities of competence. In *Observing Systems*. Seaside, CA: Intersystems Publications.

Acknowledgments

Although Michael and I have taken somewhat different paths in our meanderings through the chaotic landscape, several guides have helped us keep on track. Some of the people who have provided support, criticism, advice, and encouragement, either directly or through their work, deserve our acknowledgment. First, our thanks to Larry Vandervert and Fred Abraham who organized the first "Society for Chaos Theory in Psychology" conference in San Francisco in 1991. It was there that we were first introduced and where the third member of our team, Bill McCown, joined us in forming a trio of like-minded people interested in pursuing a fascination with nonlinear dynamics. The following year at the "Chaos Society" conference, the three of us were formally brought together by Tom Levine when he chaired a panel presentation with us.

Bill McCown, in his inimitable way, arranged our first presentation for the American Psychological Association national conference in 1992. We have had the great pleasure of joining Bill in presenting our work on chaos theory to the APA every year since then at the annual conventions. Thank you Bill. We want to recognize and thank APA divisions 1, 3, 12, 16, 17, 20, 24, 26, 29, 37, 42, 45, and especially 43 (Family Psychology) for sponsoring our presentations at the APA conventions.

Others who have played significant roles in guiding me include Robin Robertson, Tom Masters, Mark Michaels, Steve Proskauer, Laurie Fitzgerald and the Denver Chaos Club, Ray Hawkins, and Marty Dubin. Certainly, each of the contributors to this volume have enlightened and influenced our thinking in the area of chaos theory. We are enormously grateful for their involvement in this project and thank each of them for their time, effort, interest, and commitment to making this book a reality.

Finally, as anyone who has written a book knows, it is in itself a chaotic process. To all of my family, friends, colleagues, students, teachers, and pets, my most deeply felt thanks for giving me your support as this work emerged.

Linda Chamberlain

This is a book about clinical practice, and therefore, it seems only appropriate to give thanks to those who have guided my development as a clinician. Fortunately, I have been graced with many wise and empathetic guides along the way, such as Rosemarie Bowler, Ricardo Carrillo, Eduardo Duran, Kim Faulkner, Robert Fisher, Doris Gilbert, Gary Goldenberg, Ruth Goldman, Claudette Heisler-Scott, Allan Jacobson, Evelyn Lee, Betty Magers, Robert Morgan, Alex Nemeth, Richard Recor, Saul Siegel, Charolette Sky, May Tung, and William Vlach.

As with any project, one must acknowledge those whose support and guidance are less visable in the final product. First, thanks must be made to John Holderegger, Kim Faulkner, Cay Cox, Linda Bennet, Cloyd Cornia, Wendy Slagowski, John Knopf, and Sue Regnier at Cornerstone Behavioral Health and Mountain Regional Services. These individuals have gone out of their way to support me on this project and others, and without their tolerance of my absence, and the additional time and expense this work produced, my contribution to this book would have not been possible. On a personal note, my thanks to the ongoing support of my wife Shelli, as she has endured the process of yet another book. Our good friends and family also deserve thanks for the support they have afforded us, the Bütz family, Kim and Terry Faulkner, the Fenton family, Mark Takata and his family, and Carolos and Ann Wagner.

Many thanks to our editor, Elaine Pirrone, for not only her patience, but her bravery in taking on texts that address this controversial topic. Also, our gratitude for Kerry Stanley's help in getting the text into "publishable" form.

                                                                                    Michael R. Bütz

Part One

An Introduction to Chaotic Systems

The journey begins in Part I (Chapters 1 and 2), by exploring the basics of chaos theory and non-linear dynamics. These two chapters will provide an overview of basic concepts and tenets of chaos theory that will resurface throughout this book. The terminology that is common in describing nonlinear phenomena and the dynamics of interactive, interdependent systems are the main attractions on this part of the path. Once the language and patterns of observation have been conquered, Chapter 2 examines the relevance of these concepts for clinicians.

Throughout this book, the authors have attempted to "be gentle" with those readers who may not have approached the territory of pure science for some time. As clinicians, we are aware that our training and work are often focused more on the theories and techniques unique to psychotherapy. Be assured—more familiar therapeutic themes and issues will be the focus of later chapters. We believe, however, that the scientific foundation that is being established by those studying nonlinear dynamics has clear implications for how we observe, understand, and interact with others as therapists. The perspective of chaos theory as it applies to human behavior and psychotherapy is still being developed. We hope that clinicians who read this book will allow themselves to question the foundations of the phenomena they observe and not push ahead too quickly to find applications. Stay with the theory for awhile and try the perspective it offers. For many of us, it has opened up incredible new territory.

Chapter 1

An Introduction to Chaos and Nonlinear Dynamics

Linda Chamberlain

"The future is disorder. A door like this has cracked open five or six times since we got up on our hind legs. It's the best possible time to be alive, when almost everything you thought you knew is wrong"
Valentine (p. 48). In *Arcadia* by Tom Stoppard.

In case no one has told you yet, reality is shifting. The platform that social scientists have stood upon for more than a century is breaking apart. This pronouncement will strike terror in the souls of many readers, and joy or relief in the souls of others. It is the goal of this book to make the journey into the realm of chaotic dynamics as non-threatening and illuminating as the authors' journeys have been. Welcome to chaos and complexity. Leave some assumptions behind for now; they will always be there for you if you want them back after your adventure. In this first chapter, you will be introduced to strange attractors, uncertainty, phase space, non-linearity, punctuated equilibria, butterfly effects, fractals, and other basic concepts that you will encounter in other chapters. As with any journey into new territory, learning the language will help prepare you for encounters with those who inhabit this chaotic landscape.

If you are like many in the social sciences, the realm of "hard" science and the demands of empiricism may be intimidating. Designing empirically solid experiments with human subjects has been daunting at best and often, simply impossible. Most of us have known throughout all of our training and careers that we were working with conditions and variables that (at best) loosely fit the criteria demanded by experimental models. As I once noted in conversation with a microbiologist, it is difficult in psychology to have finite, "clean" results since we generally can't kill our subjects once we have completed the experiment and reached the outcome we want. The empirical goal of objectivity has been a major stumbling block. Human beings are simply too complex to fit the mold of traditional, "objective" experimentation. As Gregory Bateson (1972, p. 47) noted in a metalogue:

Daughter: What does "objective" mean?

Father: Well. It means that you look very hard at those things which you choose to look at.

D: That sounds right. But how do the objective people choose which things they will be objective about?

F: Well. They choose those things about which it is easy to be objective.

D: So it's a subjective choice?

F: Oh yes. All experience is subjective.

D: But it's *human* and subjective. They decide which bits of animal behavior to be objective about by consulting human subjective experience. . .

F: Yes—but they do try to be not human.

The basis for scientific inquiry first began to shift when Albert Einstein (1954) delivered evidence which challenged the Newtonian view of a mechanistic universe. The Newtonian goal of discovering comprehensive, immutable laws that would unfailingly govern all phenomena and would allow us to predict and modify the course of natural processes began to crumble under the weight of relativity. Although still largely deterministic in nature (hence, Einstein's fervent wish that God not play dice with the Universe), relativity set the stage for profound changes in scientific tradition. Perhaps the most important shift was that the observer was introduced back into the system. Objectivity as a part of the scientific process was challenged. Even the most rigorous of scientific endevours, physics, could no longer remove the observer from the data.

The second blow to traditional science came from quantum theory. Quantum science certainly buried even deeper the notion of objectivity, and it sounded an even louder death knell for the world as machine. A major tenet of quantum theory explains that an irreducible degree of randomness is a fundamental feature of nature. Therefore, experimental data and results will fluctuate to an unavoidable extent. "All elementary events occur at random, governed only by statistical laws" (Hebert, 1985, p. xii). Quantum processes are inherently unpredictable such that it is impossible to determine from moment to moment how a system or an element in a system will behave. If that is true for the behavior of such a fundamental element as light, how can that not be true for human behavior? Quantum physics began to weave together the dynamics of chance and predictability in a context-dependent tapestry. It became clear that data gathered out of context was incomplete, particularly if the context did not include the effect of the observer. The idea of spontaneous, unpredictable events was embraced by quantum theory. It began to appear that God did indeed play dice with the Universe.

These challenges to traditional, empirically-based scientific paradigms, coupled with the advent of the computer and the ability to "crunch" vast amounts of data, led to the birth of chaos theory. Chaos is an epistemology based on a concept of reality which, instead of being intrinsically orderly, stable, and equilibrial, is seething with spontaneous change, irregularity, disorder, and chance.

The interest in chaos has generated a myriad of definitions and descriptions that attempt to capture the nature of this beast. As Ian Percival writes, "The science of chaos is like a river that has been fed from many streams. Its sources come from every discipline—mathematics, physics, chemistry, engineering, medicine, and biology . . ." (Hall, 1991, p. 16).

In retrospect, it is apparent that the interest in chaotic dynamics arose simultaneously in almost every field of scientific study. Pieces of the theory that will be outlined came from meteorologists, paleontologists, biologists, physicists, mathematicians, computer engineers, economists, astronomers, and chemists. Chaos theory is the combination of ideas and research from many diverse scientists. As Robin Robertson notes (Robertson & Combs, 1995), "Chaos theory has begun to emerge as any true symbol emerges, from all directions at once, from the 'most complex and differentiated minds' of our age" (p. 14).

So what exactly is chaos and chaos theory?

"Chaos theory is the qualitative study of unstable aperiodic behavior in deterministic nonlinear dynamical systems" (Kellert, 1993, p. 2).

"Chaos is persistent instability" (Percival, 1991, p. 12).

". . . chaos is a science of process rather than state, of becoming rather than being" (Gleick, 1987, p. 5).

". . . complex behavior that seems random but actually has some hidden order" (Freeman, 1991, p. 78).

". . . complex behavior, produced by simple, deterministic rules, is called chaos" (Cohen and Stewart, 1994, p. 190).

Each of the contributors to this book will offer further definitions regarding the nature of chaos and chaos theory. It should, however, be clear from the definitions already given that chaos theory seeks to investigate areas that have previously been avoided or ignored by science. Traditionally, physics and the other sciences have focused on, "the very big and the very small. The universe: the elementary particle. The ordinary-sized stuff which is our lives, the things people write poetry about—clouds-daffodils-waterfalls—and what happens in a cup of coffee when the cream goes in—these things are full of mystery . . ." (Stoppard, p. 48). Newtonian or classical science is based on simplification, and its effectiveness lies in dealing only with areas in which phenomena can be reduced to fragments amenable to the methods employed to analyze data. As Appleyard notes, "The entire scientific edifice, for all its hermetic inaccessibility to the uninitiated, is a vast monument to simplification" (1992, p. 141). Chaos theory is a human-sized science, a paradigm that deals with the behavior of complex, interactive systems without relying on the reductionistic principles previously employed by empiricism.

The question of whether psychology can be a "true" science has been debated almost since its formation as a separate discipline. Perhaps the dilemma is not so much whether psychology is a science or not, but whether psychology has found or created an appropriate model from which to pursue, gather, and process information. The vantage point of empiricism, from which psychologists have attempted to observe human phenomena, may have constricted our ability to develop a more comprehensive understanding of behavior and the process of change in human beings and human systems.

Chaos theory and the study of non-linear systems offers an alternative model for observation and understanding in psychology. Since chaos theory provides a broader perspective for many fields of science, it "offers unique possibilities for unifying psychology" (Robertson & Combs, 1995, p. 3). Natural and human systems contain essential elements of uniqueness, randomness, and irreversibility. Part of what differentiates theorists in chaos science is that they "jump from the paradigm of things to the paradigm of pattern" (Keeney, 1983, p. 95). As Robertson (1995, pp. 12–13) outlines, chaos theory has a direct relevance for clinical psychology, particularly in three of the basic principles it proposes. First, change isn't always linear. "A" doesn't always or only lead to "B". In addition, small fluctuations in a behavior or sequence can have large effects. This will be further expanded in the description of the "butterfly effect" or sensitive dependence on initial conditions. Second, determinism and predictability are not the same. When there is feedback in a system, deterministic equations can lead to unpredictable results or chaos. Finally, in systems that experience chaotic or "far-from-equilibrium" periods (essentially, all natural, biologically based systems), change is not necessarily related to external causes; these systems can "self organize" at a higher level of organization.

In order to look further at these ideas and others that are encompassed in the theory of non-linear dynamics, it may be useful at this point to learn the language that can guide you through the territory. Chaos theory is rich in symbolism and metaphor. Perhaps this is true of chaos more so than other scientific paradigms because science is finally looking at the human level of experience, where language and story are important tools in communicating. Certainly, there are exquisite, complex mathematics that have been generated by the study of chaos which may interest many readers. It is the purpose of this book, however, to simplify those concepts in order to make them more available to clinicians who may not have an extensive mathematical background. So, welcome to the incredible stories that comprise the non-linear, chaotic view of the world.

THE LANGUAGE OF CHAOS

Before wandering too much further down the chaos path, it may be helpful to acquaint the reader with some basic terms and concepts that will be encountered in other chapters of the book. Chaos and complexity theory are certainly works in progress, and the different aspects of the general theory described here are not exhaustive. This section should provide a beginning point of reference for further examination and a basis for understanding some of the ideas that form the core of non-linear systems dynamics.

"The Butterfly Effect", or Sensitive Dependence on Initial Conditions

It seems likely that an idea has truly captured the public attention when it is used as the basis for a car commercial. The ad begins with a butterfly flapping its wings in the jungle which adds turbulence to a storm system that is brewing which then generates rain clouds over a wide area of the hemisphere including the stretch of road on which the relieved driver of a new, special traction, better visibility car is making her way home. The idea is that even very tiny, distant events or effects can profoundly impact circumstances in our lives.

In much of the literature on chaos, sensitive dependence is referred to as the "butterfly effect." The term "butterfly effect" came from a description of a possible chain of linked events described by a meteorologist. In 1960, Edward Lorenz, a meteorologist at the Massachusetts Institute of Technology, was working on a computer generated model weather program. His goal was a common goal of most meteorologists at that time: to clarify the natural laws that were at work in creating weather patterns so that the weather would be more predictable. Although the repetitions of patterns were never quite exact, there was clearly a recognizable structure to the model his computer generated and he was able to see familiar patterns arise over time. He was able to graph many of the different aspects of the weather (i.e. winds, temperatures) and see order in the patterns, even though there was no exact repetition.

In 1961, however, he wanted to replicate a segment of the program in order to examine the data more carefully. Instead of starting the whole program again, he began at a mid-point near the phenomena he wanted to examine. In the initial program, he had used six decimal places, the number:.506127. In his input for the segment replication, he used only the first three decimal places:.506. He had assumed that the difference—one part in a thousand—would be inconsequential. This assumption proved to be incorrect. The two patterns began the same but at one point began to clearly diverge and become two very different patterns.

Newtonian science would have predicted that the small change in the initial conditions would have had some effect, but that the effect would stay minimal and the patterns would remain largely similar. In linear scientific theory, a small change in a standard pattern should produce only an equivocally small fluctuation. Lorenz, however, realized he had not simply produced some type of computer error that could be overlooked as accidental. He recognized that the "butterfly effect" was no accident. The butterfly effect—the theory that a butterfly stirring the air today in Peking can transform storm systems next month in New York— became known technically as "sensitive dependence on initial conditions." The understanding that even minute differences in input can quickly become over- whelming differences in output is a cornerstone of chaos theory. Lorenz also rec- ognized that "crisis points," where a fluctuation could occur, exist everywhere in natural systems.

Strange Attractors

Strange attractors began their existence as mathematical terms that helped explain why smoke from a cigarette finds a patterned swirl as it curls up from the first puff and why flooding water finds its point of ebb and flow. Briggs and Peat (1989) eloquently describe attractors as "creatures that live in a curious abstract place called 'phase space'" (p. 31). It is a beast that exists at the juncture between turbulence and order. Later in their book, they define strange attractors as turbulence; the turbulence that "breaks up orderly systems and causes disorder to boil across our landscape" (Briggs and Peat, p. 45). As seen in David Ruelle's (1980) writing, it seems difficult even for mathematicians not to wax poetic when describing strange attractors:

> I have not (yet) spoken of the aesthetic appeal of strange attractors. These systems of curves, these clouds of points, suggest sometimes fireworks or galaxies, sometimes strange and disquieting vegetal proliferations. A realm lies here to be explored and harmonies to be discovered. (p. 126).

Strange attractors are thought to be the foundation for the hidden order in natural systems. DiBello (1990) notes, "The strange attractor acts like a magnet constraining systemic variables to lie within (these) given ranges" (p. 1). Bütz (1992) helps to simplify the concept by stating that, "An attractor simply is what it sounds like, something that attracts this or that" (p. 10). He goes on to describe strange attractors as nonlinear and fractal in nature. This differentiates them from other types of attractors (e.g., higher and lower frequencies on an oscillator) that are fixed point, limit cycle attractors. Patterns in strange attractors are never repeated exactly, but they do exert some limits on the activity in a system.

Strange attractors exist in a mysterious place called "phase space." Phase space was a mathematical term that allowed physicists to visualize many numbers simultaneously.

> They take the situation of the system at an instant as a point in what they call a 'phase space' so that in phase space the complete state of knowledge about a dynamical system at a single instant in time collapses to a point. That point is a dynamical system— at that instant. (Albert, 1990, p. 109).

The images generated by strange attractors have an immediate recognition factor for most people. It is a complex image of an infinity symbol. In strange attractors, the trajectory or behavior of the subject never repeats exactly, but there is a pattern that begins to emerge with repetition. As previously noted, chaos is a science of pattern, not discrete events.

As a way to adapt the idea of phase space to a social science perspective, the notion of "phrase space" is suggested. Phrase space is the pattern of communication that establishes both problems and solutions in relationships. Because human behavior is most significantly impacted and influenced by our interactions with

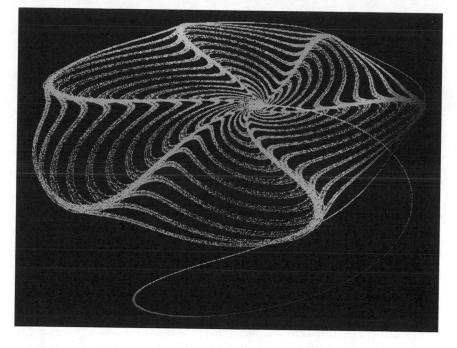

Figure 1   Strange Attractor. From *Strange Attractors: Creating Patterns in Chaos*, by Julien C. Sprott. New York: M&T Books. Copyright 1993. Reprinted with permission.

others, strange attractor patterns in human dynamics tend to be created by the balance of opposing "pulls" or attractors that we experience in our communications with others. The concept employs the broadest sense of the term "communications" so that it encompasses any involvement or activity that takes place between people, not just spoken or written language. The term also includes the internal dialogue or relationship that we maintain with others; our unexpressed thoughts and feelings as they relate to people we encounter. For example, in intimate relationships, it seems that most communication between parties is an expression of fear or love, of closeness or distance, of desire or despair. The strange attractor is created as both parties attempt to balance the energy devoted to each of these areas.

Uncertainty and Unpredictability

According to new science theory, the empirical goals of predicting and controlling change are illusions fostered by the artificial nature of the experimental dialogue science has relied on for its examination of phenomena. The search for the "grand unifying theory" in psychology relies on the belief that human behavior is predictable. Does abandoning an empirically-based science require an admission that a comprehensive explanatory theory is unattainable? According to Prigogine & Stengers' (1984) model, an all-encompassing theory that can control and predict how a system will change is an impossibility. In linear relationships, equations are solvable. There is predictability and stability. Time is considered reversible, such that the system can be taken apart and put back together without assuming that the elements have been changed by the passage of time. In the system of mathematics, a 3 is a 3 is a 3 and its value is not affected by the passage of time. This is a factor which is crucial to empirical science.

Experimental science relies on replicability and predictability in order to establish validity. However, natural systems cannot be "solved" and cannot be understood in isolation from their context. Replicability becomes problematic due to the irreversibility of time. All natural systems change through the passage of time such that they cannot be taken apart and put back together in the same way. Changes implicit in the passage of time include maturation and aging in all life forms. Complexity is real, not just multiple levels of simplicity. Also, elements are not equivalent across systems or sub-systems. "Nonlinearity means that the act of playing the game has a way of changing the rules" (Gleick, p. 24).

Platt (1970) states that "It is not at all clear whether self-structuring hierarchical jumps of this kind can be to any appreciable degree anticipated or guided" (p. 47). The unpredictability of change in systems makes calculation and empirical investigation difficult, but also creates a richness and potential for higher levels of organization. Determinism can offer some predictions for how a system maintains a homeostatic level, but not how, when, or what will begin the process of disequilibrium or the structure of the new order that will result from disturbance in a system. As Auerswald (1987) points out, " 'new science' formed a basis for a new set of rules that could be used to define a universal reality" (p. 323). But it is a reality in which predictability, equilibrium, reversibility, control, and dualism (separation of events into cause and effect, stimulus and response, and/or individual and environment) are no longer the central elements.

Clinicians are certainly aware of the inherent unpredictability of human behavior. Although people's behavior tends to be constrained by past experience, personality factors, learning, and other determinants, trying to accurately predict exactly when a person will make a suicide attempt or whether they will commit a specific crime in the future is generally an impossible task. Because all natural systems display complexity, they are potentially unknowable to an irreducible degree.

Self Organization and Dissipative Structures

Maturana and Varela (1988) describe the dynamics of self organization through the concept of "autopoesis." Autopoesis describes the ability of biological units (such as people) or natural systems to couple with diverse environments in a manner that makes them continually self-generating. They state that "the most striking feature of an autopoietic system is that it pulls itself up by its own bootstraps and becomes distinct from its environment through its own dynamics" (p. 47).

Essentially, as dynamic systems move further from equilibrium, new structures and new types of organization in the system can emerge spontaneously. On an individual basis, consider the example of mutations that arise and provide some advantage to the unique entity, such that the mutation helps with adaptation, and therefore increases the likelihood of that particular individual reproducing so that the mutant element will become more established in the species. These new dynamic states are a result of autopoesis; the dynamic interaction of a given system and its surroundings or context. This allows the system to move from chaos or disorder to a new order. New orders are established when a system interacts in some new way either within itself or with the environment or both. Because of the complex cognitive abilities of humans, new ideas that change behavior provide the feedback necessary for new orders to be established and cultures to emerge. Prigogine and Stengers (1984) described these newly ordered structures as "dissipative structures" to emphasize the constructive role of dissipative processes in their formation (p.12).

Self-organization is a part of the pattern that emerges when small fluctuations in a system are amplified. Certainly, the experience of transition that humans periodically experience in life is captured by this concept. As Robertson (1995) notes, "the whole fabric of a person's life interacts with his or her total environment, and something new emerges that wasn't predictable from previous behavior" (p.13). Although past behavior is generally the best predictor of future behavior, spontaneous leaps into new patterns of thought, affect, and action are an essential aspect of being human. If this were not so, psychotherapy would be a useless pursuit. We would all be doomed to constantly repeat whatever we learned as our inital reaction to any life event.

One of the important aspects of the idea of self-organization is that it emerges when systems are in chaos. During periods of stability, systems tend to maintain whatever pattern is in place and functional. The process of change is inextricably linked to disruption, disorder, confusion, and irregularity: chaos. Only when there is sufficient unrest in a system is it likely to be amenable to transformation. How often do people come to a therapist when everything in their lives are going just fine? It is during periods of chaos, when the old "structure" or approach to solving problems and coping with life no longer works, that people are able to make significant leaps out of previous patterns into new behaviors.

"Punctuated Equilibria" and Bifurcations

As already indicated, chaos theory postulates spontaneity in the process of change as opposed to an ordered, step-at-a-time, gradual process. People, like other complex, dynamic systems, do not usually change in gradual increments, but in discontinuous leaps. The term "punctuated equilibrian" comes from Stephen Jay Gould's (1980) arguement against Darwin's slow, orderly evolutionary process. Gould proposed that there is equally convincing evidence for cataclysmic change in the evolution of species. Punctuated equilibria is based on the relatively sudden appearance of species. Instead of arising gradually through minute changes from their ancestors, new forms of life appear "all at once and fully organized or formed as a different species" (p. 182).

Specifically, this paradigm suggests that change in systems occurs in leaps following a gradual accumulation of stresses that a system resists until it reaches a breaking point. As already noted in the description of dissipative structures, the farther from equilibrium a system moves, the greater its perception of differences in the external world. Although the buildup of stress or confusion in the system may be gradual, the transition to a different order may be comparatively swift. How the system will reorganize and at what point a steady state will resume is unpredictable. Once the bifurcation occurs and a new behavior or form is introduced, the system will magnify that difference and transform itself until some more adaptive level is reached. Exactly what the bifurcation point will be or when it will occur is impossible to predetermine. One can't assume how much difference it will take to make a difference.

The bifurcation point, or critical moment or crisis point, is where chaos and order meet. The term "bifurcation" is often used in chaos theory to describe the dynamic that initiates a transformation. Near the point of bifurcation, chance plays a significant role. After the bifurcation occurs, systems become more settled and deterministic until the next bifurcation. In order to more clearly picture the concept of bifurcation, Goerner (1995) uses the example of the different types of gait that horses exhibit. "Each gait represents a completely different organization of leg motion. The transition between gaits occurs in a sudden reorganization ... walk to trot, trot to gallop" (p. 24).

Irreversibility

The final essential paradigm in chaos theory is the concept of irreversibility. A long-standing challenge in physics grew out of the second law of thermodynamics, the law of entropy. Entropy introduced the elements of time and irreversibility to mechanistic science. Entropy has been popularly thought of as the measure of disorder in a system. According to this second law, the "machine" of nature could not function unchanged through time, and the longer it ran, the more chaotic its functioning would become. Therefore, there is an irreversible process which is dependent on the direction of time. In Newtonian physics, the laws of nature served to maintain equilibrium and order. Irreversible processes such as entropy were nuisances or aberrations in a naturally lawful, stable, and orderly universe. The nature of empirical inquiry and scientific experimentation is certainly based on the repetition and replication of data gathered from the manipulation of phenomena. Theoretically, time should have no effect in changing the outcome of an experiment that has been properly designed and implemented. In fact, it is this "reversibility" or capacity to replicate that lends credibility to the results of empirical studies.

From the perspective of chaos theory, it is the spontaneous and irreversible that are of interest. Systems in nature are historically determined since they are changed by the passage of time. Natural systems collect information over time that is stored and exerts an effect on both their current and future activity. It is impossible for a natural system to "start over again" or return to baseline. Time cannot be reversed, nor can the inevitable changes that occur in systems over time. Eggs cannot be unscrambled, a broken vase will not spontaneously resume its previous shape, babies cannot re-enter the womb.

EXPLORING CHAOS

Now that you are equipped with some of the basic concepts and language of chaos, an exploration of the relationship of chaos theory and psychotherapy can commence. Depending on one's theoretical orientation and training, some of the chapters will begin in familiar territory and lead into innovative applications of nonlinear dynamics. It is our hope that you will find the paradigms offered by chaos theory to be both intellectually stimulating in relation to your conceptualization of human behavior, and useful in formulating treatment strategies and interventions with your clients.

Each of the chapter authors has a unique voice. All of the contributors have been captivated by the relevance, richness, and beauty of chaos theory as it relates to human development and behavior. Perhaps you will find that chaos theory raises important philosophical questions or transforms your concept of the nature of human life and experience. Whether you find yourself experiencing a "bifurcation" that changes your perspective on human nature in some significant way, or simply discover novel ways of observing and understanding human behavior, we hope you will find your journey into chaos to be curious, enlightening, and mentally invigorating. As Valentine, Tom Stoppard's character in *Arcadia*, says about chaos theory, " It makes me so happy. To be at the beginning again, knowing almost nothing" (p. 47). Have a good trip!

REFERENCES

Albert, M. (1990). *Chaos: A new order.* Unpublished manuscript.

Appleyard, B. (1992). *Understanding the present.* New York: Anchor Books.

Auerswald, E. H. (1987). Epistemological confusion in family therapy and research. *Family Process, 26*(3), 317–330.

Bateson, G. (1972). *Steps to an ecology of mind.* New York: Ballantine Books.

Batten, M. (August, 1988). Charting life's unpredictable pathways: Stephen Jay Gould. *The Cousteau Society Calypso Log, 15*(4), 14–17.

Bohm, D. & Peat, F.D. (1987). *Science, order and creativity.* New York: Bantam Books.

Briggs, J., & Peat, F. (1989). *Turbulent mirror.* New York: Harper & Row.

Bütz, M. (1992). *Chaos theory, psychology's new friend?* Unpublished manuscript.

Cohen, J., & Stewart, I. *The collapse of chaos.* New York: Viking.

DiBello, R. (1990, December 31). Personality as a strange attractor. *The Social Dynamicist.* p. 1.

Einstein, A. (1954). *Ideas and opinions.* New York: Bonanza Books.

Freeman, W. (1991). The physiology of perception. *Scientific American*, 78–85.

Gleick, J. (1987). *Chaos: Making a new science.* New York: Viking.

Goerner, S. (1995). Chaos, evolution, and deep ecology. In R. Robertson & A. Combs (Eds.), *Chaos theory in psychology and the life sciences*, (pp. 17–38). Hillsdale, NJ: Lawrence Erlbaum Associates.

Gould, S. J. (1980). *The panda's thumb: More reflections in natural history.* New York: W.W. Norton & Co.

Hall, N. (1991). *Exploring chaos: A guide to the new science of disorder.* New York: W.W. Norton & Co.

Hebert, N. (1985). *Quantum reality: Beyond the new physics.* New York: Anchor Press/Doubleday.

Keeney, B. (1983). *Aesthetics of change.* New York: The Guilford Press.

Kellert, S. H. (1993). *In the wake of chaos.* Chicago: The University of Chicago Press.

Maturana, H., & Varela, F. (1988). *The tree of knowledge: The biological roots of human understanding.* Boston: New Science Library.

Percival, I. (1991). Chaos: a science for the real world. In N. Hall (Ed.), *Exploring chaos: a guide to the new science of disorder*, (pp. 11–21). New York: W.W. Norton & Co.

Platt, J. (November, 1970). Hierarchical growth. *Bulletin of the Atomic Scientists*, 2–4 & 46–48.

Prigogine, I., & Stengers, I. (1984). *Order out of chaos: Man's new dialogue with nature.* New York: Bantam Books.

Robertson, R., & Combs, A. (Eds.). (1995). *Chaos theory in psychology and the life sciences.* Hillsdale, NJ: Lawrence Erlbaum Associates.

Ruelle, D. (1980). Strange attractors. *Mathematical Intelligencer*, 2, 126–137.

Stoppard, T. (1993). *Arcadia.* London: Faber & Faber.

Chapter 2

Chaos and the Clinician: What's So Important About Science in Psychotherapy?

Michael R. Bütz & Linda Chamberlain

"All that I insist upon is the idea that the activity of the first psychological system is directed towards securing the free discharge of the quantities of excitation, while the second system, by means of the cathexes emanating from it, succeeds in inhibiting this discharge and in transforming the cathexis into a quiescent one, no doubt with a simultaneous raising of its level"

Sigmund Freud (1900, p. 599).

Some readers may be wondering why this book has been devoted to the topic of integrating a new set of scientific theories into clinical practice. What does science have to do with clinical theory and psychotherapy? The quote above from Freud is pretty scientific—it sounds like physics. In the Preface and Chapter 1, we set forth that empiricism, and other associated ideas, would be challenged by the set of notions expressed in this book. Still, what do science and research methods have to do with therapy other than helping us to delineate certain treatments and measure the effectiveness of their outcomes? These are legitimate questions, and the answers might be surprising.

THEORY AND THE THERAPIST

First, at least according to the dominant training model in psychology since 1948, clinicians aspire to become scientist-practitioners. This training focus is referred to as the Boulder Model. The name came from the location of the conference where it was determined that psychologists should be both scientists and practitioners if they were going to be able to use research effectively in their clinical work. The divergence from empiricism, one of the central models for scientific research in psychology and other social sciences, means that a radical shift must take place in what is considered valid research. More descriptive models and qualitative methods are called for that focus on pattern instead of number, concepts instead of details. This shift might be compared to the shift in the 1980s from behaviorism to cognitive models (Mahoney, 1991; Baars, 1986).

Shifts of this magnitude are frequently referred to as paradigm shifts (Kuhn, 1962/1970). Because the concept of a paradigm shift has been applied to almost every slight theoretical change or novel idea that has emerged in the social sciences, it is difficult to entertain the notion of a true revolution in science and what that means for psychology. For many scientists, the paradigm shift from empirical science to chaos science is equivalent to moving from a flat world to a global theory. Lorenz's "butterfly" has stirred the same magnitude of change in the world as Newton's "apple." Incorporating nonlinear dynamics into our view of the cosmos changes forever the manner in which we understand phenomena.

Chaos theory, and the host of concepts associated with it, is considered the third great scientific revolution of this century (Vandervert, 1996). Unlike relativity and quantum models, however, chaos and complexity theories are clearly relevant to the study of human behavior. Chaos theory emerged from several fields encompassed under the natural sciences. Biology, meteorology, paleontology, and economics all made contributions. Although physics and mathematics play a seminal role in the construction of chaos theory, the science of nonlinear dynamics is not limited to these realms, as was more the case with earlier scientific paradigms. Why are scientific notions so important for clinicians to understand?

Citing Freud at the beginning of the chapter was no whim, as he is often credited with founding the profession of psychotherapy. Freud's theories had a scientific underpinning that can be clearly grasped even in that short quote. His theories were developed in accordance with notions about the scientific study of neurology and biology at the turn of the century. In fact, ideas about the transformation of energy ran all through his work and formed part of the foundation of his theory. Freud was not alone in the effort to align contemporary scientific theory with the dynamics he witnessed in his clients. Jung, Freud's early associate, was also deeply concerned with how energy was transformed—one of the crucial questions being studied in physics at that time. Jung wrote an entire volume on the topic titled "The Structure and Dynamics of the Psyche" (1969). Studies of this nature were not limited to individual psychotherapy as a modality.

Family therapy, from its very inception as a field, borrowed heavily from contemporary science to study the dynamics of communication in families (Bütz, Chamberlain, & McCown, 1997; Bateson, Jackson, Haley, & Weakland, 1956). Cybernetics and general systems theory provided a framework and impetus for the founders of family therapy (as discussed further in Chapters 6 and 10). Most clinicians trained in family systems therapy have an understanding of such scientific constructs as positive and negative feedback loops, homeostasis, and deviation-amplifying processes. Furthermore, family therapists, perhaps more so than therapists working from other models, have continued to keep up with developments in the area of cybernetics and systems theory (Elkaïm, 1990; Hoffman, 1981; Selvini-Palazzoli, Boscolo, Cecchin, & Prata, 1978; Watzlawick, Beavin, & Jackson, 1967). Certainly, other theoretical orientations have been aware of and incorporated developments in science. The important thing for clinicians to understand, however, is that many established psychotherapy orientations have their basis in science—the science that was prevalent at the time they emerged. The *Zeitgeist*, or general trend of thought and feeling that characterize an era, does apply to science and scientific endeavors. Phenomena that scientists choose to study, deem unimportant, or ignore, and the conclusions that are drawn from data, are as vulnerable to the Zeitgeist as the clothing that is in fashion.

Clinicians must recognize that if they are working from outdated notions of scientific dynamics, their concepts of therapeutic processes and change may be outmoded as well. Not only might the notions be outdated, they may even be dangerous or counterproductive. When significant new theories, discoveries, or inventions emerge from science, a lack of awareness on the part of any scientist, social or otherwise, can lead to a "flat world dilemma." Clinicians that are not exploring the implications of nonlinear dynamics will soon find themselves living in a flat world while others circle the globe. Some who are embedded in the linear models of radical behaviorism may still be treating people as if they were machines. That is one reason this book is important for clinicians. We do what we do in therapy because the model was extracted at some point from the science of the day. If we do not adjust our models when new information becomes available, we live in a flat world. New understandings that emerge from the enterprise of science do have a direct effect on the formulation of our images regarding what it means to be human. Finally, chaos and complexity theories have produced a set of ideas that help explain human behavior and experience, rather than hindering us.

This book is an attempt to bring the emerging edge of scientific theory to the clinician so that new understandings of nonlinear dynamics can influence their practice. These ideas offer a different conceptualization of human beings, our relationships, and our developmental process across the life span. If we are not working with simple stimulus-response driven entities or beings governed by the conservation and release of innate energies, what are we working with in our clients?

A BRIEF VENTURE INTO HISTORY AND SYSTEMS IN PSYCHOLOGY

Our journey begins at a trailhead where one can see dozens of different paths all leading to the same point in the distance. Some of these paths clearly lead through a wide variety of terrain and ecosystems, whereas others appear to have only a few representative environments that roughly approximate the diversity and detail of the other trails. The first widely varied paths represent a thorough examination of the history and systems of social science dating back to different points in the past. The second, more characteristic, set of trails provides a sample of nodal points in social science over the past century, hitting only the highlights of theoretical developments.

Books have been written to simply address one path (Freedheim, 1992) or one aspect of these paths (Ellenberger, 1970), and volumes have been devoted to only one of the disciplines in social science (Koch, 1959). Consequently, given the nature of this text, we have chosen the shorter more representative path to guide the reader along in order to illustrate the different conceptualizations of human development. Other paths have been described and revised elsewhere (Bütz, 1992 and 1997). This one will begin at the turn of this century when the whole notion of psychotherapy emerged.

SCIENCE AND THE PSYCHOTHERAPY OF THE TWENTIETH CENTURY

At the beginning of this century, there was an almost dizzying explosion of thought in science with innumerable ideas appearing on the scientific scene that had a richness and diversity only recently appreciated outside scientific circles. Human beings were learning to fly higher and faster than birds, outrun horses in automobiles and trains, and dive under the seas. At the same time, the seeds for what would be called quantum theory were beginning to germinate. Philosophy, the right arm of science, was also expanding. Science and philosophy became more entwined, as in quantum physics, when scientists had to confront the philosophical implications of their explorations.

Human beings were rapidly moving away from a reliance on natural systems (like the horse) by creating machines (like the automobile), and there was a great difference between the two types of systems. Natural systems were "open systems." That is, they continued to integrate new information and develop along an evolutionary path. Machines, on the other hand, were "closed systems" that, once produced, contained all the information they would need to function and did not evolve. Instead, from the moment they were produced, there was a progressive downward spiral until the machine finally broke down (a phenomena known as *entropy*). It could be fixed, but it was never as "good as new." We cannot make such a statement about a human infant or an Aspen seedling—they continue to grow and become more complex as they interact with their environments. In many instances, however, machines were the model that social scientists chose to approximate human behavior.

At that time in history, not only were explorers going out into the world, but some turned inward—toward our own existence. One such explorer was Sigmund Freud. His early studies in physiology and neurology led him down a path that slowly, some five years after he had received his medical degree in 1881, turned toward the mind. These early studies afforded Freud a unique perspective from which to study psychological processes, one that was well grounded in what was considered "contemporary" scientific theory. Freud's studies in psychology are well known by many, but not generally well understood. Both the translation of his work (Bettelheim, 1982), and Freud's expectation that readers would devote themselves to the study of his entire works with each consequent revision of his theory (1914), have proven to be impediments to many modern students.

Freud's model is often described to undergraduate psychology students as being based on the dynamics of hydraulics. Yet few texts, if any, actually describe Freud's model as hydraulic. Even basic texts (Carson & Butcher, 1991; Ornstein & Carstensen, 1992) describe his model as one of tension reduction (Hall & Lindzey, 1978, pp. 44–46). The misconception that Freud's was a hydraulic model may have arisen from some authors' attention to the notion of conservation of energy in physics (Hall, 1954), whereas Freud himself was unmistakable about the foundation of his theory (1900, pp. 537–538).

Nevertheless, let's entertain the notion that the mind operates according to hydraulic principles, as some people assert. There are a few basic assumptions that follow. First, the mind is a closed system. Second, pressure from outside redistributes the contents of the system until a certain equilibrium of pressure is reached. Third, when this pressure is relieved, the system returns to its former state. With just these three assumptions about hydraulic dynamics, it becomes clear that a hydraulic model of the mind is absurd.

First, if the system is closed, how does it integrate new information and initiate change? Essentially, the mind could not develop since it would be cut off from the environment around it—nothing could get in. There is some truth to the notion expressed in the second point that pressure from outside forces changes the dispersal of contents on the inside. But, so what? If one drops a sealed canister from the top of a thirty story building, pressure from the outside will change something on the inside here too. Pressure from the outside and change on the inside transpire in human beings through the act of perception. Perception occurs through both awareness of a novel stimulus in the environment, and the recognition of some emotion, feeling, or thought arising spontaneously from within. Not only do human beings respond to pressure from the outside, but also to pressure from the inside. People experience a far more complex set of perceptive responses than a hydraulic model affords us. The final notion is that systems return to their former state once the tension is reduced. Particularly in Freud's system where there are conscious and unconscious contents, this connotes that with pressure, one becomes more unconscious and without it one is more conscious (or vice versa). Perhaps it is an acceptable hypothesis that under pressure, one has to become more conscious in order to respond to the environment. Once the pressure is off, however, the model implies that one becomes just as unconscious as he or she was before. Is this possible?

Readers are encouraged to simply consider their own experience in the world and compare it with this model. Also, it is implied that systems, be they human or other life forms, may return to an earlier state. Many people wish to return to a certain age; the "if I only knew then what I know now" lament. Of course, this cannot happen. But with this hydraulically based, simplistic notion of human psychological processes, to reverse experience is possible. It is clear, however, that developmental processes are irreversible, and cannot be undone. Individuals, couples, and families will often present for therapy expressing a desire for "things to go back to the way they were." Yet, no one is the same person he or she was yesterday or the day before. Each has accumulated some new experience or information and is forever altered in the process. You can't learn less.

Given this very brief consideration of some of the problems with a hydraulic model of human psychological processes, let's get to what Freud actually said. He was very clear on the topic of psychological processes. Even though his system is very complicated, his basic ideas can be outlined through a few concepts. First, the concepts of primary and secondary processes, at a rudimentary level, distinguish automatic defenses from manual defenses. Primary process' main job is to defend the individual against being overwhelmed by experiences in the environment, whereas secondary process is sort of a manual override that responds to experiences at a more sophisticated level. In so doing, the ego becomes involved in the process. So, in Freud's model these two processes mediate one's experience of the world.

One might compare this difference to the experience of walking the same path day after day with little attention to the details, and then suddenly noticing a change in the environment such as a fallen tree or a new building that he or she needs to examine. We have two processes, one meant for maintenance, and therefore primary, and one for processing stimuli that require more attention, the secondary. Freud felt the reduction of tension was the single most important notion that described these processes, and so he said "Reflex processes remain the model of every psychical function" (1900, pp. 537–538). A reflex constitutes a discharge of tension similar to putting one's hand on a hot burner, and without thinking about it (secondary process), the hand is withdrawn (primary process).

Freud did not consume himself with studies of physics, rather, he studied physiology and neurology. Consequently, he had a different approach to the study of psychological processes and used these models as the basis for his theories. Even at this very elementary level, the true difference between Freud's theoretical system and the hydraulic model is clear. We are talking about an open system that integrates experience and grows from it. Examination of nonlinear dynamics that operate in the process of free association, and the emergence of symbolic material in dreams, further promotes psychodynamic theory as an open system (Bütz, 1997). The emerging experiences, described in associations and dreams, are typically unpredictable and difficult to describe except in terms of patterns and symbols.

A contemporary of Freud's, and a man with whom one of the most consuming dialogues about psychology occurred early in this century (McGuire, 1974), was Carl Jung. Jung's early focus was on sorting out the dynamics witnessed in his clients by comparing those dynamics with models known to him through the science of his day. These undertakings occupied him early in his career after his break with Freud, the first full statement of his investigations being his essay "On Psychic Energy" written between 1912 and 1928 (Jung, 1969, p. V). These studies led him down unexpected paths, and through uncharted territory in the social sciences. Jung's research even went so far as to delve into quantum physics, where he conversed with such eminent figures as Wolfgang Pauli (Jung, 1969, pp. 437–440).

Scientific notions that were referenced throughout Jung's explication of Analytical Psychology included equilibrium theory and the second law of thermodynamics (1969, pp. 2, 3, and 49). Though not exact, Jung's use of this model was applied to his ideas about how the personality developed over time. He used the model of equilibrium to describe how his theory of psychological types (1971) developed, stating, "The psyche is a self-regulating system that maintains its equilibrium just as the body does" (Jung, 1966a, p. 330). Jung described his psychological types (e.g., introverted or extroverted) as a developmental process. The task, considering equilibrium, is to become more extroverted (inferior function) later in life when one is predisposed to being introverted (superior function). Superior and inferior functions reflected in these types indicated a movement toward equilibrium (1971), or a compensation toward psychic equilibrium (1966a; 1966b). Ultimately, the goal is to find a balance between these polarities—to be able to move between the two types with equal ease—to achieve a sort of equilibrium.

Jung later went beyond this with his explorations into mythology. He found that theories based on equilibrium and entropy were limiting—they were closed system models. In particular, entropy, or the second law of thermodynamics, describes closed systems running down as they use up their internal sources of energy. Entropy is often referred to as an index of the degree of disorder in a system, or how far the system has run down. Only recently (Prigogine & Stengers, 1984) has this set of theories on equilibrium been revised and integrated into an open systems model. Jung's psychological types can be considered an equilibrium based theory, where his notion of the "Self" may be seen as the midpoint of the personality (1966b, p. 365) whereby all the contents of the psychic system are used up. From Jung's investigations into equilibrium dynamics we are able to place his theory in the light of our current discussion. "Inasmuch as the intellect rigidly adheres to the absolute aim of science it cuts itself off from the springs of life" (Jung, 1971, p. 86).

The models put forth by Freud and Jung represent psychodynamic models that emerged early in this century. There were certainly other notions about human behavior and its relation to science evolving at this time. "Give me a dozen healthy infants, well-formed, and my own specified world ... and I'll guarantee to take any one at random and train him to become any type of specialist I might select." These were the words of John Watson (1914, 1925), who believed that a scientist should only be concerned with "observable behavior." Aspects of being human that were not observable, that were part of the internal "black box" of the mind, were unimportant. These theories were promoted by behaviorists whose views were predicated on empirical findings—"hard data." Watson was one of the first, and most vehement proponents of this view.

Some forty years later, another important figure emerged in this movement: B.F. Skinner. Skinner accepted Watson's behaviorism with some differences, but, the basis of the assumptions he espoused hinged on the notion that "order is not only a possible end product; it is a working assumption which must be adopted at the very start" (Skinner, 1953, p. 6). Even though many behaviorists have a substantial knowledge of biology, these are mechanical, Newtonian ideas predicated on the belief in a predicable, orderly universe—a universe that operates like a machine. Skinner even followed some of the writings of Henri Poincaré (Hall & Lindzey, 1978, p. 640), a prominent figure in chaos theory (Briggs & Peat, 1989). Nevertheless, he proposed that order must be the "working assumption." A common element of most research in behaviorism is that it happens in a "laboratory," a controlled environment, a specified world. In considering these purely scientific notions, one analog emerges—the machine.

Machines are expected to operate in controlled environments, they are supposed to behave in an orderly fashion, and people are supposed to be able to "fix" them if they break. First, the environments in which human beings operate are never controlled; they do not function in a closed system. That is what made Lorenz' discovery so fantastic (1963)—that a variable as tiny as a butterfly in a weather system could throw all the assumptions and predictions about the developing weather dramatically awry. Second, nonlinear dynamics have established that the world is not orderly or predictable. It is impossible to begin with Skinner's basic assumption. Third, the notion that one can "fix" something so it is like new is based on the assumption of a reversible world. Human beings and other organic processes cannot be undone. They, like time (Davies, 1995; Prigogine, 1980), are irreversible. While the ideas noted do not encompass all of behaviorism, they do point out the underlying assumptions on which Watson and Skinner based their work. Just as we cannot observe every butterfly in the atmosphere, we cannot observe every act in a laboratory, and certainly not in a natural environment. This model of human behavior is outdated. People are not machines (Bütz, et al., 1996), and they have never been machines. It was simply one way to attempt to view human behavior.

There were few theoretical options available to psychotherapists during the middle of this century which connoted a more organic, holistic, and open systems view of human nature. As will be discussed in Chapter 7, the humanistic and existential schools of thought arose out of the disparity those theorists perceived between existing psychological theories and the experiences of their clients. Humanist theories were established on philosophical grounds and based on what was adaptive in human behavior.

At roughly the same time, another model was also developing. Systems theory emerged from several different places, but the message was the same: communication is important. How these theorists came to understand the dynamics of communication, and the family as a "system" have noticeable roots in the scientific models of this century. Elsewhere (Bütz, et al., 1996), it has been proposed that from its inception, family systems therapy has evolved through five paradigm changes. Here, we will briefly review two of these paradigms and note for the reader that Bateson, Jackson, Haley, and Weakland's theory on the double bind

(1956), in part, came out of their investigations of Whitehead and Russell's theory of logical types (1927) and Korzybski's notions about map territories (1948). Those ideas challenged these theorists to re-think communication dynamics in terms of paradoxical communication. The two paradigms that we will explore are cybernetic theory (Wiener, 1961) and general systems theory (von Bertalanffy, 1968).

Jay Haley (1959) was one of the first to explore the implications of cybernetic theory for family therapy, having worked with his colleagues in Palo Alto on these and other ideas (Bateson, 1972). Basic to cybernetics was the notion of feedback in mechanical systems (Wiener, 1961), and how through differences in feedback, communication is changed. While feedback will be specifically discussed in Chapter 16, the notion was to move from paradoxes in communication (Bateson, et al., 1956) to a pattern consisting of positive and negative communication. Affirming types of communication and negating types of communication both constitute feedback. For example, someone might say "the sunset is pretty," and another person responds "yes it is." This is a positive feedback loop, where one message affirms the other. Hence, the notion of feedback loops moved out of mechanical science and into human communication.

Still, there was a basic problem with this analogy. It is mechanical and compares humans to closed system models. Binary communication can only go two ways whereas human communication is much more complicated (as will be explored further in Chapter 5). The common analogy was that of a thermostat, which switched on when the sensor was either too hot or too cold and used that information as feedback to regulate the system. Nevertheless, this took systems theorists a step further down the road of uncovering family system dynamics. The next step, general systems theory, returns the clinician to familiar territory. The analogy is not of machine, but that of biological development. In actuality, it is more a leap than a step.

Ludwig von Bertalanffy's (1968) theory of general systems was introduced to clinicians when Watzlawick, Beavin, and Jackson integrated the concept into family therapy in their book, *Pragmatics of Human Communication* (1967). The key to general systems theory was that it was based on the premise that biological organisms are very different from machines because they transform. What von Bertalanffy's work did was move social scientists from a model of machines back to a model of biological life forms. As noted, life forms evolve and become more complicated with time, whereas machines, once produced, decay with time. As a result, von Bertalanffy proposed two states for biological life forms—steady and transformative states. Steady states referred to more stable, and yet evolutionary, periods of existence where systems continue to develop even though they have the appearance of stability. Transformative states connote an entirely different process where systems became unstable in their evolution, and through this instability, the system transforms. Watzlawick and his colleagues believed that families also made themselves over again in the face of environmental stressors through the act of communication. Families transform through communication. With the inclusion of this model, we begin to approximate the human condition where we make ourselves over again; we transform. Those periods in our lives where we feel that we "know ourselves" are steady states. But, those periods in our lives that seem to dominate, where we are struggling with who we are or who we will become, are transformative states. For us, these descriptions begin to sound more like the clients with whom we work.

Even with the great advantages brought about by general systems theory, there was one weakness—it did not describe transformative states very well. It was presented as though, "we know the transformative states are there, but we don't know what they look like." This is exactly where chaos, complexity, and the new physics come into the picture. These theories explain the process of transformation, its shape, its evolutionary path. Describing the process of transformation from a number of different philosophical and theoretical perspectives is what the remainder of this book offers.

REFERENCES

Baars, B. J. (1986). *The cognitive revolution in psychology.* New York: The Guilford Press.

Bateson, G., Jackson, D. D., Haley, J., & Weakland, J. H. (1956). Toward a theory of schizophrenia. *Behavioral Science, 1*(4), 251–264.

Bateson, G. (1972). *Steps to an ecology of mind.* New York: Ballantine.

Bettelheim, B. (1982). *Freud and man's soul.* New York: Vintage.

Briggs, J., & Peat, F. D. (1989). *Turbulent mirror.* New York: Harper & Row.

Bütz, M. R. (1992). The fractal nature of the development of the Self. *Psychological Reports, 71,* 1043–1063.

Bütz, M. R. (1997). *Chaos and complexity, implications for psychological theory and therapy.* Washington, DC: Taylor & Francis.

Bütz, M. R., Chamberlain, L., & McCown, W. G. (1997). *Strange attractors: Chaos, complexity, and the art of family therapy.* New York: John Wiley & Sons.

Carson, C. R., & Butcher, J. N. (1992). *Abnormal psychology and modern life* (9th ed.). New York: Harper Collins.

Davies, P. (1995). *About time: Einstein's unfinished revolution.* New York: Simon & Schuster.

Elkaïm, M. (1990). *If you love me, don't love me.* New York: Basic Books.

Ellenberger, H. F. (1970). *The discovery of the unconscious: The history and evolution of dynamic psychiatry.* New York: Basic Books.

Freedheim, D. K. (1992). *History of psychotherapy: A century of change.* Washington, DC: American Psychological Association.

Freud, S. (1900). *The interpretation of dreams.* New York: Modern Library.

Freud, S. (1914). *The standard edition of the complete psychological works of Sigmund Freud.* London: The Hogarth Press.

Haley, J. (1959). The family of the schizophrenic: A model system. *Journal of Neuroses and Mental Diseases, 129,* 357–374.

Hall, C. S. (1954). *A primer of Freudian psychology.* New York: Mentor.

Hall, C. S., & Lindzey, G. (1978). *Theories of personality.* New York: John Wiley & Sons.

Hoffman, L. (1981). *Foundations of family therapy: A conceptual framework for systems change.* New York: Basic Books.

Jung, C. G. (1966a). *The practice of psychotherapy.* (Hull, R. F. C., Trans.). (2nd ed.). Princeton, NJ: Princeton University Press.

Jung, C. G. (1966b). *Two essays on analytical psychology.* (Hull, R. F. C., Trans.). (2nd ed.). Princeton, NJ: Princeton University Press.

Jung, C. G. (1969). *The structure and dynamics of the psyche.* (Hull, R. F. C., Trans.). (2nd ed.). Princeton, NJ: Princeton University Press.

Jung, C. G. (1971). *Psychological types* (Hull, R. F. C., Trans.). Princeton, NJ: Princeton University Press.

Koch, S. (1959). *Psychology: A study of a science.* New York: McGraw-Hill.

Korzybski, A. (1948). On structure. In A. Korzybski (Ed.), *Science and sanity.* Lakeville, CT: International Non-Aristotelian Library Publishing Company.

Kuhn, T. S. (1962/1970). *The structure of scientific revolutions.* (2nd Ed.). Chicago: University of Chicago Press.

Lorenz, E. N. (1963). Deterministic nonperiodic flow. *Journal of Atmospheric Sciences, 20,* 130–141.

Mahoney, M. J. (1991). *Human change processes: The scientific foundations of psychotherapy.* New York: Basic Books.

McGuire, W. (1974). *The Freud/Jung letters.* Princeton, NJ: Princeton University Press.

Ornstein, R. E., & Carsten, L. (1991). *Psychology: The study of human experience* (3rd ed.). New York: Harcourt Brace Jovanovich.

Prigogine, I. (1980). *From being to becoming: Time and complexity in the physical sciences.* San Francisco, CA: W. H. Freeman & Sons.

Prigogine, I., & Stengers, I. (1984). *Order out of chaos.* New York: Bantam Books.

Selvini-Palazzoli, M., Boscolo, L., Cecchin, G., & Prata, G. (1978). *Paradox and counterparadox: A new model in the therapy of the family in schizophrenic transaction.* Northvale NJ: Jason Aronson.

Skinner, B. F. (1953). *Science and human behavior.* New York: Macmillan.

Vandervert, L. (1996). Introduction. *Journal of Mind and Behavior, in press.*

von Bertalanffy, L. (1968). *General system theory: Foundations, development, applications.* New York: Braziller.

Watson, J. B. (1914). *Behavior: An introduction to comparative psychology.* New York: Henry Holt.

Watson, J. B. (1925). *Behaviorism.* New York: W.W. Norton & Co.

Watzlawick, P., Beavin, J., & Jackson, D. D. (1967). *Pragmatics of human communication.* New York: W. W. Norton & Co.

Whitehead, A. N., & Russell, B. (1927). *Principia mathematica* (2nd ed.). New York: Cambridge University Press.

Wiener, N. (1961). *Cybernetics, or control and communication in the animal and the machine.* (2nd ed.). New York: John Wiley & Sons, Inc.

Part Two

Chaos Theory and Clinical Orientations

In Part II (Chapters 3 through 7), we re-enter familiar territory via the paths of various clinical orientations. Now, the similarities and relevance that chaos theory offers these perspectives on behavior is the focus of our exploration. The editors have attempted to provide as many "friendly" paths as possible, given the variety of perspectives on human behavior and interaction that are common ground for clinicians. Of course, neither Freud nor Jung were acquainted with the concepts described in Part 1 of this book. Neither are most of the clinicians and theoreticians who founded some of the primary orientations that are basic to clinical training. It is our experience, however, that an understanding of nonlinear dynamics has enhanced and broadened the perspectives of many clinical orientations, including analytic, cognitive, humanistic, and systemic paradigms.

Notably, not all orientations have a good "fit" with chaos dynamics. In our experience, the traditional behaviorist model clearly belongs in the Newtonian, empirical science camp. That is the intrinsic foundation for behaviorism. Perhaps that explains some of the loss of popularity of the behaviorist paradigm: it isn't a good fit with complex, nonlinear, dynamic systems. The editors believe that human behavior is definitely in the realm of the new science of complexity and not that of reductionistic, empirical science.

We trust that readers will now begin to see an emergence of the new science in their once familiar territory. For us, it has enhanced and enlarged the scope of our vision and awareness. Enjoy the view.

Chapter 3

Chaos Theory and Psychoanalysis

Michael G. Moran

Researchers and theorists have begun to apply the principles of chaos theory to the study of mental phenomena, but at this time those efforts tend to be more metaphorical than concrete (Berge, Pomeau & Vidal, 1984; Eder & Remold, 1992; Hauge, 1993; Hoppensteadt, 1989; Kaplan & Cohen, 1990; McKenna, McMullen & Shlesinger, 1994; Nandrino et al., 1994; Roschke & Aldenhoff, 1992; Tritton, 1986; Tsonis & Tsonis, 1989; Wang, Pichler, & Ross, 1990). This chapter describes several scenarios in which certain metaphors of chaos theory may expand and inform clinical thinking in the psychodynamic domain, including pattern recognition, the effects of stress on defensive structure, and an understanding of the mutative effects of therapy.

This chapter aims to provide an introduction to nonlinear systems, examine the basis for seeing the mind as a nonlinear system, look at some applications in related life sciences, and cast ahead to possible research directions for chaos theory and psychoanalysis.

AN OVERVIEW OF NONLINEAR SYSTEMS

Nonlinear systems are those which are best modeled by differential equations, which are formulas that can account for the *interaction* of a system's components. The behavior of such systems can be represented fully only by such an approach, as opposed to a *summation* of the individual behaviors of its parts. There is a body of knowledge and methodology by which the nature of the apparent disorder in the evolution of certain systems, called nonlinear systems, may actually be understood as quite determined, and by rather simple underlying principles. Despite the variety of "actual matter" of the systems under study, they have analogous behavioral characteristics that can be modeled by the new science. There are several paradigms in the literature on chaos theory that have definite implications for psychoanalytic thought. These specific paradigms include *sensitivity to initial conditions, nonperiodicity, scaling, transitional states*, and *strange attractors*.

Sensitivity to Initial Conditions

As noted in Chapter One, in the evolution of a nonlinear system, tiny alterations in the beginning conditions produce profound alterations in the specifics of behavior. The principle of the "butterfly effect" (a popular title for sensitivity to initial conditions) attempts to put into words a great potential for going "off course" shown by perturbed nonlinear systems: minute changes may produce widely variant results.

Nonperiodicity

Nonlinear systems show little in the way of behavior that is exactly repetitive, or *periodic*. On a large scale of magnification, there may be recognizable patterns, but on close inspection, these systems do not repeat: they are aperiodic or *nonperiodic*. Meteorology provides an example in yearly patterns of temperature: although summers may "repeat" in that they are always warmer than other times of the year, the temperature on, say, July 16th will rarely be exactly the same from year to year, even if determined in the same geographic location. Nonperiodicity becomes more apparent at an even higher level of magnification. At 11:13 a.m. on July 16th in any given location, there would likely be an even greater variation from year to year: greater evidence of nonperiodicity. Large scale nonperiodicity confers a recognizable character to the system. But when examined in detail, on high magnification, no periodicity is seen. Nonperiodicity and sensitive dependence on initial conditions have important implications for understanding and anticipating the future behavior of a nonlinear system.

Scaling

When nonlinear systems are represented graphically, other characteristics become apparent. As the level of magnification changes, certain shapes may recur, irrespective of the dimension. The degree of magnification can be increased, but always with the recurrence of the original pattern—infinite and repeating detail filling what may at first seem to be empty space. As with Russian toy dolls, the endless repetition continues. An example comes from the field of fluid dynamics. When one examines the bottom of a creek bed through clear water, one can often see the familiar pattern of furrows, sculpted by the stream's current. The dimensions of the entire design may occupy only a few inches. When looking down on a cloud cover from the window of an airplane, the same pattern appears: sculpted furrows, again shaped by a "stream," but this time, one with power and magnitude perhaps millions of times the strength and scope of the forces operating in the river-stream bed. Same pattern, vastly different scope. Such self-similarity in stable, idiosyncratic forms, recognizable at different scales of examination is called *scaling*.

Transitional States

Nonlinear systems are capable of changing their state with the application of various kinds of energy. Examples include laminar flow turning into turbulent flow (fluid dynamics), conductor to superconductor (thermodynamics and electromagnetic theory), and nonmagnet to magnet (electromagnetic theory) (Gleick, 1987). Such changes in state are called the transition to chaos. As the transition occurs, there is often a dissipation of energy from a usable to a less usable form, as when, because of friction, the energy of motion turns into the energy of heat (Hofstadter, 1981).

Chaos theory can replicate some of the qualities of the transitional state, as well as some of the quantitatively measurable aspects of the event, such as the timing of onset and the rate of development of turbulence, or its analogue, in a system (Feigenbaum, 1980). For example, there are mathematically demonstrable similarities between the *transitional states* of a fluid undergoing the transition to turbulence, and an electromagnetic domain undergoing magnetization, even though the objects under inspection are vastly different (fluid and metal).

Those transitional states offer an occasion for the appearance of sensitive dependence on initial conditions. Consider the course of two paper cups floating on the surface of the water, upstream from a waterfall. Above the falls, assume the flow to be regular. The two cups would, if placed close together, float along in parallel and relatively predictable lines. However, as the stream passes over the falls, additional energy is released as the water is acted upon by gravity. That energy drives the system to a state transition and the behavior becomes turbulent. The transition to turbulence exhibits chaotic dynamics, and the cups that were adjacent to each other above the falls will very soon be driven apart in an unpredictable manner. In a second run of the experiment, and with only small changes in the initial placement of the cups above the falls, the resulting below-falls positions of the cups would be incalculably different compared to those of the first run. This is sensitive dependence on initial conditions.

The reader may wonder whether what is lacking in this predictive task is simply a computer of adequate power, or measuring instruments of accuracy adequate to permit better determinations of the positions above-falls. Could observers not then successfully predict downstream, below-falls behavior and cup location? Is the problem described only a practical one, some day to be solved by an evolution of computer power and measurement capacity? The answer is "no." Chaos imposes limitations on the ability to predict the behavior of certain kinds of systems, and this limitation is one that will never be overcome (as noted in Chapter One). Kellert (1993) provides an excellent discussion of the relevant scientific philosophy.

Strange attractors

The graphic representations of nonlinear systems may be familiar to any reader who has come across pictures of fractals, or of their geometric cousins, *strange attractors*. Fractals are stacks of two-dimensional sheets displaying a self-similar packing structure, and when rendered into computerized color pictures, they unfurl a crystalline, convoluted ornateness that has come to be associated with the field of chaos.

Strange attractors bear a close relationship to fractals in that they are graphic, but also have a temporal dimension. Fractals are static representations; strange attractors (as noted in Chapter One) exhibit the mathematically generated behavior of a system over time, and show fractal geometry. That is, they appear to be layered on the two dimensional page in a manner that suggests an attempt to eke out one more dimension (for example, more than two, less than three, thus a fragmental dimension). No actual chaotic system could ever be perfectly represented by such a model because of the principle of sensitive dependence. Strange attractors, however, allow researchers the opportunity to model the spatial and geometric aspects of a system for a qualitative appreciation of its nature.

Any nonlinear system with *dissipative* characteristics will have a strange attractor. The forces driving the system are countered by ones that are dissipative. An everyday example would be the dissipative force of friction working against the momentum of a simple pendulum (Tritton, 1986). As the friction increases, especially late in the decay phases of a pendulum's cycle, chaotic behavior appears (even with a simple pendulum), and can be modeled with a strange attractor.

The attractor is a spatial representation of the modeled path of the system, with each point's coordinates accounting for some quantitative aspect of the system at that moment. As the characteristic changes, the point moves and describes a line or curve. The force of the attractor works in a somewhat opposing manner to sensitive dependence, attracting the system's activity toward itself. At infinite time the attractor acts as the asymptotic limit on the influence of initial conditions.

THE MIND AS A NONLINEAR SYSTEM

Although mental phenomena may intuitively seem to fall within the domain of nonlinear systems, it is important to examine those phenomena that suggest such a conclusion. If within mental phenomena, nonlinear interaction of variables, sensitive dependence on initial conditions, nonperiodicity, scaling, transitional states, and strange attractors are evidenced, it is fair to assume that the mind is a system for which nonlinear differential equations could be useful in creating qualitative models of behavior. The discussion that follows is of necessity a metaphorical one. Without quantifiable variables that can be plotted and examined, the mathematical proofs of chaotic phenomena and the existence of strange attractors must wait.

Most psychoanalytic models of the mind assume an interdependence to mental phenomena. The psychoanalyst, and any other psychodynamic clinician, takes for granted the interactive nature of the various affective, verbal, and motoric manifestations of mental activity that the patient displays or relates to him in any session (Moran, 1991). For a working construction of the patient's mental presentation, the clinician must consider these variables and many more, and the manner in which they affect each other. A simple "adding up" of the manifest activities would produce an inadequate or stilted picture of the patient. No case conference participant could accept a "sum" of behaviors as a realistic portrait of a patient. When listening to or reading such a presentation, clinicians always listen for and expect of the presenter some kind of assessment which takes into account, for example, how the patient reacted to awareness of his own affective state, and how affect impinged on motor behavior in the session. What comment within the session led to what mood? How did that memory arise from the combination of both the mood and the body posture?

The model of the mind that most closely approximates linearity, although it is only an approximation, is that topographic, which does emphasize a summation of unconscious pressures on the mind, with a kind of resulting vector of behavior, affect, or verbalization. Mental activity, from this perspective, is related in an almost linear fashion to the distance of the operative mental content from consciousness. But even this attempt to find linearity is hopelessly reductionistic. Most clinicians would be unsatisfied with an explanation of patient behavior that failed to take into account both the unconscious and conscious *interactions* of mental forces. One can reasonably conclude an interactive tendency of the mind.

Sensitive dependence on initial conditions seems to be a characteristic of historical objects (Gould, 1983), and history itself (Kellert, 1993). Even though "history books teem with examples of small events that led to momentous and long-lasting changes in the course of human affairs" (Kellert, 1993), therapists may still cling to the notion that they do not have to account for small amounts of vagueness in the measurements of a system's behavior. Such clinging leads to the belief that human behavior can be fractionated as a collection of individual entities with nonrelational properties, and, can thus be successfully specified as to allow useful prediction.

Most clinicians would agree that a "useful" prediction of very specific mental phenomena is so difficult that when able to make one, they are surprised. From the seemingly small events in a patient's developmental history, to the contemporary events in the therapeutic process and current life, the abundant sensitivity of behavior to initial (or, in the real-time clinical sense, "ongoing") conditions is apparent. Even when colored by neurotic interpretation, clinicians often believe that patient who says, "If only she had accepted my offer, my life would be different!" Even without grandiose regard for our own interpretations, we can claim to see changes in a patient for whom an interpretation was well-timed and well-dosed.

The *near*-periodicity of mental phenomena often brings the patient to treatment. The neurosis, with its repetitively operating fantasies driving behavior, affect, and perception, create the "stuck" experience, the sense of meaninglessness and frustration, or their variations, which bring many patients to a psychotherapist. The neurosis might be seen as acting like a strange attractor in mental life. Neurosis pulls the system toward repetition, gives behavior some of its predictability, and contributes to the "shape" of a personality. Because of the princi-

ple of sensitive dependence, the neurosis cannot generate perfectly repetitive behavior: the minutiae of mental life are too numerous, and their eventual influence
too great because of their multiplicative effects, for mental life to be completely
predictable. Indeed, that property of the multiplying effects of sensitive dependence is enough to make "intractably complicated behavior ... appear even in
mathematically simple systems" (Kellert, 1993).

Evidence of *scaling* appears in the self-similarity of mental processes of the
patient (and the therapist–patient dyad) at several levels of magnification. Recurrence of patterns is the bread-and-butter of psychodynamic psychology. The idiosyncratic "signature" of a patient's personality shows itself in the broad sweep
of the synopsized case history (perhaps the lowest level of magnification), within
the conduct of a single session's summarized activity, within the defensive and
expressive activities of a dream, and even down to the level of a single slip (a high
level of magnification) (Moran, 1991).

The *transitional states* of chaos theory have referents within psychoanalysis.
An example of one kind of non-incremental change in the therapeutic context
occurs during the achievement of insight. The patient, with a certain suddenness,
feels different to the clinician, and often to himself. Rarely is there a gradual
accumulation of insight, or a sense that the patient is moving across a smooth
spectrum toward increased awareness (Moran, 1991). Rather, it is a qualitative
change in the patient's state. Located within different levels of abstraction one
can also note changes in ego state ("state" obviously having distinct but similar
meanings depending upon the context), and in self and other representations. The
essential feature of this capacity of dynamic nonlinear systems is the thorough
qualitative change in the system. As can be understood from the examples (and
there could be many others) a patient-system may have many different states of
relatively stable behavior. State change need not always connote clinical disorder
or disorganization.

Therapists actually rely on the presence of nonperiodicity and the principle
of sensitive dependence as bases for hope and constructions of the potential for
change. The patient is not doomed; smaller or larger differences in experience,
understanding, insight, self-object functions (and many other kinds of forces),
can make a difference. Indeed, the patient may be surprised by the realization that
any sense of inevitable repetition is itself only one more fantasy to be understood,
because *exact repetition is impossible.*

The forces of psychic determinism thus operate through the momentum of
the past history and the relatively stable collection of defense and operating fantasies (regarding self, object, the functioning of the world, fate, and many others).
Such forces operate to attract the patient's behavior, feelings, and perceptions
toward certain events and outcomes that have global predictability. Mr. X demonstrates obsessive behavior today, and will likely demonstrate such behavior—to
the point that he will still be recognizable as himself—even a year from now.
Those forces may one day be modeled with a strange attractor, and allow a level of

pattern recognition and qualitative experimental prediction that for now remains metaphorical and behavioral.

The perturbations created by interpretations, insight gained, empathy experienced, and even of increased awareness alter the trajectory of the patient's mental phenomena. A series of events experienced consciously is not the same as when experienced unconsciously. Even the passage of time alters the patient, alters everyone. The patient here today is not the patient who will show up for tomorrow's session, and she will not have exactly the same therapist. Even that insight can be liberating (and, of course, terrifying), and that therapeutic and existential fact is predicated on sensitive dependence and nonperiodicity.

Let us look specifically at metaphorically modeling mental phenomena with the principles of chaos theory. Using the model of a strange attractor of a patient's mental system activity, one can speculate about how neurosis acts on the system, and how to use interpretations and the experience of the therapy to counter that action. Neurotic (or chronic characterologic) behavior acts as an attractor that pulls the system toward less dimensionality—that is, toward more stereotypy. The evolving activity of such a mental strange attractor would appear in the form of a tendency to lose dimensions. A three-dimensional attractor might develop into a two- or one-dimensional attractor. The experiences of stress or anxiety, or any other intensely dysphoric mood might also act in this same way, driving the system toward a less complex, less sophisticated version of itself. The altered strange attractor might then appear less complex. This happens with any person under stress: everyone becomes a caricature of himself. The reduced complexity of the strange attractor's geometry is the spatial analogue of what is experienced with the patient: less trust, less creativity, less self-tolerance, or less of whatever trait tends to vanish most quickly for that patient as he adopts a simplistic way of experiencing himself and the world.

THERAPEUTIC ACTION

Could a strange attractor serve also as a model of the therapeutic action of psychoanalysis? With our efforts at creating a safe therapeutic environment, clinicians hope to enable the patient to experience himself, the therapeutic relationship, and the world in a progressively less defensive manner, and thus allow the chance for novel experiences. Therapeutic interventions, in whatever form they take, may all be seen as continually trying to perturb the patient's experience just enough to promote a gain in consciousness. Clinicians adjust the dosage and timing of interventions in hopes of reducing the threats that come with being awakened: threats of humiliation, sadness, loss, or of novelty itself. A patient who is relatively awake to new experience may then assimilate it and be less frightened by the possibility of its future enactment, since its threatening meaning will have been changed ever so slightly by the therapeutic episode.

If the patient—the "system"—is represented by a strange attractor, its lines describe paths and a shape in phase space that display the ongoing expression of clinical dimensions on which to focus. *Phase space* is "the space whose axes are the coordinates of [the clinical dimensions]" and within that space is a "*phase trajectory* which is a curve . . . representing the evolution of the system" (Berge, 1984). Thus, in a three-dimensional attractor one might graph the evolving interrelationship between measurements of (1) a patient's affective state, (2) transference hostility, and (3) volume of speech (leaving aside for the moment the non-trivial tasks of giving these variables measurable values!). Any three variables could be picked, as long as they are quantifiable. One might decide to make measurements, and plot points in phase space every five minutes thereafter, or at the beginning of every session, or at the end to the narration of every dream. As long as there was a consistent nature to the interval, the representation would have coherent meaning. With enough time and points, a shape would eventually appear: the strange attractor for that patient. The study of the geometry of the attractor (its topology) gives a qualitative grasp of the patient's behavior, and that geometry would be idiosyncratic and recognizable for that patient. Points lying on paths very close to each other, if followed over time, would eventually diverge and trace widely disparate paths, thus displaying sensitive dependence. That trait (nonperiodicity) would make exactly repeating paths nonexistent, but the overall "picture" of the patient from the attractor would tend to remain recognizable over time. There would also be blank space on the graph, without points or tracings. That is, the distribution of tracings would not be random or scattered throughout phase space. Most of the paths and points would be confined to a space near the attractor.

Theoretically, one could predict that the study of the effects of therapeutic interventions would show a gain in complexity by the strange attractor of the patient over time. The increased complexity takes the form of a strange attractor that fills more of phase space (a topological assessment), corresponding to greater stability of the personality. For any given moment, the point representing the activity of the system would be at a coordinate whose volume in phase space had been increased as a result of therapy. Even with those therapeutically-induced changes, the system retains its recognizable shape. There is still an operating attractor: the system has not become random or erratic even though it is now more complex and unpredictable. Some interventions might be predicted to be so intense as to produce a state transition that manifests chaotic behavior. Pathologic forces would exert dissipative effects, and the dimensional complexity of the patient's strange attractor would decrease during such phases.

In order to accurately model this kind of evolution and change, one would need (1) a selection of valid dimensions of mental activity along which to measure change over a large number of time points, and (2) a quantitatively valid measure of the activity in those dimensions. If such capacities were available, it might be possible to experimentally model the transition of state changes, such as "without insight" to "having insight," or "without object constancy" to "having object constancy," or "positive transference" to "negative transference." Each transition might display chaotic features: period doubling, followed by apparently erratic and highly complex trajectories, as the researcher experimentally varies the parameter under study.

It is important to note that "chaos" has no inherent psychological bias in this context. There is no "good chaos" and no "bad chaos," there is only "chaos"— part of the transition between certain states for nonlinear systems. The clinical and experiential implications of the dimensions under study would determine whether there were associated adverse or positive emotional consequences of the state transition.

PSYCHOLOGICAL STUDIES INFORMED BY CHAOS THEORY

Studies in psychological and psychoanalytic applications of chaos theory remain predominantly conceptual, but some are worth special mention (Bütz, 1992). Galatzer-Levy (1978) conducted an early exploration of the interrelationship between complex mathematics and psychoanalysis that assessed the utility of mathematical models of the mind. Spruiell's (1993) paper is a thoughtful and thorough examination of the sciences of complexity, and places psychoanalysis squarely among them. The term "chaos" retains an unfortunate connotation associated with *dis*-order and, by implication in a psychological context, with psychopathological states. This connotation may account for what appears to be a recurrent emphasis on equating deterministic chaotic phenomena with adverse clinical manifestations, such as "a state of overwhelming anxiety", and the appearance of such questions as "is there chaos in schizophrenia?" (Schmid, 1991).

Pediaditakis (1992) suggests that borderline states reflect the "emergence of a pathological order as the system becomes an oscillating one", an interesting metaphorical construction, consistent with cardiologic and electroencephalographic models of pathophysiology that have a mathematical basis, as described in Doyon (1992) and Garfinkel, Spano, Ditto, and Weiss (1992). Another group that also takes a metaphorical tack concludes that chaos theory reveals both normal development and chaos theory to be creative processes open to chance, choice, and meaningful coincidences and governed by harmonious and conflictual interactions between opposites (Sabelli & Carlson, 1991).

One author uses the concepts of self-similarity and scaling in a metaphorical application of Daniel Stern's (Stern, 1987) *representations of interactions that become generalized* (RIGs) (Lonie, 1991). Lonie understands RIGs to occur at various levels of enactment and various levels of magnification, and attempts to integrate the notion of RIGs with information theory to facilitate modeling in psychotherapy efficacy research. Another group uses the concept of bifurcations from chaos theory to inform a re-reading of Freud, and thereby, to expand our understanding of repetition compulsion and transference (Priel & Schreiber, 1994).

There have been a few mathematically-based approaches to psychotherapy using nonlinear dynamics. Redington and Reidbord (1992) have analyzed autonomic nervous system activity in a psychotherapy session, and assert the establishment of nonlinear characteristics of chaos in the patient's cardiac activity. This finding was not new. However, they went on to identify chaotic behavior in heart rate patterns associated with psychologically meaningful events. This discovery suggests the existence of a "psychophysiologic attractor."

Langs and Badalamenti (1994) sought chaotic attractors in their examinations of the "how" of communication within sessions. Their interest lies in the process and manner, rather than the content, of communicative exchange. A "deep determinism" emerged that they were able to characterize as "laws" governing human communication.

CONCLUSIONS

These exciting explorations suggest we are on the way to the clarification of useful principles of modeling psychotherapeutic behavior, both of the patient and therapist, with the advent of chaos theory. Nonlinear dynamics may offer psychoanalysis a bounty of riches by providing the basic elements for constructing useful theoretical models. Psychoanalysis, a science that has been long considered "nebulous" and "soft" seems now to be taking its place alongside a number of sciences of the inanimate and animate worlds that are best modeled by chaos theory. The continued integration of psychoanalysis with chaos theory may ultimately equip researchers with the tools for models on which innovative qualitative experiments may be conducted and allow novel insights into mental phenomena.

REFERENCES

Berge, P., Pomeau, Y., & Vidal, C. (1984). *Order within chaos: Towards a deterministic approach to turbulence.* (Laurette Tuckerman, Trans.). New York: John Wiley & Sons.

Bütz, M. R. (1992). Chaos, an omen of transcendence in the psychotherapeutic process. *Psychological Reports, 71*, 827–843.

Doyon, B. (1992). On the existence and the role of chaotic processes in the nervous system. *Acta Biotheoretica, 40*(2–3), 113–119.

Eder, J., & Rembold, H. (1992). Biosemiotics—a paradigm of biology. Biological signalling on the verge of deterministic chaos. *Naturwissenschaften, 79*(2), 60–67.

Feigenbaum, M. J. (1980, Summer). Universal behavior in nonlinear systems. *Los Alamos Science, 1*, 4–27.

Galatzer-Levy, R. (1978). Qualitative change from quantitative change: Mathematical catastrophe theory in relation to psychoanalysis. *Journal of the American Psychoanalytic Association, 26*(4), 921–935.

Garfinkel, A., Spano, M. L., Ditto, W. L., & Weiss, J. N. (1992). Controlling cardiac chaos. *Science, 257*(5074), 1230–1235.

Gleick, J. (1987). *Chaos: Making a new science.* New York: Viking Press.

Gould, S. J. (1983). Quick lives and quirky changes. In *Hen's teeth and horse's toes* (pp. 56–65). New York: W. W. Norton & Co.

Hauge, A. (1993). Chaos and fractals: Are these of interest to medical science? *Tidsskrift for Den Norske Laegeforening, 113*(30), 3678–3685.

Hofstadter, D. R. (1981). Mathematical themas: Strange attractor: Mathematical patterns delicately poised between order and chaos. *Scientific American, 245*(5), 22–43.

Hoppensteadt, F. C. (1989). Intermittent chaos, self-organization, and learning from synchronous synaptic activity in model neuron networks. *Proceedings of the National Academy of Science, USA, 86*(9), 2991–2995.

Kaplan, D. T., & Cohen, R. J. (1990). Is fibrillation chaos? *Circ Res, 67*(4), 886–892.

Kellert, S. H. (1993). *In the wake of chaos.* Chicago: University of Chicago Press.

Langs, R., & Badalamenti, A. (1994). Psychotherapy: The search for chaos and the discovery of determinism. *Australian & New Zealand Journal of Psychiatry, 28*(1), 68–81.

Lonie, I. (1991). Chaos theory: A new paradigm for psychotherapy? *Australian & New Zealand Journal of Psychiatry, 25*(4), 548–560.

McKenna, T. M., McMullen, T. A., & Shlesinger, M. F. (1994). The brain as a dynamic physical system. *Neuroscience, 60*(3), 587–605.

Moran, M. G. (1991). Chaos theory and psychoanalysis: the fluidic nature of the mind. *International Review of Psychoanalysis, 18*(2), 211–221.

Nandrino, J. L., Pezard, L., Martinerie, J., El, M. F., Renault, B., Jouvent, R., Allilaire, J. F., & Widlocher, D. (1994). Decrease of complexity in EEG as a symptom of depression. *Neuroreport, 5*(4), 528–530.

Pediaditakis, N. (1992). Deterministic nonlinear chaos in brain function and borderline psychopathological phenomena. *Medical Hypotheses, 39*(1), 67–72.

Priel, B., & Schreiber, G. (1994). On psychoanalysis and non-linear dynamics: The paradigm of bifurcation. *British Journal of Medical Psychology.*

Redington, D. J., & Reidbord, S. P. (1992). Chaotic dynamics in autonomic nervous system activity of a patient during a psychotherapy session. *Biological Psychiatry, 31*(10), 993–1007.

Roschke, J., & Aldenhoff, J. B. (1992). A nonlinear approach to brain function: Deterministic chaos and sleep EEG. *Sleep, 15*(2), 95–101.

Sabelli, H. C., & Carlson, S. L. (1991). Process theory as a framework for comprehensive psychodynamic formulations. *Genetic, Social & General Psychology Monographs, 117*(1), 5–27.

Schmid, G. B. (1991). Chaos theory and schizophrenia: Elementary aspects. *Psychopathology, 24*(4), 185–198.

Skinner, J., Molnar, M., Vybiral, T., & Mitra, M. (1992). Application of chaos theory to biology and medicine. *Integrative Physiological & Behavioral Science.*

Spruiell, V. (1993). Deterministic chaos and the sciences of complexity: Psychoanalysis in the midst of a scientific revolution. *Journal of the American Psychoanalytic Association, 41*(1), 3–44.

Stern, D. (1987). *The representational world of the infant.* New York: Basic Books.

Tritton, D. (1986). Chaos in the swing of a pendulum. *New Scientist, 24*, 37–40.

Tsonis, P. A., & Tsonis, A. A. (1989). Chaos: Principles and implications in biology. *Computer Applications in Bioscience, 5*(1), 27–32.

Wang, L. P., Pichler, E. E., & Ross, J. (1990). Oscillations and chaos in neural networks: An exactly solvable model. *Proceedings of the National Academy of Science, USA, 87*(23), 9467–9471.

Chapter 4

Chaos, Energy, and Analytical Psychology

Michael R. Bütz

"It is the spirit of the chaotic waters of the beginning, before the second day of Creation, before the separation of opposites and hence before the advent of consciousness. That is why it leads those whom it overcomes neither upwards nor beyond, but back into chaos."

(Jung, 1970, p. 252)

Indeed, we have returned to chaos, ostensibly not in its mythological form, but through the doorway of scientific inquiry in regard to energy and transformation. A host of theories have been titled chaos theory (Gleick, 1987; Yorke, 1975), and share the stage with similar notions about nonlinear dynamics such as complexity theory (Kauffman, 1995; Waldrop, 1992) and the new physics (Davies, 1989). But, chaos theory, and the fresh approaches that have followed, harken this culture back to the notion of chaos as a mythological concept and one that describes the dynamics inherent in energy transformation (Bütz, 1995a). While these comparisons may not be as precise as others, as spanning the vast distance in this culture between science and myth is an arduous enterprise, nonetheless an analogical journey into this material will be traversed as even the scientific application of these notions to modern psychotherapy is tenuous (Bütz, Chamberlain, & McCown, 1997; Burlingame & Hope, 1996; Burlingame & Bloch, 1996). So, it is here at this crossroad between science and mythology, that recollections about Carl Gustav Jung's theory of Analytical Psychology come to mind.

As Jung went about the business of developing his ideas on Analytical Psychology, one central concern was energy. He was interested in the dynamics of energy within the psychic system, how it emerged, how it was channeled, how it was transformed. Early in the development of his theory he looked to the science of his day for examples of how other fields were dealing with the issue of energy.

Like Freud (1900, 1949),[1] he relied on contemporary models to explain how these dynamics unfold (Jung, 1969). In this vein, Jung even went so far as to consult with the eminent quantum physicist Wolfgang Pauli (Jung, 1969, pp. 437–440, 963; 1959, Vol. 9, p. ii) in these deliberations. Yet, despite the depth of his inquiry into the matter of energy, contemporary models proved insufficient to describe the dynamics he was witnessing in his patients. The outcome was Jung turning away from the scientific theory of his day, and instead directing his attention toward mythology for answers (1969). A common theme arose out of his studies in this area, that chaos preceded transformation, and that chaos was the prima materia of creation. There, an entirely different set of possibilities opened to him, which ultimately were described in his theories on the collective unconscious and archetypes. Still, it was his inquiries into the arena of myths that captures one's attention when considering Analytical Psychology, chaos, and complexity theory.

Like other scientists, Jung found the scientific models of his day limiting, and searched for a way to elucidate the dynamics he was observing in his clients. Chaoticians and complexologists also found themselves grappling with similar conundrums, and sought better heuristic models that commented directly on their experience of phenomena (Bohm, 1980; Capra, 1983; Feigenbaum, 1978; Jantsch, 1980; Kauffman, 1995; Lorenz, 1963; Mandelbrot, 1977; Prigogine, 1980). And here, how Jung's path crosses with this set of theories starts to become clear. His explorations into mythology lead him to a remote and rarely trodden path by Westerners that is now becoming recognized through the host of scientific notions that comprise chaos and complexity theory as well as the new physics. The deep and penetrating heuristic that both approaches share is that of transformation through a process of nonlinearity, complexity, or chaos toward a more adaptive form of existence.

JUNG'S INQUIRIES INTO THE PAST, TO UNDERSTAND THE FUTURE

It is widely known that Jung was Freud's crown prince in the psychoanalytic movement afoot early in this century, and that it was Jung whom Freud had professedly chosen to be his successor. However, great divides rose up between these men over the issue of sexualized energy, libido (Ellenberger, 1970; Jung, 1961a; McGuire, 1974). For Jung, libido meant more than just a sexual expression (Jung, 1969, pp. 56–59; Jung, 1961b, pp. 102–128), and he knew full well that when he presented this position to Freud it would be at the cost of their relationship (Jung, 1961b, p. 167; McGuire, 1974, p. 522). But, in essence, this was the first step Jung

---

[1] But, where Jung looked to physics, Freud sought answers from the fields of biology and neurology, with which he was already familiar (Freud, 1900, pp. 598–599). The two men took different paths, but came to somewhat similar conclusions about how dynamics unfold (Bütz, 1997). Where Jung eventually sought answers in mythology, Freud continued to pursue biology and neurology deductively to find this path (1949).

made on the path that eventually led him toward mythology and the concept of *mana*.

Other changes followed, and Jung outlined his change in attitude from those in Western science to a more mythologically derived standpoint in the distinctions he makes between the "mechanistic" and "energic viewpoints" in his essay *On psychic energy* (1969). There, the Western concept of energy is interwoven with the more mythological concept of mana (Jung, 1969, pp. 123–130, 441; 1966, pp. 108, 375–380). Mana was often used interchangeably with energy, though mana was a more qualitative description, while energy was more quantitative in nature (Jung, 1969, p. 441). Robertson (1992, pp. 192–193) also points out that mana had a more archetypal/mythological connotation, than did energy. Energy was more common, while mana was reserved for descriptions of archetypal phenomena. Jung notes how mana was, in essence, a precursor to the Western concept of energy: "We cannot escape the impression that the primitive view of mana is a forerunner of our concept of psychic energy and, most probably, of energy in general" (Jung, 1969, p. 128). In making this distinction, Jung acknowledges setting off on a path divergent from the one taken up by Western science at the time. Energy or mana for Jung was not a "thing," but rather an ineffable substance that flowed through matter, in some ways akin to the notion of "chi" in Asian mythology. Still, lest Westerners attribute these somewhat odd, rather so called primitive notions to other cultures, he points out that Westerners also fall prey to this phenomena (1969, p. 341). These dynamics are indeed universal, as his theory on archetypes and the collective unconscious depicted.

By making his viewpoint clearly distinct from what he described as the "mechanistic," the one most closely aligned with the more linear view held by scientists in his day, Jung opened a path for himself to explore how energy flowed, and to think about such basic notions as cause and effect. As the reader may recognize, the notion of "synchronicity" diverges markedly from such linear notions (1969, pp. 440–441), and Jung made his feelings known on the relationships of cause, effect, and linearity:

"The causal–mechanistic view sees the sequence of facts, *a-b-c-d*, as follows: *a* causes *b*, *b* causes *c*, and so on. Here the concept of effect appears as the designation of a quality, as a 'virtue' of the cause, in other words, as a dynamism. The final–energic view, on the other hand, sees the sequence thus: *a-b-c* are means towards the transformation of energy, which flows causelessly from *a*, the improbable state, entropically to *b-c* and so to the probable state *d*" (Jung, 1969, p. 58).

Others at the time who described similar problems with the notion of a universe of linear cause and effect were the theorists working with quantum realities such as Wolfgang Pauli. So, here it becomes clear how different his notions were compared with the more mechanistic theories prominent in his day. His ideas about mana, the movement of energy, and the like, were indeed unusual for that time in Western thought. But, even more unusual were his ideas about transformation and adaptation. These ideas were more closely tied to mythology than to

Western science, and expressed a more organic notion of development not fully described until much later in the century (von Bertalanffy, 1968).

Of the mythologies Jung looked to for answers in this domain, few were explained with equal detail to those of the alchemists (Jung, 1967a). In the essay, *An account of the transference phenomena based on the illustrations to the "Rosarium Philosophorum"* (Jung, 1966), he explained the process of transformation by using what is referred to as the Rosarium Philosophorum (1550). The alchemists had laid out a developmental process that fed back on itself; it was a recursive process symbolized by the uroboros (Jung, 1968, p. 404). Though different, the representation in the stages of the Rosarium Philosophorum also connoted this type of developmental process. These processes featured the creation of new forms out of the degradation of existing forms, and metamorphosis through a mysterious process involving the transformation of energy. The alchemists' attention to the notions given in the Rosarium Philosophorum and the uroboros are not only progressive processes that bring out anxieties about death and other existential issues, but they are recursive as well, where by facing death, one is preparing for a new life.

A BRIEF ALIGNMENT OF JUNG'S UNDERSTANDING OF MYTHS WITH THE SCIENCE OF CHAOS

For the seasoned Analytical Psychologist, a great many parallels will come to mind that will not be explored here. Rather, this chapter is a substantially abridged treatment of the subject, with only rudimentary parallels delineated, given the nature of this text. With this much said, a comparison of some of the ideas in chaos theory, such as bifurcations, period-doubling routes to chaos, and self-organization, with Jung's explorations into alchemy are called for. As the reader will recall from Chapter 1, a bifurcation connotes the system diverging from its customary path, moving away from an existing order. A period-doubling route to chaos indicates that the system has continued to diverge from its accustomed path further and further with each passing moment, ultimately resulting in a state of chaos. As noted before, there is no ability to predict a system's movement in this state, nor what course it will take in the future. Yet, apparently after all of these dynamic motions away from order, in the midst of chaos, the system finds a new order, a more adaptive form of existence as it self-organizes. By careful examination, one is able to see these more scientific notions in the mythological forms presented originally by the alchemists, and prepared for the contemporary reader by Jung. By comparing the two, the value of Jung's explorations into mythology may become clear to the reader.

Taking on the notion of a bifurcation first, mythologically this was described through an individual losing touch with himself, becoming what appears to be two people. This occurs as an individual encounters unfamiliar experiences, and previously hidden aspects of himself. In such a process an individual is forced to assess those aspects of himself known already, and yet come to grips with a new form, one unfamiliar to him—some aspect of his unconscious which now presents itself. While not exact, and more generalized, Jung described one such encounter through the alchemical metaphor of the King and Queen, in the Rosarium Philosophorum.

The Rosarium Philosophorum describes ten stages of transformation, the first of which is The Mercurial Fountain, and it is "the basis of the opus" (1966, p. 402), the beginning, "the state of chaos" (1966, p. 404) from whence this process is inaugurated.[2] From this beginning, nine other stages emerge, the second of which is the King and Queen; this is the initial separation, and simultaneously, the most basic union of opposites. Basic, in that these opposites represent the masculine and feminine forms so central in Jung's theories on integrating opposite components of the personality. At the same time, however, in the representation of the King and Queen the left hands are joined, and this connotes, as Jung states the "(sinister) side is in the dark, the unconscious side" (1966, p. 410). So, not only does this stage indicate the inexorable nature of the role that the masculine and feminine aspects of personality play in differentiating, but that the roots of unconscious exploration lie here as well (Jung, 1966, pp. 422–424). In essence, a bifurcation is felt, in this mythological sense, as a divergence from the sense that one has known of the conscious ego, where that aspect of the personal unconscious is represented in the opposite sex, and the encounter with the unconscious symbolized by the joining of the King and Queen's left hands. Still, this bifurcation is not simply represented as a break with the known and an encounter with the unconscious, but rather, as a mysterious healing process also. In the representation of the King and Queen, one also needs to keep an eye on the right hands through which a complicated message is conveyed. The right hands of these figures hold what is called an "ogdoad" or a "totality, for something that is at once heavenly and earthly, spiritual or corporeal . . . that is to say in the unconscious" (Jung, 1970, Vol. 14, p. 8). This particular ogdoad is comprised of five flowers with three branches, one held by a dove, with all three branches intersecting so as to connect the King and Queen in the totality. Therefore, while the left hands indicate an encounter with the unconscious, the right hands indicate that this encounter is one that is consistent with the whole of the opus, the entirety of the journey, and consequently a mysterious holistic developmental process.

One finds that a bifurcation, described in mythological form, takes on a depth, a meaning, that transcends system dynamics when symbolic of the human experience (Bütz, 1997). Consequently, an admittedly terse consideration of just one of these periods in the mythology of the alchemists indicates that human beings conceptualize the transformation of energy as a symbolic process—that it is represented in myths and symbols. As in the beginning with The Mercurial Fountain, it has both the power of chaos, and also in its waters, the seeds of creation. The

---

[2]However, the process, as noted above, is recursive. It is merely given as a beginning, to comfort those who need a beginning and an end. The recursive nature of these processes, again, are connoted by the uroboros—a winged dragon eating its tail. This figure is one of the oldest in alchemy, and one that represents the full process, without a beginning or an end, an ongoing process.

movement of energy, then, must be understood in symbolic form if one is to understand how it has been referred to in myth. Energy takes on mysterious forms. Where on the one hand it appears sinister, something evil must be lurking about, while at the same time the dynamics associated with it have something of the heaven and the earth. In its mythological reference, it is a total process. And, this is precisely the value of the new theories discussed in this book. Chaos, complexity, and the new physics conceptualize systems as a total holistic process, where nonlinear dynamics are an inherent aspect of a system's repertoire of dynamics—of its development.

It has been mentioned above that there are eight more stages outlined in the Rosarium Philosophorum, but that only two other processes will be discussed—a period-doubling route to chaos, and self-organization. Seven of the eight stages connote a period-doubling route to chaos, including what Jung has described as The Naked Truth, Immersion In The Bath, The Conjunction, Death, The Ascent Of the Soul, Purification, and The Return Of The Soul. Self-organization, as a culmination of this process, is described, not surprisingly, as The New Birth. As the reader has no doubt surmised, describing all the stages that make up a period-doubling route to chaos in the form of this mythology would take a good deal more space than has been dedicated to this particular aspect of the book. Therefore, only certain stages will be mentioned, while others will be alluded to with specific citations that may assist the reader in exploring these notions further.

Considering a period-doubling route to chaos and this mythology, one cannot help but notice that each stage of this process takes one further and further away from the original notion of who one once was. The Naked Truth portrays a process where one must deal with himself and the encounter he has had honestly, putting aside vices such as arrogance and the like. The individual is called on to face his or her shadow with the honesty of nakedness, and as such in this mythology, start on a spiritual path (Jung, 1966, pp. 450–452). The weight of the encounter becomes clear, and the divergence from old ways also becomes clear as the process moves from being naked before the truth to Immersion In The Bath. This act is also a monumental step away from the safety of the existing conscious ego, whereby the individual risks dissolution of him or herself by entering the very waters of The Mercurial Fountain. This is reminiscent of Jung's other mythological explorations, such as what is referred to as *the night sea journey* (Jung, 1967b, pp. 308–310). Here, a critical threshold is crossed mythologically, and may speculatively be described analogically as a continuum limit (Coveney & Highfield, 1990, pp. 209–214) where the system verges on chaos. This stage, and the next stage that follows, The Conjunction, indicates an encounter with the personal unconscious that allows the two notions of the self to co-exist in these struggles. Struggles that are likened to competition, as the now archaic conscious ego grapples with the less known and more unconscious aspect of the personality (Bütz, 1992, 1993).

The next stage, Death, indicates that the older conception of the conscious ego is no longer viable, and must be integrated with that aspect of the personal unconscious in order for the individual to adapt to the current environment. This is that stage at which many clients will have dreams of dying, or will relate such a fear in therapy. Indeed, in this comparison, in entering this stage, human beings have the subjective experience of wading into the chaos or standing on the precipice of a limitless void. Jung points out this most existential experience by paraphrasing the alchemists: "No new life can arise, say the alchemists, without the death of the old" (1966, p. 467).

The stages that follow may be analogically compared to the way many theorists describe chaos, where the seeds of the new organization are forming amidst what appears to be random behavior. These stages are The Ascent Of The Soul, Purification, and The Return Of The Soul. In these instances, some comparisons may be made with how systems appear to use an immense amount of energy during a chaotic period as it moves about filling up the space of a strange attractor in its attempt to find a new order. And so, one is able to speculatively compare the movement of the soul from the individual to heaven, and then its return, to a process of seeking new information outside of the realm of the conscious ego (Bütz, 1997). The return, then, is a return with new information to assist the individual in adapting. However, in the mythological example there is an attribution to divine intervention, as the soul now has the pure form of energy—"the divine gift of illumination" (Jung, 1966, p. 484). This divine gift is information, nothing else, simply information found in the emotional/intellectual search tracked through phase space. Information, knowledge, and the like is the food of the psyche that feeds the development of the individual. Considering these notions, The Return Of The Soul is little more than the return of a sense of a coherent self. This return is the sense that the ego may be able to integrate the two notions represented in the conscious ego and personal unconscious. Hence, the seeds of the new organization, and this new sense of self, begin to take form.

Last, consider self-organization as the transformation itself, where the image of a hermaphroditic figure, the unarius, emerges as an integration of half man, half woman (Jung, 1966, pp. 306–307), what Jung describes as The New Birth. This new birth is simultaneously referred to as both the denarius and the unarius, where one is the completion of the work—the perfect number ten—while the other represents unity (Jung, 1966, p. 525). The notion of numerical significance combined with the notion of psychological significance cannot be missed here, as it was an ongoing theme throughout the opus in symbolic form. While it was not commented on in this chapter, the notion of number and development has been dealt with elsewhere (Bütz, 1995b; Robertson, 1989). Here, number parallels the developmental process, where it is at once a mystical union of two—the tenth stage of the opus and the culminating point for the entire process. The number ten here is very interesting, as it feeds back on itself, thereby beginning the process again at the first stage. As Jung states, "everything has grown from this One and through this One" (1966, p. 527). He thereby invokes again the notion of the uroboros that fertilizes itself and gives birth to itself as a complete and ongoing process.

What Jung found in his explorations into mythology was a process very similar to those discovered by scientists working with nonlinearity, chaos, and complexity. Though not an exact replica, as is the case with most developmental processes in life, Jung's description of a transformative process is remarkably similar. And, this is the essence of the appeal of this new set of ideas—the process described is roughly universal.

"I CAN'T GO BACK TO THE WAY I USED TO BE, CAN I?"

If the process being described in this text is universal, then it should have broad application to any number of therapeutic interactions, and in the pages to follow, one such example will be given. The case presentation is about a young woman learning to separate from her family, and it shares the commonalties many experience at different phase-of-life problems which typically invoke some sort of existential experience. This young woman's experience is no different, and the quotation used as the title for this section of the chapter aptly comments on another attribute of chaotic systems—they are irreversible (Prigogine, 1980). The case begins when Dorothy, a young European American woman, presents for therapy stating, "I don't want to be like my family any more." She was twenty-four at the time, a single parent with two daughters ages four and five, and experiencing a great deal of discomfort in social situations. "I just don't understand stuff. My family says it's one way, but everyone around me seems different." She still had close contact with her former husband since their divorce three years earlier, and her biological family was very close interpersonally, living some eighty to a hundred miles away from each other. Using Barber's distinction between cohesion and enmeshment (in press) to describe their dynamics, the family can fairly be portrayed as enmeshed by mention of the manipulative controlling dynamics found there.

Some brief exchanges between Dorothy and her therapist will be provided to succinctly illustrate the processes described above. Below is a caveat from the first session, where Dorothy is describing her problems to her therapist, Mr. Hodge.

> Dorothy: Well, I'm here, I guess—no, I'm sure, because I don't want to be like my family any more, it's just all too strange and I know my children are influenced by it. I can hear myself say something, and it sounds just like my parents. And, I think to myself, "Oh my God, this can't be happening . . . , I sound just like them." I'm not sure how to change all this, but I don't want to turn out like my mother, and I don't want my children to turn out like me.
>
> Mr. Hodge: Why is that?
>
> Dorothy: I just feel like I haven't done very well in life. I mean, I'm twenty-four, have gone to some college, and working at the job I'm working at, and well, my friends—I know they're screwed up—and so that must mean something about me, and I don't want to screw up my kids.
>
> Mr. Hodge: What has happened now that has made you feel this way?

Dorothy: Well, I just saw my mother with my kids, and was really irritated with her, and then I thought, 'I wonder if I'm any different with them. I wonder how other people see me with my children.' I know I'm different from my family, 'cause of some of my friends. But . . . but, a . . . I don't feel like who I want to be either.

In the above passage, it becomes clear that Dorothy has not only taken a different path than earlier in her life, but that this change was prompted by the realization that she wants to be different from the pattern of interactions laid down by her family. She had become aware that she wanted to change, not only for herself, but for her children. And, in doing so, she had become aware that she was no longer the Dorothy she used to be, but not yet clear about the type of person she wanted to become. Having entered therapy, since neither she nor her family had ever been in therapy before, was choosing a different path—bifurcating from existing patterns of behavior. Something had welled up from her unconscious when she witnessed the interaction between her mother and her children, but what "that" was did not become clear to her until the end of the process.

She had been making good progress in therapy. The session below is an excerpt from the twelfth session in which Dorothy became aware that her perspective on life had forever changed.

Dorothy: You know, a while ago I told my parents how I felt about things, and my brother and sister, both, told me how they felt about what I said. They were not happy, and it wasn't bad enough facing my parents about this stuff, but them too. My sister told me how upset my mother was, and that she just didn't understand why I couldn't let things go. So, I guess, now not only will my father not talk to me, but my sister tells me that my brother doesn't want to speak to me either. Telling people you don't like what they do is really tough (she begins to cry quietly). I just thought they'd be able to handle this a lot better than they have. I mean, I'd just like to have a life of my own. Is that too much to ask? And now I'm getting all this guilt from them. My youngest asked me, "why is Grandma mad at you? Is she mad at us too?" What do I say to that?
Mr. Hodge: So, this process of carving out a life for yourself has become more difficult, and it seems your family is pulling out all the stops?
Dorothy: Yeah, it sucks. At times I wish I could just say, "sorry I made your lives messy," and go back to the way it used to be. But, that would be miserable too. So, I guess what you're saying is that I can't go back to the way I used to be, can I? Once you see things a certain way, you can't go back and not see them anymore can you?
Mr. Hodge: Mm, it seems that way now, doesn't it? Do you think there's another way to go about it?
Dorothy: Ugh, no I don't think there is. I was just hoping for some magical solution I guess.

Dorothy had presented with a rather depressed mood and mixed sensorium, as could be witnessed in certain aspects of the dialogue in the first session. Between the first session and this one, it is apparent that she had cleared these hurdles to some degree, and the presenting problem had solidified around a need for her to separate from her family, to find her own way as an adult emerging from an enmeshed family environment. By her report in earlier sessions, family members were in regular phone contact on a daily, sometimes hourly basis. In setting boundaries with her family, so that she could have a life that was more independent, Dorothy had endured a number of attacks from not only her immediate family, but extended family as well. But, with the confrontation she alludes to above, she dove into what the alchemists referred to as "the bath," and entered the process of separating fully. At times rueing the day, she now describes seeking a solution to her dilemma: figuring out how to still have some sort of relationship with her family, and have an adult life. Now she was past the phase of period-doubling, diverging more and more from her family, and was instead, in the chaos. Her mood fluctuated between anxiety and depression, as she continued to steadily pull away from the depressive mood that had engulfed her at the beginning of therapy.

Dorothy regained the energy necessary to confront her family, and move on towards carving out an adult life for herself. It is clear that she had not negotiated integrating these two desires though, so organizing this experience into a new form was going to take some time. It was not until the twenty-sixth session in therapy that it became apparent that she was beginning to emerge from this process.

It is worthy to note that ending therapy prematurely (as some in brief modalities and others with financial interests at heart have suggested) would surely have had negative consequences, and likely would have proven more costly both emotionally and financially for everyone concerned. Metaphorically, it would have been similar to cutting a butterfly out of its cocoon before the entire metamorphosis had transpired, and therefore, the process would have produced an immature organization (Bütz, 1997; Bütz, et al., 1997). This may have started Dorothy on a path of incomplete organizations, and a regular ongoing need for therapeutic interventions. And, equally likely, she may have become more depressed than she was when she started therapy.

Fortunately, ten, or even twenty sessions, were not a limitation that had to be dealt with in this therapy, and Dorothy was able to work through this process to an acceptable degree for both herself and to the satisfaction of Mr. Hodge. While she had a difficult time sorting through adult romantic relationships, and the ongoing relationship she had with her former husband, she was eventually able to carve out a niche where she had both an adult life for herself and her children, and also a transformed relationship with her family. One does not usually find a singular moment when the birth of a new organization occurs in therapy, as therapy occupies only a few hours in a client's life over the course of a month. Rather, these organizations or adaptations typically occur at spontaneous moments outside the office, and this was the case for Dorothy as well. The session below is from the twenty-eighth session in therapy, as Dorothy went about explaining what occurred.

Dorothy: I was talking with some of my friends, some of the new friends I've made lately, and they brought up something about their parents. I'm not even exactly sure what it was, but she was saying something about her father and it occurred to me that I had treated Byron (her former husband) just like my mother treated my father. And, and . . . a, my father and Byron both did not want to be around us when we did that. I remember thinking, "I'll make it so he can't do that" or "I'll make him feel guilt," and you know I used to watch my mother do that to my father and it used to make me so mad. I couldn't believe I did that too, and my father didn't want to be around that kind of stuff and neither did Byron. I think that's one of the reasons we got a divorce. Sure, he did stuff too, but it was this stuff that drove me crazy about my family, and I think it's sorta what my mom did with Thomasina that made me so mad.

Mr. Hodge: Could you say more about what "that" is that you are talking about?

Dorothy: Oh, that, well you know, a . . . no, you don't know, otherwise you don't ask. A . . . it's a, like when you feel you're all tied up by words, and I just felt like I could see the words my parents used to tie me up for so long. Like I was tied up in knots, and it didn't occur to me that I tied people up in knots too. I used to do it a lot more than I do now, but it just pissed me off that I did it too.

Mr. Hodge: You mean like trying to control people?

Dorothy: A, ooh . . . yeah that's it, just like my parents tried to control me.

Mr. Hodge: So how does that make a difference?

Dorothy: Well, now not only have I started to see the words my parents, and brother and sister, use to tie me up, but I can also see how it used to make people, especially men, not want to be around me. I think that's the difference, okay, the control thing like my folks. That's the difference. I don't feel like I need to control people any more, and I'm not sure if I ever could.

The issue then, like in this text, was about control and wishing she had more control of her world. It was only when Dorothy realized that she had been tied up, controlled by words her whole life, that she no longer felt the need to control others. It was significant that she was able to appreciate it by appreciating the dilemma of her father and Byron. Significant, in that, this insight came through understanding the opposite sex, the opposite, meaning her own unconscious—her masculine side. This allowed her to integrate this aspect of her own shadow, and adapt to the adult world around her by reducing her felt need to control others with words and guilt. And, in turn, she did not allow herself to be controlled in these ways either, mainly by her family. Dorothy's energy then was able to be refocused, no longer did she need to channel such vast amounts of energy into defending herself against the enveloping words of her parents, nor did she have to expend so much energy in attempts to capture others with such words. This adaptation transformed Dorothy on a number of levels, allowing her to go about her adult life, while at the same time maintaining her relationship with her family in a different way.

CONCLUSIONS

The descriptions offered here diverge from the precision of binary mathematical formulas, and instead call upon the reader to ponder issues in a more qualitative manner. This has been the suggestion for chaoticians as well, as it is a visual science (Garfinkel, 1983) of phase portraits (Sprott, 1993) and fractals (Mandelbrot, 1977). The human experience is full of such symbolically rich phenomena, the least of which are the myths through which people live. Exploring Jung's venture into mythology for answers about the dynamics of change, and comparing it to contemporary science's chaos theory, has hopefully fleshed out the similarities that co-exist across the expanse of Western science and the ancient mythology of the alchemists. As he stated, we must "be content with the mere resemblance to one another" (1969, p. 442). Jung's path cut across this expanse, and the Analytical Psychology he developed in the process remains a rich source for further explorations as this culture evolves from the self-representation of a machine to that of a symbolic organism. Perhaps, just perhaps, chaos, complexity, and the new physics have opened a doorway through which the Western mind will be able to appreciate the value of the unconscious and the culture's myths, whereby clinicians will understand their ancient message that energy is not a thing, but a process of interactions.

REFERENCES

Barber, B. K. (1996). Family cohesion and enmeshment: Different constructs, different effects. *Journal of Marriage and the Family*.

Bohm, D. (1980). *Wholeness and the implicate order*. New York: Ark.

Burlingame, G., & Hope, C. (1996). Dynamical systems theory and social psychology: The promise and pitfalls. *Psychological Inquiry, in press*.

Burlingame, G., & Bloch, G. J. (1996). Complexity theory: A new direction for psychoneuroimmunology. *ADVANCES: The Journal of Mind-Body Health, 12*(1), 16–20.

Bütz, M. R. (1990, August). *Chaos, an omen of transcendence in the psychotherapy process* (long version). Society for Chaos Theory, 1st Annual Conference: San Francisco, CA.

Bütz, M. R. (1992). Chaos, an omen of transcendence in the psychotherapy process. *Psychological Reports, 71*, 827–843.

Bütz, M. R. (1993). A model of developmental transformation: Process, perspective and symöbia—a view of symbols in chaos. *Studies in Psychoanalytic Theory, 2*(2), 3–18.

Bütz, M. R. (1995a). Chaos theory, philosophically old, scientifically new. *Counseling and Values, 39*(2), 84–98.

Bütz, M. R. (1995b). Emergence in Neurological Positivism, and the algorithm of number in Analytical Psychology. In R. Robertson & A. Combs (Eds.), *Chaos theory in psychology and the life sciences*. Hillsdale, NJ: Lawrence-Erlbaum Associates.

Bütz, M. R. (1997). *Chaos and complexity, implications for psychological theory and therapy*. Washington, DC: Taylor & Francis.

Bütz, M. R., Chamberlain, L., & McCown, W. G. (1997). *Strange attractors, chaos, complexity and the art of family therapy*. New York: John Wiley & Sons, Inc.

Capra, F. (1983). *The turning point: science, society, and the rising culture*. New York: Bantam Books.

Coveney, P., & Highfield, R. (1990). *The arrow of time, a voyage through science to solve time's greatest mystery*. New York: Fawcett Columbine.

Davies, P. (1989). *The new physics*. New York: Cambridge University Press.

Ellenberger, H. F. (1970). *The discovery of the unconscious, the history and evolution of dynamic psychiatry*. New York: Basic Books.

Feigenbaum, M. (1978). Quantitative universality for a class of nonlinear transformations. *Journal of Statistical Physics, 19*, 25–52.

Freud, S. (1900). *The interpretation of dreams*. New York: Modern Library.

Freud, S. (1949). *An outline of psycho-analysis*. New York: W. W. Norton & Co.

Garfinkel, A. (1983). A mathematics for physiology. *American Journal of Physiology, 245*, 455–466.

Gleick, J. (1987). *Chaos: Making a new science*. New York: Viking-Penguin.

Jantsch, E. (1980). *The self-organizing universe, scientific and human implications of the emerging paradigm of evolution*. New York: Pergamon Press.

Jung, C. G. (1959). *Aion: Researches into the phenomenology of the self* (Hull, R. F. C., Trans.). (2nd ed.). Princeton, NJ: Princeton University Press.

Jung, C. G. (1961a). *Freud and psychoanalysis*. (Hull, R. F. C., Trans.). Princeton, NJ: Princeton University Press.

Jung, C. G. (1961b). *Memories, dreams, reflections*. New York: Vintage.

Jung, C. G. (1966). *The practice of psychotherapy*. (Hull, R. F. C., Trans.). (2nd ed.). Princeton, NJ: Princeton University Press.

Jung, C. G. (1967a). *Alchemical studies*. (Hull, R. F. C., Trans.). (2nd ed.). Princeton, NJ: Princeton University Press.

Jung, C. G. (1967b). *Symbols of transformation*. (Hull, R. F. C., Trans.). (2nd ed.). Princeton, NJ: Princeton University Press.

Jung, C. G. (1968). *Psychology and alchemy*. (Hull, R. F. C., Trans.). (2nd ed.). Princeton, NJ: Princeton University Press.

Jung, C. G. (1969). *The structure and dynamics of the psyche*. (Hull, R. F. C., Trans.). (2nd ed.). Princeton, NJ: Princeton University Press.

Jung, C. G. (1970). *Mysterium coniunctionis*. (Hull, R. F. C., Trans.). (2nd ed.). Princeton, NJ: Princeton University Press.

Kauffman, S. A. (1995). *At home in the universe*. London: Oxford University Press.

Lorenz, E. N. (1963). Deterministic nonperiodic flow. *Journal of Atmospheric Sciences, 20*, 130–141.

Mandelbrot, B. B. (1977). *Fractals: From, chance, and dimension*. San Francisco: W. H. Freeman & Sons.

McGuire, W. (1974). *The Freud/Jung letters*. Princeton, NJ: Princeton University Press.

Prigogine, I. (1980). *From being to becoming—time and complexity in the physical sciences*. San Francisco: W. H. Freeman & Sons.

Robertson, R. (1989). The evolution of number. *Psychological Perspectives, 20*(1), 128–141.

Robertson, R. (1992). *Beginner's guide to Jungian Psychology*. York Beach, ME: Nicolas-Hays.

Rosarium. philosophorum. Secunda pars alchimiae de lapide philoophico vero modo praeparando . . . Cum figuris rei perfectionem ostendentibus. Frankfort on the Main: 1550.

Sprott, J. C. (1993). *Strange attractors, creating patterns in chaos*. New York: M & T Books.

von Bertalanffy, L. (1968). *General system theory, foundations, development, applications*. New York: Braziller.

Waldrop, M. M. (1992). *Complexity, the emerging science at the edge of order and chaos*. New York: Simon and Schuster.

Yorke, J. (1975). Period three implies chaos. *American Mathematical Monthly, 82*, 985–992.

Chapter 5

Cognitive Psychology and Chaos Theory: Some Possible Clinical Implications

William McCown, Ross Keiser, & Anthony Roden

COGNITIVE PSYCHOLOGY AND CHAOS THEORY

Chaos theory is an advanced field of mathematics that involves the study of systems that have the potential for constantly changing. Psychology, with its traditional emphasis on reliability and stability, has neglected the most interesting aspects of human behavior, namely, behavior that does not remain constant (Keiser & Kreymer, 1997). Because of this bias, traditional psychology, especially in fields such as cognitive and personality psychology, has reached the position of what the late Hans Eysenck (personal communications, July 1993) referred to as "a perpetual crisis of triviality." This may be because the simplest questions regarding the causes of human behavior have already been answered, while the more important and genuinely interesting inquiries about who we are and what we do are discretely avoided (Langs & Badalamenti, 1993). One reason they may be avoided is that such study involves understanding and interpreting the immense complexities of human change (Abraham, 1995; Mangan, 1982). This has been an ability that behavioral scientists have lacked until recently.

However, chaos theory allows us to study systems that change (Loye, 1995). These systems are often referred to as "dynamical" and include people and their complex skein of behaviors (Abraham, Abraham, & Shaw, 1991). Chaos theory allows us to make qualitative predictions and descriptions of heterogeneous systems that shift in seemingly random and unfathomable manners (Abraham & Shaw, 1991). By this point in the book it should be clear that the concepts of chaos theory, while comparatively new to traditional Western sciences, are as ancient as the reflexive process of thought (Bütz, Duran, & Tong, 1995).

Despite the fact that incontrovertible evidence for chaotic functioning in many complex biological systems remains controversial (Rapp, 1995), it is clear that chaos theory has influenced a number of areas of behavioral science in general and psychology in particular (e.g., Abraham, Abraham, & Shaw, 1991; Langs &

Badalamenti, 1993; Vandenberg, 1995). This parallels similar trends in the natural and life sciences, where the impact of chaos theory has been even more dramatic (Devaney, 1992; Waldrop, 1992). What was once viewed as a faddish intellectual pursuit by a few mathematical eccentrics has now become mainstream science, as is indicated by the professional journals devoted to nonlinear research and even the number of "chaos-based" articles that are finding publication in traditional scientific journals. In other words, chaos theory is here to stay (Casti, 1992), as is the broader finding that spontaneous order often occurs out of unstable conditions in complex systems during critical periods (Kauffman, 1993).

CHAOS AND COMPUTATIONAL NEURAL NETS: A PRINCIPAL APPLICATION TO COGNITIVE PSYCHOLOGY

Perhaps the most well-known application of chaos theory to cognitive psychology is that of neural nets and their relevance to the new field of computational cognitive neurosciences. A series of conferences, beginning in 1993 and supported in part by the National Institute of Mental Health, the National Science Foundation, and the Office of Naval Research, have been organized around interdisciplinary issues regarding the broad range of research approaches and issues in nonlinear dynamics and brain functioning. These meetings have brought together experimental and theoretical neuorobiologists, computer scientists, mathematicians, physicists, and cognitive psychologists. Throughout this unusual professional synthesis, the emphasis has been on how biological neural systems compute. This is a topic now intimately connected with nonlinear dynamical systems theory, or the study of chaos. Not surprisingly, this area of research is of foremost interest to many cognitive psychologists, inasmuch as it may help provide more useful models of actual human thinking and learning.

Just as chaos theory is not new, the ideas involved in computational neural systems are not particularly novel. Instead, they are an example of how newer scientific discoveries can reframe and elucidate older, previously perplexing results (Amit, 1989). For example, in the 1890s the famed Spanish neuroanatomist Ramon y' Cajal first suggested a concept uncannily similar to what we now refer to as neural nets—neurons working together in a linked and somewhat orderly pattern (Shepherd, 1991). In 1943, the neurologist McCulloch and his mathematician colleague Pitts, at the Massachusetts Institute of Technology, demonstrated that a neural network could perform Boolean algebra. In a very technical paper (1943) they showed that elementary neural networks could be combined to produce binary output.

Whether this was the birth of artificial intelligence (AI) or not remains controversial. Ironically, however, the results were interpreted by an eager generation of researchers to indicate that humans act like linear computers (Carlson, 1994). For almost 40 years, the metaphor of the linear computer as a model of human thought became quite popular (Casti, 1992). This is a concept that is now, quite fortuitously, rejected by an increasing number of cognitive psychologists.

According to the philosopher of science, Wallace (1972), the behavioral sciences continually ignore their most important contributions, only to rename and rediscover them in later generations. In the cognitive science literature, an excellent example of this occurred with the works of the Canadian psychologist, Hebb (Gray, 1991), whose contribution to the physiology of learning overshadowed his notion of a "dynamic conceptual nervous system." As early as the 1940s, Hebb (1980) postulated that memories are stored by the multiple strengthening of synapses between numerous strings of related neurons. Hebb's work illustrated to psychologists that at least some aspects of the previously verboten black box of the brain could be understood. It also suggested that patterns of connections, rather than specific singular linkages, allowed the brain its flexibility and its plasticity following injury. Unfortunately, in the flurry of computational cognitive psychology that was to follow, Hebb's notions of the brain performing complex pattern analyses was to be one of his least influential theoretical statements. Hebb believed that the brain was able to work nonlinearly and sequentially, with numerous neurons connected in ever-shifting patterns. This is a notion we now refer to as massive parallel processing and is common in the study of supercomputers (Langs & Badalamenti, 1993).

In the 1950s, Rosenblatt (cited in Amit, 1989) designed and built actual machines called perceptrons, based in part on Hebb's theories, but more strongly influenced by McCulloch and Pitts' ideas. Yet as Minsky and Papert (1969) noted, the amount of information the Rosenblatt/McCulloch/Pitts perceptron could learn was quite limited. Furthermore and most damning to these interesting, simple attempts at "thinking machines" is that the perceptron requires an inordinate amount of time to learn. In fact, the amount of time required for it to learn simple behaviors is actually too much time to make it a useful model of even primitive psychological processes. For a while, it appeared that cognitive psychology was doomed to permanently reseal the black box of human thinking. However, as Hebb (1980) and many others have noticed, the utility of the perceptron is limited only if computations are occurring sequentially and linearly, and not in an interactive network, as Hebb had previously specified.

It is arguable what contributions the perceptron has made to the complex field of AI. However, it is quite clear that AI hit somewhat of a theoretical "brick wall" during the 1970s and 1980s (McNeil & Freiberger, 1993). Its basic problems were apparently unsolvable, and consequently its contributions, both mathematical and technological, were fairly trivial. Two separate paths—though not necessarily mutually exclusive—have emerged to solve these difficulties.

The best known are attempts to model brain functioning using attractor neural networks. This is a concept derived explicitly from chaos theory (Amit, 1989; Abraham, Abraham, & Shaw, 1991). The word attractor to the chaotician has a special meaning: Attractors are functions with slopes less than 1, which "pull" other nearby points closer to them. According to Amit, attractor neural networks are, "A network of interacting formal neurons", "with a high degree of feedback, whose dynamic is governed at long times by attractors" (p. 481). The work of Amit and others has done much to illustrate how attractors can make perception, recognition, and even recall, possible in the highly noisy system we call the human brain (e.g., Sulis, 1995).

The applications of neural networks, just like traditional AI, have primarily been used to model human and more complex animal behavior. However, unlike a traditional neural functional approach (e.g., Luria, 1973; Sonnier, 1992), the guiding belief has been that mathematical patterns may explain the dynamics of behavior in a more satisfactory method than previous reductionistic methods. There are a variety of types of neural networks that are based on the perceptron, the most common being the multilayer perceptron. These are "feedforward" neural networks that are trained with standard back propagation algorithms. Like humans, they can learn from experience. In fact, they only learn from experience. They learn how to transform input data into a predefined response, almost like humans attempt to problem-solve solutions for their environments. However, like the successful human problem solver, once they have "figured out the correct response" they can exhibit extraordinary flexibility in optimal statistical classification. Most neural networks in commercial use today involve multilayer perceptrons. The interested user can consult any number of perceptron home pages on the World Wide Web to find out about advances in commercial technology and the newest theoretical innovations.

Neural networks can also model common and less uncommon abnormal behavior. For example, Amit (1989), based on an idea from a colleague, demonstrated how neural networks can simulate the rare condition of prosopagnosia, which is the inability of otherwise normal persons to recognize familiar faces (Luria, 1973). Hoffman (1987) showed how neural nets may rather simply model the complex disorders of mania and schizophrenia.

Neural networks have also provided numerous commercial applications. Computer programs based on neural networks have been applied to areas from soil analysis to predictions of horse racing winners. (Indeed, a lively portion of the Internet is devoted to the modeling of nonlinear data that is required by the professional horse racing handicapper!) Neural networks build models by learning patterns in the data. Because such methods do not impose linear equations across data, such networks can better handle nonlinear or "noisy" data, the type of data that is likely to be found in real life. Unfortunately, such approaches require a vast amount of data, as does almost any system that attempts to analyze nonlinear phenomena.

To date, our modest contributions to modeling of abnormal behavior have been to attempt to illustrate how the early experiences of rapidly evolving neural nets can sensitize them to a condition similar to the "classic" neurotic behavior that is often seen in clinical patients (e.g., Eysenck, 1953, 1970; Horney, 1950). Although no longer used in official psychiatric nomenclature, the concept of neurosis has a long, and very fruitful history (Eysenck, 1970, 1993). For a number of reasons, neurosis is paradoxical. First, the patient recognizes the absurdity of his or her behavior, yet continues the very behavior that is considered unusual. Secondly, sometimes even severe cases of neurotic behavior spontaneously disappear; in some cases, however, the same behaviors may intensify through time. Third, it is often easily treatable, though some cases appear much more intractable (Horney, 1950; Eysenck, 1993).

Over 50 years of research now suggest that certain personality traits are associated with the acquisition of neurotic behavior (Costa & McCrae, 1989; Digman, 1989, 1990). Quite naturally, this personality trait has been labeled "Neuroticism," a term that gained popularity with the classic work of Hans Eysenck (1953). Recent emphasis in behavioral genetics has been on heredity, especially of broad and relatively stable personality traits discovered through factor analysis. Many of these major personality factors have large heritability coefficients. For example, it is estimated that 60% to 80% of individual differences in extroversion are due to genetic factors (Eysenck & Eysenck, 1985).

Neuroticism is an exception to this tendency of "superfactors" having a high heritability. Only about 25% of the variance of Neuroticism is inherited (Eysenck & Eysenck, 1985). Still more confusing is the fact that within-family variance of Neuroticism is much greater than between-family variance. In other words, there is little evidence that specific child-rearing styles or family dynamics contribute to neurotic behavior. Instead, it appears that idiosyncratic and unrepeatable events act as formative frameworks that sensitize persons to experience relatively neutral events as potentially harmful (Eysenck & Eysenck, 1985; Gray, 1991).

M. W. Eysenck (1992) has provided the most comprehensive cognitive psychological model of anxiety and the broader construct of Neuroticism. He postulates that persons who are anxious or neurotic (a) consistently process neutral stimuli as threatening, and (b) consistently process threatening stimuli more efficiently than non-threatening stimuli. This cognitive model compliments the physiological model of Gray (1991), illustrating how physiology makes such cognitions possible but not necessarily inherent.

The personality dynamics of elevated anxiety or chronic neurosis have been relatively easy to model with neural nets. Recall above that discrete or isolated events may serve as a seminal framework for developing neurotic behavior. A network with as few as one feedback loop can produce dramatic computer simulations of periodic or chronic anxiety and avoidance. Interestingly, depending where the "critical negative event" is introduced, the unlearning that occurs with this network may approximate the spontaneous recovery seen in a variety of neurotic conditions, or may become self-reinforcing and impossible to extinguish. In other words, it is very easy to model a neural network that resembles either curable or intractable neurotic conditions, depending on whether the type of fixed point is attracting, repelling, or neutral. Actually, this model may indeed correspond to reality, inasmuch as a mathematical function acts similar to the locus coeruleus— the small structure next to the fourth ventricle that contains only 15,000 cells

(Carlson, 1994). The locus coeruleus acts as a general amplifier or augmentation system for directing attention of the organism towards potentially threatening information. For example, this structure can raise or lower the ability of individual rats, dogs, or humans to respond to potentially threatening aspects of the environment.

Up to a critical point, our mathematical model of the locus coeruleus will gradually decrease its response to environmental "threats." In other words, it will provide for the natural extinction of neurotic behavior, a phenomenon long noted in the psychotherapy literature (Eysenck & Eysenck, 1985). On the other hand, once mathematical values exceed a particular control parameter, the system becomes self-reinforcing, as sometimes occurs in posttraumatic stress disorder, where symptoms seem to spontaneously disappear, and then, to emerge strong and more intensively over time (Johnson & McCown, 1997). A simple equation modeling an eventually increasing function (e.g., (f) $X = X^2 - .5X$) can often approximate delayed traumatic stress.

It is also possible to model a computational neural network that may explain why long-term therapy is necessary and desirable, at least for some clients. It is easy to mathematically model behaviors that are highly similar to the "eventually fixed" point orbits seen in nature. Points that show this orbital behavior do not start off stable, but after n iterations become fixed. In mathematics, iterations means repeating a function over and over again, with each subsequent value being iterated or refed into the equation. A simple example of this is the function $f(x) = x2$, where the fixed point soon becomes 1. An infinite family of more complex functions converge much slower to orbit stability or relative stability. Assuming that psychotherapy can help stabilize such fluctuating systems (Bütz, Chamberlain, & McCown, 1997)—perhaps by reducing or augmenting seed values in iterative equations, as is necessary—simple mathematical models can show how long-term therapy is not only desirable, but also, in many cases necessary. In fact, we have used these models to successfully argue with managed mental health care for additional therapy sessions for people who would have otherwise been prematurely terminated!

Does this speculative approach have any immediate practical clinical application? We think so, although we are only at the preliminary stage of determining the usefulness of the concept of chaotic attractors to psychiatric problems. Thinking about addiction in terms of chaos theory may provide a very useful language for both understanding and making qualitative predictions regarding the behavior under treatment. For example, a fixed-point neural net encourages addicting by "pulling in" nearby close points, resulting in a condition where the addiction becomes generalized to different situations. Similarly, a repelling-point neural net attractor does the reverse. After a few iterations, a nearby point will be pushed far away from the repelling neural network.

An example of one case that we have treated from our clinic illustrates the potential value of this application of chaos theory to addictions. The client being treated was a person from a fundamentalist religious background who oscillated between prolonged periods of binge gambling and drinking and intense periods of repentance and spirituality. A simple neutral fixed-point attractor function, $f(x) = x - x^2$, is a convenient mathematical approximation to the wildly vacillating behaviors of this client. This equation was actually generated by examining long portions of the client's behavior and "number crunching" them into algorithms that account for the most variance. A number of curve-fitting programs are commercially available and almost any is satisfactory.

Neutral fixed points are found where the function's slope is equal to 1 or -1 (Çambell, 1992). Translating this into an application of neural net theory, where a neural net remains inflexible about behavior, it maintains the capacity of wild and unpredictable fluctuation. In the case of the client in question, his attitudes towards drinking and gambling were as prohibitional as possible, which in the past often predicted a relapse. Again, on the basis of computational neural net theory, this makes sense, since neutral attractors occur when the function's slope is equal to either 1 or -1 (Casti, 1992).

In this case, we performed what would be considered a paradoxical intervention. Despite the fact that the individual client's behaviors were staunchly anti-gambling and prohibitionist regarding alcohol use, we actually encouraged him (under supervision) to play video poker, one of his favorite games while on a gambling spree. Naturally, he lost, as do video poker players in the longer run, though for the purposes of treatment, this outcome was irrelevant. However, by forcing changes in his otherwise rigid neural net regarding gambling and drinking, we reasoned we were producing a repelling fixed point, which occurs when the absolute value of a slope is greater than one. By tempting the potentially wildly vacillating client and allowing him to experience his weakness, his neural net changed. This, we hypothesized, produced a less attracting fixed point. A six-month follow-up on this client revealed he has moderated his attitude about others alcohol use and gambling, but remains personally abstinent.

Chaos theory, combined with the notion that decisions are made by computational neural nets, may one day provide us the opportunity of determining what type of treatment should be administered, and perhaps more importantly, when it should be administered. With this client we had a variety of treatment options— almost all involved reinforcing the notion that gambling and drinking were bad for him. However, these options would do nothing to change the functional slope of the neutral attractor and its wild bifurcation. By moderating his prohibitionist attitudes, we were able to reduce extreme bouts of behavioral fluctuation. Using the language of chaos theory, by making the neural network more flexible, we were able to reduce the probability of relapse.

FUZZY LOGIC: A SECOND MAJOR COGNITIVE APPLICATION OF CHAOS THEORY

Some of the limits to the application of AI are being overcome by a number of theorists who have combined the concept of neural nets with a different set of theories—those of the oxymoronic-sounding notion of fuzzy logic (Kosko, 1991). Fuzzy logic is an engineering, mathematical, and logical orientation that defies much of traditional Western thinking about categories (Zadeh, 1965). Not surprisingly, though developed primarily in the United States, major practical applications have occurred in Japan (Terano, Asai, & Sugeno, 1994), a culture that is much friendlier to the cognitive assumptions necessary for an understanding of fuzzy systems.

From the time of Plato, Western thought has assumed that ideas and words have crisp, rigid boundaries (Kosko, 1991). Aristotle's Laws of Contradictions and Excluded Middles, a cornerstone of Western thought (Vandenberg, 1995), are a vestige of the Platonic idea that at the basis of every concept is a unique and singular Form, or an ideal type. Each individual word—at least as seen by persons of Western culture, such as logicians and most scientists—is a discrete entity, a non-overlapping Venn diagram (McNeil & Freiberger, 1993). Ideally, words should have one, and only one meaning. Indeed, a large portion of 20th Century philosophy was directed towards the notion that metaphysical and meta-ethical questions would disappear once crisp definitions were provided for concepts being discussed. This concept is called "ordinary language philosophy" and proved to be much less useful in philosophy than initially expected (Wallace, 1971).

One of the legacies of ordinary language philosophy that has permeated contemporary psychology is the concept of "operational definition." This notion first advanced around the turn of the previous century, and was held in disrepute by most philosophers of science (Casti, 1992; Loye, 1995). Fuzzy logic takes a more Zen-like approach, actually eschewing operational definitions (Kosko, 1991). The seemingly simple concept of fuzzy logic is that a cognitive "item" can belong to several different classes simultaneously. Furthermore, such an item can have partial membership in any particular class. For Western thinkers this concept is often difficult to comprehend, but it is commonly understood by Native Americans and people of Eastern philosophical orientations.

A simple example will clarify fuzzy logic. Consider this question "Is a woman who is 5'7", tall?" Intuitively we all would say "Maybe. It depends on to whom she is being compared . . ." In other words, she is partly in the class of tall people, partly in the class of those of average height. However, according to traditional mathematical set theory, such an answer is not tolerated; truth-value is binary. The woman either belongs to the class of tall people or non-tall people. However, fuzzy logic says people can be simultaneously short, moderately tall, and very tall. It depends on to whom they are being compared at any particular time (Kosko, 1991).

For almost 25 years, cognitive psychologists have had experimental data indicating that people think in terms modeled by fuzzy logic. Rosch (1973, 1975), in an ingenious set of experiments, demonstrated that people are able to recognize words as being "similar to" or "partly in" a particular category. For example, we see a tomato (which technically is a fruit) as "kind of like a fruit, kind of like a vegetable." The boundaries for the observer regarding tomatoes are fuzzy. An orange, on the other hand, is more prototypically recognized as a 'purer' fruit," with boundaries less fuzzy. A similar experiment can be conducted in less than five minutes in any Introduction to Psychology class, yet its implications are astounding to many traditional scientists. People do not categorize words in crisp, mutually exclusive classes, but maintain a fluidity of categorical organization.

Rosch (1975) further demonstrated that human categorization of cognitive concepts form a hierarchy, with three fuzzy tiers: superordinate categories, basic categories, and subordinates. People begin forming concepts in the middle and add them up to form larger ones. Furthermore, reaction times in classifying less prototypical items are substantially slower. In other words, the fuzzier a concept is, the more trouble we have recalling and classifying it.

Rosch's (1975) research has direct applicability to fuzzy logic. Fuzzy logic has already found a number of very practical engineering applications. These include sophisticated bread-making machines, subways, and even cars that park themselves, all based on a minimal set of algorithms involving fuzzy calculus (McNeil & Freiberger, 1993). Yet for some reason, applications of the fuzzy logic paradigm to the field of cognitive abnormal psychology have lagged.

Our present research in fuzzy logic was prompted by pilot studies performed by the authors earlier in the 1990s. At the time we were interested in the hypothesized tendency of chronic procrastinators to demonstrate difficulty in shifting cognitive sets. This has nothing to do with "set shifting" as is normally thought of in neuropsychology (e.g. Lezak, 1983), but is a much more subtle process. It is best illustrated by a simple experiment, readily performable by anyone who has a friend who is a chronic procrastinator. Ask your procrastinating friend what he or she is doing at any particular time. You will observe a tendency for them to identify their behavior either on a more subordinate category (e.g., "sitting here at the computer") or a more superordinate category (e.g., "organizing the rest of my life") than your more punctual friends. Eventually, we found that this was restricted to a subset of procrastinators, those whose procrastination was related to impulsiveness, rather than to neurotic tendencies or perfectionist traits (McCown, Keiser, Johnson, Roden, & LaCroix, in press).

Fuzzy Logic and Impulsivity

We have now begun to consider whether impulsiveness is related to an inability to "shift cognitive sets" from a lower order behavior (or less fuzzy set) to a higher order conceptualization. Impulsivity is the tendency to habitually act without thinking (McCown, Johnson, & Shure, 1993). Impulsivity has multidetermined biological, psychosocial, and psychological causes; very similar behaviors are found in persons with low cerebral spinal fluid levels of serotonin, people who have received brain injury to prefrontal areas, and in children who have experienced extreme stress from abuse or war. Regardless of etiology, psychotherapy can assist impulsive patients in gaining insights about their behaviors and in obtaining practice in thinking-through the consequences of their actions.

Based on Gray's (1991) theory of impulsiveness, we hypothesized that two biopsychological "source traits" are important for determining behavioral impulsiveness. These include (1) Elevated sensitivity to present environmental indices of rewards (probably mediated through the nucleus acumbens and the ventral tegmental areas), and (2), a decreased sensitivity to future signals of punishment. Neuropathways which mediate insensitivity to harm-avoidance are better understood than reward systems, and include the so-called "septo-hippocampal" system, the ascending noradrendergic projections which extend to the prefrontal areas (Carlson, 1994; Gray, 1991; Zuckerman, 1995).

As a result of elevated reward-sensitivity in combination with poor harm-avoidance, impulsive people have an information processing bias which (1) maximizes information regarding present rewards or positive states, and (2) minimizes environmental information regarding signals of future punishment (or problems). The seemingly illogical and often perplexing behaviors of people who habitually act without thinking can be partly explained by these two informational processing biases, which are probably equally rooted in biology and experience.

Not surprisingly, then, two different subtypes of impulsivity have been found (Dickman, 1993). Functional impulsivity is related to verve, spontaneity, and affability. Dysfunctional impulsivity is related to disinhibition, aggressiveness, substance abuse, and other negative social behaviors. Evidence suggests that functional impulsivity closely resembles extroversion or outgoingness, while dysfunctional impulsivity is a more complex phenomenon to pin down psychologically and behaviorally (Zuckerman, 1995).

Recently, we began a series of experiments applying fuzzy logic to the study of impulsiveness. We compared three popular theories of impulsive behavior, using the paradigm of fuzzy logic to test hypotheses generated from these theories. Three cognitive theories of impulsivity are popular in the literature and are reviewed by Dickman (1993). The first is an arousal theory (Eysenck, 1953), that states that dysfunctional impulsivity is related to cortical underarousal. The second is associated with the immense experimental work of Barratt (1993) and states that impulsivity is related to an inability to maintain a consistent cognitive tempo. Dickman's own theory postulates that impulsivity is related to an inability to focus attention.

One of our experiments involved digitizing the head movements of impulsive and non-impulsive subjects while they performed cognitively demanding tasks. Dysfunctional impulsivity is related to a less stable attractor for head movement. Using Sprott and Rowlands' (1992) Chaos data analyzer we examined this digitized data. Behavior from impulsive subjects was mathematically chaotic, as evident by both a positive Lyapunov exponent and a moderately high fractal dimensionality. Data for non-impulsive subjects did not show a positive Lyapunov exponent, a major test for the presence of chaos.

More relevant to the discussion regarding fuzzy systems is the ability of high- and low-impulsive subjects to generate appropriate fuzzy categories. In this task, subjects are asked to progressively abstract "upwards" from what they are doing. For example, they might be sitting in a chair. In one experiment (McCown, Keiser, Borderloin, & Roden, in press), our subjects were asked to conceptualize or describe their behavior with progressively higher purpose. Data were analyzed with traditional analyses of covariance, controlling for extroversion, which can be related to verbal fluency, and also controlling for verbal intelligence.

Our findings converged to indicate that dysfunctionally-impulsive persons have difficulty generating fuzzy categories (McCown, Keiser, Borderloin, & Roden, in press). Furthermore, the latencies in time to shift from one category to another are slower for dysfunctionally-impulsive subjects. This is partial support for both Dickman's and Barratt's theories. On a cognitive level, impulsive people get "stuck" and can only think of their behavior in one way. The reason they may have difficulty self-monitoring is that they cannot shift fast enough to observe their behaviors from the perspective of others. This may also explain why impulsiveness is paradoxically related to "absentmindedness." Both the preoccupied professor and the impulsive criminal forget where their keys are because they are self-absorbed and have difficulty thinking at the "appropriate" level of fuzziness. However, they are self-absorbed for very different reasons.

From a physiological basis, it also makes sense that impulsive persons may have particular difficulty with "fuzzy" concepts. Impulsive behavior is related to low levels of serotonin, a neurotransmitter also targeted to attention (Zuckerman, 1995). This phenomenon becomes even more pronounced for categories that are fuzzier. When concepts are less crisp and situations are less obvious, the ability to generate additional and higher order categories is slower still. Fuzzy concepts apparently involve more attention and mental energy, as judging by the slower reaction times of dysfunctionally-impulsive people in generating such categories. Persons with extreme difficulty in generating alternatives appear to respond "concretely," a phenomenon well-documented in the neuropsychological literature for people with neurobehavioral compromise (Grant & Alves, 1987). The apparent paradox of how brain injury produces both cognitive concreteness and also impulsivity becomes less mysterious if we examine exactly what types of thoughts or behaviors impulsive people have trouble maintaining with flexibility.

CLINICAL IMPLICATIONS

Bütz, Chamberlain, and McCown (1997) have reported an experiment with a form of family therapy that can be seen as an application of fuzzy logic theory. Their goal was to help families that were overly undifferentiated, which they conceptualized as resembling fractals. This case was successfully treated and the family reached a better level of organization and functioning. Based on this case study and our laboratory experience, we speculate that a potentially useful treatment for impulsive persons might involve a similar approach. We are now experimenting with training highly dysfunctional persons to conceptualize their behavior (1) as more abstract, and (2) from multiple perspectives. While such training may be more commonly undertaken and accepted for persons who have neurobehavioral compromise (Anderson, 1994) or overt brain trauma (Grant & Alves, 1987) we believe that it is appropriate to frame substantial behavioral change as a rehabilitative process.

An example is a 14-year-old youth that has been arrested several times for stealing money from neighbors. Apparently, most of this money goes to support a gambling habit of several hundred dollars per week, which he gleefully spends in the back rooms of quasi-legal video parlors. According to his scores on Costa and McCrae's (1989) popular five-factor test, this youth is neurotic, outgoing, very closed to new experiences, highly disagreeable, and not very conscientious. His intelligence is in the normal range, and he is sullen and uncooperative. Many clinicians would have seen him as untreatable and refused to work with him.

Our tactic was not to attempt insight or behavioral therapy. Instead, we thought we would experiment with having him conceptualize his gambling (which was essentially an act of continuous button pressings) in a number of different ways. When placed in front of a simulation video poker machine, the client showed extreme latency in generating alternative descriptions of his behavior, finding it very difficult to conceptualize his behavior as anything but "winning money . . . having fun . . . betting."

Eventually he was able to produce a number of alternative descriptions of this behavior. These included, "Sitting here . . . wasting money . . . doing something mindless." Several sessions focused on getting him to generate alternative descriptions of his behaviors, in order, we hypothesized, to transform his neural net and to allow him to think more "fuzzily" about his behavior. At last contact, over a year ago, the youth was reportedly abstaining from gambling and found the idea of video poker, "kind of boring . . . in fact almost repulsive." He has also been in no further legal trouble.

EPISTEMOLOGICAL IMPLICATIONS

Additional research will be necessary to determine whether such treatment has any effectiveness with a group of patients that are known to be recalcitrant to long term changes (Ferrari, Johnson, & McCown, 1994). But perhaps more important for the clinician than any specific individual finding in the "science of chaos" is the new attitude towards the scientific method that chaos theory is now mandating. Rapp (1995) argues that the epistemological changes associated with chaos theory are permanent. Popper's (1965) long-held notion of science progressing by a series of falsifications is no longer as tenable during this genuine paradigm shift (e.g., Kuhn, 1970).

It is likely that this new science of chaos will itself remain in flux for some time (Abraham, 1995). Where theory produces results that are meaningful or somehow useful, they will be refined and retained and ultimately will produce some type of data. Where such results are not forthcoming, subdisciplines that have endorsed chaos will probably become more esoteric and "literary," with increasing stagnation and internecine warfare among adherents. However, to date, chaos theory appears to hold an untapped ability to contribute to cognitive, and perhaps also to clinical, psychology (Ruelle, 1991).

Acknowledgments

Thanks is due to a number of colleagues in Mathematics and Physics departments, as well as in Psychology, and to the three anonymous outside readers who made helpful suggestions on earlier versions of this manuscript.

REFERENCES

Abraham, F. (1995). Dynamics, bifurcation, self-organization, chaos, mind conflict, insensitivity to initial conditions, time unification, diversity, free will, and social responsibility. In R. Robertson & A. Combs (Eds.), *Chaos theory in psychology and the life sciences*. Hillsdale, NJ: Lawrence Erlbaum Associates.

Abraham, F., Abraham, R., & Shaw, C. (1991). *A visual introduction to dynamical systems theory for psychology*. Santa Cruz, CA: Aerial Press.

Abraham, R. H., & Shaw, C. D. (1991). *Dynamics: The geometry of behavior*. Redwood City, CA: Addison-Wesley.

Amit, D. J. (1989). *Modeling brain function: The world of attractor neural networks*. Cambridge & New York: Cambridge University Press.

Anderson, R. (1994). *Practitioner's guide to clinical neuropsychology*. New York: Plenum.

Barratt, E. (1993). Impulsive behavior: Integrating paradigms. In W. McCown, J. Johnson, & M. Shure (Eds.), *The impulsive client: Theory, research and treatment*. Washington, DC: American Psychological Association Press.

Bütz, M., Chamberlain, L., & McCown, W. (1997). *Strange attractors: Chaos, complexity, and the art of family therapy*. New York: John Wiley & Sons.

Bütz, M., Duran, E., & Tong, B. (1995). Cross-cultural chaos. In. R. Robertson & A. Combs (Eds.), *Chaos theory in psychology and the life sciences*. Hillsdale, NJ: Lawrence Erlbaum Associates.

Çambell, A. B. (1992). *Applied chaos theory: A paradigm for complexity*. San Diego, CA: Academic Press.

Carlson, N. R. (1994). *Physiology of behavior* (5th ed.). Boston: Allyn & Bacon.

Casti, W. (1992). *Reality rules: Vol. 1*. New York: Pergamon Press.

Costa, P. T., Jr., & McCrae, R. R. (1989). *The NEO-PI/NEO-FFI manual supplement*. Odessa, FL: Psychological Assessment Resources.

Devaney, R. (1992). *A first course in chaotic dynamical systems: theory and experiment*. Redwood City, CA: Addison-Wesley.

Dickman, S. (1993) A cognitive theory of impulsivity. In W. McCown, J. Johnson, & M. Shure (Eds.), *The impulsive client: Theory, research and treatment*. Washington, DC: American Psychological Association Press.

Digman, J. M. (1989). Five robust trait dimensions: Development, stability, and utility. *Journal of Personality, 57*, 195–214.

Digman, J. M. (1990). Personality structure: Emergence of the five-factor model. *Annual Review of Psychology, 41*, 417–440.

Eysenck, H. J. (1953). *The structure of human personality*. New York: John Wiley & Sons.

Eysenck, H. J. (1970). *The structure of human personality* (2nd ed.). London: Methuen.

Eysenck, H. J. (1993). Cicero and the state-trait theory of anxiety: Another case of delayed recognition. *American Psychologist, 48*, 114–115.

Eysenck, H. J., & Eysenck, M. W. (1985). *Personality and individual differences: A natural science approach*. New York: Plenum.

Eysenck, M. W. (1992). The nature of anxiety. In A. Z. Gale & M. W. Eysenck (Eds.), *Handbook of individual differences: Biological perspectives*. New York: John Wiley & Sons.

Ferrari, J., Johnson, J., & McCown, W. (1994). *Procrastination and task avoidance: Theoretical and clinical perspectives*. New York: Plenum.

Grant, I., & Alves, W. (1987). Psychiatric and psychosocial disturbances in head injury. In H. S. Levin, J. Grafman, & H. M. Eisenberg (Eds.), *Neurobehavioral recovery from head injury* (pp. 232–262). New York: Oxford University Press.

Gray, J. A. (1991). *The neuropsychology of anxiety: An inquiry into the functions of the Septo-hippocampal system* (2nd ed.). Oxford: Oxford University Press.

Hebb, D. O. (1980). *Essay on mind*. Hillsdale, NJ: Lawrence Erlbaum Associates.

Horney, K. (1950). *Neurosis and human growth*. New York: W. W. Norton & Co.

Hoffman, R. E. (1987). Computer simulations of neural information processing and the schizophrenia-manic dichotomy. *Archives of General Psychiatry, 44*, 178–186.

Johnson, J., & McCown, W. (1997). *Family therapy of neurobehavioral disorders: Integrating neuropsychology and family therapy*. Binghamton, NY: The Haworth Press.

Kauffman, S. (1993). *The origins of order: Self-organization and selection in evolution*. New York: Oxford University Press.

Keiser, R., & Kreymer, R., (1997). *Measuring change and stability: The practitioner's guide to learning the Rorschach*. New Orleans, LA: North Shore Press.

Kosko, B. (1991). *Neural networks and fuzzy systems*. Englewood Cliffs, NJ: Prentice Hall.

Kuhn, T. (1970). *The structure of scientific revolutions* (2nd ed., enlarged). Chicago: University of Chicago Press.

Langs, R., & Badalamenti, A. (1993). *The physics of mind*. New York: Ballantine.

Lezak, M. D. (1983). *Neuropsychological assessment* (2nd ed.). New York: Oxford University Press.

Loye, D. (1995). How predictable is the future? The conflict between traditional chaos theory and the psychology of prediction, and the challenge for chaos psychology. In R. Robertson & A. Combs (Eds.), *Chaos theory in psychology and the life sciences*. Hillsdale, NJ: Lawrence Erlbaum Associates.

Luria, A. R. (1973). *The working brain*. New York: Penguin.

Mangan, G. (1982). *The biology of human conduct: East-west models of temperament and personality*. Oxford: Pergamon Press.

McCown, W., Johnson, J., & Shure, M. (1993). An overview of impulsivity. In W. McCown, J. Johnson, & M. Shure (Eds.), *The impulsive client: Theory, research and treatment*. Washington DC: American Psychological Association Press.

McCown, W., Keiser, R., Johnson, J., Roden, A., & LaCroix, A. (In press). Impulsiveness and difficulties in latency of recall and recognition associated with chronic procrastinators. *Personality and Individual Differences*.

McCown, W., Keiser, R., Borderloin, A., & Roden, A. (submitted). *Chaotic behavior in movements, and problem-solving abilities of dysfunctionally impulsive college students*.

McCulloch, W., & Pitts, W. (1943). A logical calculus of the ideas imminent in nervous activity. *Bulletin of Mathematical Biophysics, 5*, 115–133.

McNeil, D., & Freiberger, P. (1993). *Fuzzy logic: The discovery of a revolutionary computer technology—and how it is changing our world*. New York: Simon & Schuster.

Minksy, M., & Papert, S. (1969). *Perceptrons*. Cambridge, MA: MIT Press.

Popper, K. (1965). *Conjectures and refutations: The growth of scientific knowledge* (2nd ed.). New York: Basic Books.

Rapp, P. (1995). Is there evidence for chaos in the human central nervous system? In R. Robertson & A. Combs (Eds.), *Chaos theory in psychology and the life sciences*. Hillsdale, NJ: Lawrence Erlbaum Associates.

Rosch, E. (1973). Natural categories. *Cognitive Psychology 4*, 328–350.

Rosch, E. (1975). Cognitive representation of semantic categories. *Journal of Experimental Psychology: General, 104*, 192–233.

Ruelle, D. (1991). *Chance and chaos*. Princeton, NJ: Princeton University Press.

Sonnier, I. L. (Ed.). (1992). *Hemisphericity as a key to understanding individual differences*. Springfield, IL: Charles C. Thomas.

Shepherd, G. M. (1991). *Foundations of the neuron doctrine*. New York & Oxford: Oxford University Press.

Sprott, J., & Rowlands, G. (1992). *Chaos data analyzer*. New York: American Institute of Physics.

Sulis, W. (1995). Naturally occurring computational systems. In. R. Robertson & A. Combs (Eds.), *Chaos theory in psychology and the life sciences*. Hillsdale, NJ: Lawrence Erlbaum Associates.

Terano, T., Asai, K., & Sugeno, M. (Eds.). (1994). *Applied fuzzy systems* (C. Aschman, Trans.) Boston: AP Professional Press.

Vandenberg, L. (1995). Ripples of Newtonian mechanics: Science, theology and the emergence of the idea of development. *The Journal of Mind and Behavior, 16*, 21–34.

Waldrop, M. (1992). *Complexity: The emerging science at the edge of order and chaos*. New York: Simon and Schuster.

Wallace, W. (1972). *Causality and scientific explanation* (2 vols.). Ann Arbor, MI: The University of Michigan Press.

Zadeh, L. (1965). Fuzzy sets. *Information and Control, 8*, 338–353.

Zuckerman, M. (1995). *Behavioral expressions and psychobiological basis of sensation seeking*. Cambridge: Cambridge University Press.

Chapter 6

Systems Theory and Chaos Dynamics

Linda Chamberlain & William McCown

Perhaps of all the theoretical orientations in psychology, clinicians who are trained to think systemically may be "naturals" for incorporating some of the paradigms introduced by chaos and complexity theory. Systems theory has historically embraced the concept of nonlinearity in the process of change. Moreover, systems theory in the social sciences is more directly linked to paradigms from other sciences than most other orientations. Most clinicians who are trained as family therapists are exposed to cybernetics and general systems theory, which serve as the foundation for communication and family systems approaches in psychotherapy. Just as in systems theory, chaos science seeks to understand the behavior of complex systems with interrelating parts. In addition, as systems theorist Nicholas Rizzo (1972) notes, "A modern psychology must be constructed with principles consistent with organismic biology ... Human psychology can abandon its zoomorphic, robotomorphic, atomistic models which, in effect, have degraded, mechanized, and bestialized man" (pp. 143 & 144).

Clearly, families qualify as complex systems. It is easy to understand, therefore, that several of the concepts within chaos theory are similar to the assumptions that form the basis of family systems theory. For a more comprehensive examination of the relationship of general systems theory to chaos theory and the influence of these ideas on family therapists, the reader is directed to previous work by the authors (Bütz, Chamberlain, & McCown, 1997; McCown & Johnson, 1993). It may be intuitive for family therapists to accept the idea proposed by chaos theory that the behavior of complex systems is not linear and is constantly changing in ways that are not completely predictable. Clinicians working with families can attest to the fact that there are limits to what can be predicted regarding a family's behavior. As Johnson and McCown (1996) note: "Theories of chaos and complexity actually demonstrate that at times it may be impossible to predict anything about family behavior" (p. 258).

CHAOS AND SYSTEMS THEORY

In chaos science, the theory proposes that systems are inherently more complex, spontaneous, and individualistic than previously thought. Rather than a reductionistic science that attempts to experimentally repeat results in order to make predictions, chaos focuses on understanding and describing the inherently unpredictable, random, and holistic nature of nonlinear systemic functioning. Scientists are beginning to realize that "randomness is interweaved with order, that simplicity enfolds complexity, complexity harbors simplicity" (Briggs & Peat, 1989, p. 43). It is a theory that focuses on change, process, and pattern rather than stability, causality, and control.

Several of the basic ideas in chaos theory have clear implications for family and systems theory. According to chaos theory, even very tiny fluctuations in behavior by any part of a system can have profound effects on the structure and functioning of the entire system (see Chapter 1: "The Butterfly Effect," or Sensitive Dependence on Initial Conditions). Profound shifts in the patterns of interaction in any connected system, like a family, can be set in motion by slight differences in the behavior of any single member. A tiny difference in input can quickly become an overwhelming difference in output.

In systems theory, chaos is also described as a "far-from-equilibrium" state. As is true in systems theory, this aspect of chaos theory emphasizes that for a reorganization to occur, there must first be an increase in chaos or disorder. Some degree of randomness, confusion, and unpredictability precedes and precipitates change. The farther from equilibrium a system moves, the greater its perception of differences in the external world. Periodic instability is the foundation of adaptation and transition. The more chaotic or disordered a system becomes, the more likely it is that a spontaneous reorganization will occur that establishes an entirely different type of order. For example, on a cognitive level, new learning is only possible when old learning becomes confused or "chaotic." During periods of crisis, opportunities may suddenly appear for families to develop more effective patterns of interacting. At the edge of chaos, greater complexity can open an abundance of choices to the family that were not before available. This allows for a new order to develop that helps the family adapt and evolve.

One other significant idea proposed by chaos science is that change is not likely to be an orderly, step-by-step, slow process. Instead, changes in systems occur in spontaneous jumps (see Chapter 1: "Punctuated Equilibria" and Bifurcations). Families, like other complex systems, do not change in gradual increments, but in discontinuous leaps. Often, these leaps occur following a gradual accumulation of stresses that a system resists until it reaches a breaking point. Exactly when the leap will occur and how the system will reorganize is unpredictable. Paleontologist, Steven Jay Gould (1980) describes this phenomenon as "punctuated equilibria" and believes that the evolution of many species was spontaneous and took the form of the relatively sudden appearance of fully organized new life forms.

USING CHAOS THEORY AS A GUIDE WITH HUMAN SYSTEMS

Although cybernetics and general systems theory were helpful in providing an impetus for the development of family therapy, there are significant limitations to the application of these paradigms. Cybernetics was derived from investigations of mechanical systems, not natural or human systems. The concept of homeostasis is applicable to closed, or mechanical, systems, but does not translate to dynamic, living systems. Families, and other social groups, are open systems. It is important to understand that because they are nonlinear, dissipative, nonhomeostatic systems, groups of human beings behave much differently than machines. One implication based on this difference is that we may need to abandon our unidimensional view of what "family" means. What constitutes a thermostat is relatively easy to define; what constitutes a family is more complex. Perhaps the best definition of a family is a network of systemic relationships, characterized by a high degree of emotional involvement. This more open and inclusive definition allows for a greater variety of families to flourish. As Kauffman (1995) notes, maximal adaptation in complex social systems occurs where there is maximal diversity.

Because chaos theory emphasizes diversity and self-organization, it suggests that the notion of a "healthy" family is a dynamic quality that is emergent and different from one family to the next. The relative health of any connected group of individuals is largely expressed through the patterns and processes that it exhibits, not through adherence to a narrow set of attributes. Optimal levels of family functioning will probably be associated with an evolving diversity of behavior in members of the system. Maximal family health is dependent on the continual process of self organization that is unique to each family. This uniqueness is created through the evolution of each member's individuality. Each family follows its own internal dynamical process that unfolds through time. Every member contributes to the overall pattern of both health and pathology.

In the dynamics of human systems, these concepts empower all members of a group to be potential agents of change. All that is needed is for someone to set in motion a small fluctuation that provides some variation in the typical pattern of interaction among members. The role of "chaotician" can be assumed by even the most "powerless" member. In *Jurassic Park* (Crichton, 1990) the role of Ian Malcolm (a mathematician studying chaos theory) was to provide uncertainty about the effects that would result from introducing dinosaurs into an environment that had evolved for many centuries after their demise. Malcolm's understanding of chaos theory helped him anticipate that there would be effects and consequences that were unpredictable when a new element was introduced into the environment. For those who already think systemically, chaos is an anticipated dynamic, not some aberration or accident of poor planning.

CASE EXAMPLE: THE MILLERS

In the Miller family (names, ages, and circumstances have been changed), Marky is a chaotician par excellence. Marky is the 14-year-old son of James, who lives with his girlfriend, Terri, and her 11-year-old angelic son, Biff. According to Terri, Marky is "the spawn of Satan"—an unwashed, mumbling, pimply, awkward, abrasive adolescent. His pending visits with his father strike real terror into her heart. James and Terri have been in therapy working hard at learning to communicate better and both have made excellent progress in expressing themselves more openly to each other. Now, however, it's time for the first visit from Marky since they began therapy almost five months ago. The anticipation is enough to send their relationship into chaotic waters.

In past visits, Marky has made a point of pilfering money and little knick-knacks from Terri's dresser. Terri never deals with Marky directly; instead she complains bitterly to James about what an awful son he has and insists that he should "do something." She avoids almost any contact with Marky and openly expresses fears that he will be a bad influence on her son. James' leftover guilt about leaving Marky's mother and being his part-time father puts a definite damper on any discipline he exerts.

Marky successfully introduces a great deal of chaos into the lives of the happy couple. Although they cooperatively and adequately parent her son, Biff, they fight bitterly with each other about how to handle Marky. Their relationship, which is otherwise strong, loving, and supportive, becomes embittered, brittle, and dispensable. In preparation for Marky's summer visit of six weeks, James and Terri explored the option of a separation during that time, and even discussed ending the relationship altogether. Clearly, Marky is inadvertently pushing Terri and James to organize their relationship at some different level if they are to successfully deal with him. They must either jeopardize the relationship by splitting themselves around this issue or move in the other direction to strengthen their bonds. Instead of the breaking apart option that they had entertained during his previous visit, the therapist introduced the possibility of Terri and James devoting themselves fully to each other during his visit both by setting some pro-active rules regarding his behavior and by firmly establishing Terri as a partner in parenting Marky while he is in their home.

Their commitment to stay together during his visit, and for at least four weeks afterward, lowered the sense of chaotic randomness (will we or won't we stay together?) and set the stage for a different level of involvement from both partners. Marky's role as "chaotician" pushed the relationship to a new level of organization. His visits introduced enough (probably more than enough!) chaos in James and Terri's lives to force the couple to adopt some new order. Therapy helped introduce an alternative structure to assist their evolution through the transition. Without Marky's "help" James and Terri's relationship, although intimate, still lacked a sense of commitment. Marky's role as chaotician brought a new order to the family by formalizing Terri's role as a full partner and co-parent.

THE THERAPIST AS CHAOTICIAN

Many schools of family therapy emphasize the role of the therapist as "chaotician." Techniques such as reframing, paradoxical interventions, and symptom prescription, all increase the confusion, uncertainty, and disequilibrium in the family. Keeney and Ross (1985) have noted that it is the pattern of the constant interplay of stability and change that must be addressed by the clinician. One of the dilemmas that may be the basis for families entering therapy is that there isn't a chaotician in the house. No one is able to induce a high enough level of chaos to provoke a shift in the pattern. Therefore, the therapist becomes the chaotician.

Peggy Papp (1983) describes this essential chaos as elements of surprise and confusion that the therapist offers in order to arouse the family's curiosity and stir up their imagination. She states that "any concept which does not allow for the effect of time, sudden unexpected events, and unpredictable deviations in human behavior, is not only inadequate but therapeutically limited" (1986, p. 205). Mony Elkaïm (1981) of the Institute for Family and Human Systems Study in Brussels envisions that the task of the therapist is to try to push the system away from equilibrium, forcing it to search for a different solution. The question for therapy becomes: "How does one disrupt an arrangement that in some ways promotes family stability and instead help the family achieve a transformation that will represent a more complex integration (Hoffman, 1981, p. 167).

Chaos theory provides a strong scientific basis for the efficacy of techniques that unbalance family systems. Dislodging the patterns that become entrenched around a "problem" behavior is the key element of therapist as chaotician. For example, a family came in with the presenting problem that their five year old son, Ralphie, had been talking about suicide and death. During the interview, Ralphie was absolutely unstoppable. He interrupted every adult conversation, constantly provoked his older brother and sister, and appeared to be anything but "dead." Both parents had attempted to "talk sense to him" and get him to give up the idea of committing suicide. They spent endless hours, as did his siblings, arguing with him over how important it was for him to stay alive. Ralphie was addressed by the therapist and told that his thoughtfulness about dying was very impressive, as most children were too busy playing, having fun, or learning things to give it much thought. He was then told that he should explore the idea further by seeing what it might be like. The therapist instructed him to lie prone on the floor in a corner of the room, not make a sound, not move a muscle, close his eyes, and stay "dead" for the rest of the session. The interview with the family continued with an interruption from Ralphie in the corner after approximately 3 minutes had passed. He was reminded that "dead people can't talk" and that he could only join us if he was sure he wanted to be alive. After another 5 minutes, Ralphie had enough of "being dead," rejoined the family, and was cooperative and communicative for the rest of the session. Techniques like symptom prescription can help to create enough chaos in the pattern to allow changes to occur.

One of the disquieting elements of chaos theory is the idea of unpredictability. Once the system begins to fluctuate and move away from equilibrium, it is impossible to determine where the family will settle. The unique nature of each family means that it will transform according to its own special laws, laws at which the therapist can only guess.

There is little that a therapist can do that surpasses the family's natural ability to heal itself, once brief systemic perturbations are successfully negotiated. Families can invent far more amazing solutions than we can. An important part of the role of therapeutic "chaotician" is to identify new interactional patterns that offer some greater flexibility or potential for the family system and to encourage family members to repeat and integrate these patterns when they appear. In Ralphie's family, they were to have Ralphie spend 10 minutes "being dead" whenever he again mentioned suicide or his own death. Although he never chose to talk about his own death again, he was able to express appropriate sadness at the recent death of a favorite uncle.

CONCLUSIONS

In a relatively short period of time, chaos theory has gone from a fringe movement in the physical and life sciences to become a mainstream orthodoxy. Chaos theory is designed to investigate complex behavior and to look for underlying patterns in what appears to be random. Certainly, this has implications for clinicians working with human systems. Understanding the underlying structures and patterns in human interactions will help us to be more precise in our interventions and treatment of dysfunctional families and groups. Although chaos theory eliminates the idea of predictability and control in human systems, it enhances the concepts of description, understanding, and influence.

Chaos is everywhere. It is rapidly proving to be the third major revolution in physics in the 20th century, following in the wake of relativity and quantum physics. These scientific predecessors of chaos theory, however, did not have clear implications for human systems. The set of paradigms offered by nonlinear dynamical systems theory, chaos, and complexity, have many implications, as we have described. Chaos, when applied to family and systems therapy, does what a new paradigm is supposed to do. It answers previously unanswered questions and helps to revise our thinking about how human systems function.

Thinking about human systems and families in terms of chaos theory takes some practice; it isn't always easy. The assumptions are complex and sometimes anti-intuitive. Despite the difficulties involved, most of the concepts of chaos are well-known to family therapists. With discipline and creativity in using these new concepts, we can maximize the probability that effective systems therapy will evolve and become more vital far into the next century. As Ranier Maria Rilke (Mitchell, 1989, p. 261) so eloquently noted in his poem, "[As once the winged energy of delight]":

> To work with Things in the indescribable
> relationship is not too hard for us;
> the pattern grows more intricate and subtle,
> and being swept along is not enough."

REFERENCES

Briggs, J., & Peat, D. (1989). *Turbulent mirror*. New York: Harper & Row.

Bütz, M. R., Chamberlain, L. L., & McCown, W. G. (1997). *Strange attractors: Chaos, complexity, and the art of family therapy*. New York: John Wiley & Sons.

Crichton, M. (1990). *Jurassic park*. New York: Ballantine Books.

Elkaïm, M. (1981, July). Non-equilibrium, chance and change in family therapy. *Journal of Marital and Family Therapy*, 291–297.

Gleick, J. (1987). *Chaos: Making a new science*. New York: Viking-Penguin.

Gould, S. J. (1980). *The panda's thumb: More reflections in natural history*. New York: W.W. Norton & Company.

Hoffman, L. (1981). *Foundations of family therapy*. New York: Basic Books.

Johnson, J., & McCown, W. (1996). *Family therapy of neurobehavioral disorders*. New York: Haworth Press.

Kauffman, S. (1995). *At home in the universe*. Oxford: Oxford University Press.

Keeney, B., & Ross, J. (1985). *Mind in therapy*. New York: Basic Books, Inc.

McCown, W. G., & Johnson, J. (1993). *Therapy with treatment resistant families*. New York: Haworth Press.

Mitchell, S. (Ed.) (1989). *The selected poetry of Rainer Maria Rilke*. New York: Vintage International.

Papp, P. (1983). *The process of change*. New York: The Guilford Press.

Papp, P. (1986). *Letter to Salvador Minuchin*. In H. C. Rishman & B. L. Rosman (Eds.), *Evolving models for family change* (pp. 204–213). New York: The Guilford Press.

Rizzo, N. D. (1972). The significance of von Bertalanffy for psychology. In E. Laszlo (Ed.), *The relevance of general systems theory* (pp. 137–144). New York: George Braziller.

Chapter 7

Humanistic/Existential Perspectives and Chaos

Linda Chamberlain

Thomas Leahey (1987) notes in "A History of Psychology," that there are two kinds of social scientists; those who are the "system builders, envisioning psychology unified under a single set of principles" and those who believe that "human life is too messy, the influences on human behavior too diverse" (p. xi) to follow laws similar to those that comprise physics and other sciences. The humanistic/existential orientation to human behavior was based on the second assumption, that human behavior is intrinsically too complex to be adequately described through empirical methods and mechanistic descriptions. The paradigms that are included in chaos and complexity theory certainly support the contention that human beings are not merely complicated machines and are ill defined or understood using linear, empirical models. In this chapter, the links between humanistic/existential models and chaos theory will be examined.

Clearly, the dynamics of nonlinearity currently being described by scientists lend credence to the unpredictability, potential for change, and inherent complexity that have historically been aspects of the conceptual foundation for humanistic/existential theory. As Robertson (1995) notes, "... paradigms such as existential psychology, humanistic psychology ... and so on were viewed as outside the pale of scientific respectability" (p. 13). The mechanistic nature of physics that was part of the *Zeitgeist* when psychology emerged as a scientific discipline has severely limited what could be examined in human beings. Applying strictly mechanistic, deterministic, linear models to human nature simply doesn't work except in very limited instances. Chaos theory allows social scientists access to those aspects of human experience and behavior that were excluded for so long due to the requirements of empirical procedures. As the paradigms proposed in chaos and complexity science become more established, researchers and clinicians will no longer be required to force human nature into unnatural models.

THE HUMANISTIC/EXISTENTIAL PHILOSOPHY

Humanistic psychology developed out of several theorists' displeasure with both the psychoanalytic and behaviorist perspectives. These theorists experienced the existing paradigms as too limiting, dehumanizing, and mechanistic. The common element uniting humanists was the goal of making psychology and the social sciences more "human" than it had been in the past. They assumed that human behavior could not be adequately understood through the examination of anything other than human behavior; white rats or the most complicated of machines were not appropriate models for examining people. Humanists insisted that such phenomena as self-identity, meaning, attachment, altruism, and values were important aspects of experience that needed investigation and attention in the social sciences. Such theorists as Allport (1955), Frankl (1959), Fromm (1956), May (1969), Rogers (1951, 1961), Maslow (1968), and a myriad of those they influenced, carried the study of human behavior into more complex realms. Humanistic/existential theories stressed creativity, self-actualization, intentionalism, free choice, spontaneity, and a holistic approach as important considerations in studying humans. Their emphasis was on the uniqueness of the individual and the validity of subjective experience. Also, they "affirmed a positive attitude toward the development and preservation of human life, the dignity and value of each individual person, and the salience of human's most distinctive characteristic—rationality" (Urban, 1991, p. 202).

Most social science researchers are aware that in laboratory studies using human subjects, a minor change in any condition or variable can result in very diverse outcomes. For example, Dodds (1992) had student researchers replicate some established research studies under two conditions. First, they used subjects (college sophomores, of course) who were simply involved in the experiment without any introduction or information. With the second group of subjects, the researcher spent just a few minutes talking with the subjects before the experiment, thanking them for coming in and helping out, and assuring them that they would be given information about the nature of the experiment at its conclusion. The two conditions produced very different results. By briefly personalizing the experience for the subjects in the second group, the researcher set in motion a chain of events which resulted in very different behavioral outcomes. When such small variables influence the outcome of social research, it is not difficult to understand the dilemma of replicability. Given a dynamic system's sensitive dependence on initial conditions (as defined in Chapter 1), chaos theory would predict that any study using human (or even animal) subjects will be "messy" to an irreducible degree.

It is not surprising that a philosophy of human behavior which developed largely in reaction to the limitations of empirical models would propose that people are too complex to be adequately understood through classic forms of experimentation. Simply put, there are limits to the application of empiricism in the study of human behavior. In fact, from the framework of humanism, it is degrading and dehumanizing to equate people with machines or other non-dynamic entities. Mahoney (1989) takes exception to "scientism" as a "self-righteous, presumptuous, and exclusionary perspective on science" (p. 1374). He goes on to decry empiricists for their lack of tolerance for other types of inquiry and for the "demarcation problem" (i.e., the distinction between science and nonscience) with its suggestion that science is rational and nonscience is irrational.

As Dodds (1992) notes, there are three specific limitations inherent in using an empirical approach to understanding humans.

1   Scientists are people and therefore fallible. The scientific approach to understanding humans is hindered by the narrow-minded or subjective scientist. This subjectivity is inescapable to a certain degree;

2   Human behavior is irreducibly complex; there are too many variables to ever be able to predict individual behavior; and

3   While many human experiences are amenable to study by the scientific approach, many are not. Most behaviors cannot be separated from context.

Dodd's warnings regarding the limitations of empiricism are a reminder of the importance of having appropriate tools to use in studying subjects. Empiricism relies on the process of isolating aspects of the subject in order to control variables that might influence the factor in question. With humans, however, the issues of observer bias, behavioral complexity, and inter-relatedness to context are unavoidable complications in using traditional scientific methods. The humanist/existentialists accurately predicted what chaos science is now stating, the behavior of systems in nature (including humans) is inherently too complex to capture through traditional, reductionistic, empirical methods.

MASLOW'S SELF-ACTUALIZATION AND CHAOTIC SELF-ORGANIZATION

One aspect of humanist theory that can be further refined through an understanding of chaos dynamics is Maslow's paradigm of "self-actualization" (Maslow, 1968). Maslow describes self-actualization as a dynamic process in which the "powers of the person come together in a particularly efficient and intensely enjoyable way, and in which he (sic) is more open for experience . . ." (p. 97). In progressing toward self-actualization, a person experiences what could be described as an "edge of chaos" state in which they undergo a dynamic transformation.

Maslow focuses on peak experiences as a catalyst in the transition from one level of adaptation to the next. Creativity and spontaneity are essential components in his description of the pattern that evolves in self-actualization. Something new emerges out of the person's experience, a greater sense of self, a clearer purpose in life, a dedication to some pursuit, an enhanced sense of joy or fulfillment. These transitions to a "self-actualized state" often occur as "leaps," rather than a gradual accumulation of small changes. This dynamic is also apparent in systems at the edge of chaos.

In Maslow's book, *Toward a Psychology of Being* (1968), he defined self-actualization as:

> an episode, or a spurt in which the powers of the person come together in a particularly efficient and intensely enjoyable way, and in which he is more integrated and less split, more open for experience, more idiosyncratic, more perfectly expressive or spontaneous, or fully functioning, more creative, more humorous, more ego-transcending, more independent of his lower needs, etc. He becomes in these episodes more truly himself, more perfectly actualizing his potentialities, closer to the core of his Being, more fully human (p. 97).

Maslow's description of the emergence of self-actualization echoes throughout the writings of those studying chaotic or nonlinear dynamics.

In his book, *Complexity* (1992), life scientist Roger Lewin describes emergence in natural systems as "the principal message of the science of Complexity" (p. 191). He further describes the emergence of "an inexorable drive toward ever greater complexity and ever greater information processing in nature." The sense of natural systems becoming more fully adapted, more responsive, more creative, echos the ideas Maslow proposed when he described the process of self-actualization. Both human behavior and the behavior of natural systems thrive at the edge of chaos.

Rogers (1959) also postulated that there was an inherent actualizing tendency in all human beings. This actualizing tendency served as a self-organizing principle in guiding a person's development and behavioral expression. The importance of becoming, rather than simply being, reflects the dynamic, evolving, self-organizing dynamics that are so crucial to chaos and complexity theory. "Becoming" reflects the process of aspects of human behavior constantly coming into being that were not available earlier. "If one construes the person as standing in the midst of constant change, where one aspect becomes another, and the form of the person's being (existence) is an unfolding of succession of potentialities that become transformed into actualities, one construes the person as an instance of becoming" (Urban, 1991, p. 210).

This edge of chaos phenomenon, now generally described as complexity, is the state in which systems transform and new orders or behaviors emerge. Complexity theory is often defined as the science of emergence. Stuart Kauffman (1995) proposes that life itself is an emergent phenomenon. Others (e.g., Waldrop, 1992) have used a complexity model to describe the emergence of the mind and consciousness in humans. Anderson and Rosenfeld (1988) state that at each level of complexity, new properties appear and new laws, concepts, and generalizations are necessary.

What Maslow and Rogers have outlined in their theories of self-actualization fit very well with the paradigm of emergence and self-organization in complexity theory. The openness to novelty that characterizes the self-actualizing person is also characteristic of systems at the edge of chaos. Unlike mechanical or inorganic objects, people do not exist in some homeostatic state. Instead, an individual is in a constant state of becoming something other than what he or she is. Life is defined by activity and change. Human beings are in a constant state of creating themselves. An important aspect of humanistic/existential philosophy is that by becoming increasingly open to experience, we become more authentically human.

THE UNIQUENESS OF THE INDIVIDUAL AND STRANGE ATTRACTORS

According to humanist philosophy, every person has an equally significant thread to weave into the fabric of humanity. The value, uniqueness, and importance of each individual is paramount and unquestioned. Every human being's life represents a singular but enormously complex pattern, no two ever exactly repeating. The patterns seen in strange attractors (see Chapter 1) of periodic orbits and aperiodic paths without replication reflect the complexity of human lives. Although similar "attractor points" may exist in many people's lives (e.g., to find meaningful work, to bond with another, to create a family), no one will ever reproduce the exact pattern of anyone else's life.

The nonlinearity of the strange attractor pattern provides an appropriate, useful metaphor for the pattern of a life. Nothing is repeated, but themes and patterns emerge in everyone's unique history. The perspective of the therapist working with this metaphor certainly suits the description offered by humanists and existentialists of the nature of human change and the emergence of self. Rogers' (1961) notions of organizing principles that underlie human functioning, and Adler's (1927) notion of innate movement toward self-consistancy, both reflect the organizational complexity of the individual. This emergence, however, is not static. Change is the norm and stability, or homeostasis, generally is a consequence of some interference with the process of the emergence and creation of the self. In therapy, it is not so much the experience of change as the fear of change that creates problems. "Becoming" is an active, continual process that follows an ever divergent, but ordered path.

William James (Boring, 1929), depicted what would now be considered by chaoticians as a strange attractor pattern when he described individual consciousness as a forever changing state. He proposed that no conscious state that had once occurred could ever recur as the exact same state. Both between and within individuals there exists an irreducible level of uniqueness and unpredictability.

Humanistic science has attempted to find ways to account for the enormous complexity that each person represents. Individuals, over the course of their lives manifest many different intentions, values, patterns, and styles of behaving. Indeed, if there was not the potential for change in these aspects of behavior and personality, psychotherapy would be useless. Despite this enormous complexity, each person generally functions in a unified and organized fashion. There are some organizing principles that both guide and form people's personalities and interpretation of experience. These organizing principles are the points in the strange attractor that create a patterned life, such that we can describe a person in general terms (e.g., she's extroverted, he's sensitive, she's highly intelligent).

SENSITIVE DEPENDENCE ON INITIAL CONDITIONS AND THE UNPREDICTABILITY OF HUMAN BEHAVIOR

Although an observer may be able to make generalizations about a person's personality or behavior, it is impossible to state exactly how an individual will react in novel circumstances, or from one situation to the next. True, a professor may be extroverted when teaching her students, but she may appear self-conscious and shy when being introduced to a potential romantic partner at a singles' party. No one can be understood from fragments of his or her behavior. "Only proximal predictions could be expected, based on a thorough knowledge of where the person was at a given instant in anticipation of an immediate instant to follow, or where artificial constraints have been imposed on, or adopted by, the person as a way of forestalling the unfolding process" (Urban, 1991, p. 210).

In the humanist paradigm, the individual personality remains essentially unpredictable. "Man (sic) does not simply exist, but always decides what his existence will be, what he will become in the next moment ... every human being has the freedom to change at any instant" (Frankl, 1959, pp. 206–207). This unpredictability in chaos theory occurs in part as a result of sensitive dependence on initial conditions (see Chapter 1). Sensitive dependence means that "slightly vague knowledge of the past leads to extremely vague knowledge of the future" (Goertzel, 1995, p. 139). It is essentially hopeless to try and predict the future behavior of any system that displays sensitive dependence. Surely, human beings are the "grand masters" of sensitive dependence because we not only experience events—we remember, review, rehearse, repress, revise, and reconstruct events through our conscious and unconscious cognition. A critical argument posed by the existentialists is that because of the selectivity of experience, individuals are in a continual process of recreating what they are and what they will become. Hence, "the self is not only a product but is also a producer of experience" (Urban, 1991, p. 211). It is this consciousness and the responsibility to exercise choice or free will that becomes an "initial condition" in any circumstance. Events do not impose a structure on our lives, we construct the structure through our responses to events. The foundation for an individual's reaction to any given set of circumstances is therefore highly sensitive to initial conditions, including all of the internal conditions that are a part of that individual.

CONCLUSIONS

Fred Abraham (1995) makes the important point that psychology has "proved deficient in its own humanism" (p. 171). As he notes, "the dynamical systems view ... observes the interrelatedness of virtually all phenomena, and thus highlights a responsibility toward a healthier planet and good will among all people" (p. 171).

One aspect of science that chaos theory emphasizes is the necessity for subjects to be studied in the contextual situations through which they evolve. Robertson (1995) echos that "the whole fabric of a person's life interacts with his or her total environment, and something new emerges that wasn't predictable from previous behavior" (p. 13). It is also the case that each life affects the interwoven net of society. Our culture and community are influenced by each individual just as each individual is affected by his or her context. Context emerges from our interaction as much as our interactions emerge from context. Therefore, the role of the individual as a contributor to society becomes exquisitely important.

Science is again questioning the nature of reality. In these questions—and the answers that chaos theory proposes—lie the potential for a more humanistic psychology that blends scientific and social perspectives. The emergence of not just individual actualization but of cultural and social actualization is a common goal that nonlinearity dynamics and humanist theory can share, each strengthening and supporting the other.

REFERENCES

Abraham, F. (1995). Dynamics, bifurcation, self-organization, chaos, mind, conflict, intensitivity to initial conditions, time, unification, diversity, free will, and social responsibility. In R. Robertson & A. Combs (Eds.), *Chaos theory in psychology and the life sciences* (pp. 155–173). Hillsdale, NJ: Lawrence Erlbaum Associates.

Adler, A. (1927). *Understanding human nature*. New York: Greenberg Publishers.

Allport, G. (1955). *Becoming: Basic considerations for a psychology of personality*. New Haven: Yale University Press.

Anderson, J. A., & Rosenfeld, E. (Eds.). (1988). *Neurocomputing: Foundations of research*.

Boring, E. G. (1929). *A history of experimental psychology*. New York: Appleton-Century-Crofts.

Dodds, J. (June, 1992). *The limits of science in human psychology*. Unpublished manuscript.

Frankl, V. E. (1962). *Man's search for meaning: An introduction to logotherapy*. Boston: Beacon Press.

Fromm, E. (1956). *The art of loving*. New York: Harper & Row.

Goertzel, B. (1995). A cognitive law of motion. In R. Robertson & A. Combs (Eds.), *Chaos theory in psychology and the life sciences* (pp. 135–153). Hillsdale, NJ: Lawrence Erlbaum Associates.

Kauffman, S. (1995). *At home in the universe: The search for the laws of self-organization and complexity*. New York: Oxford University Press.

Leahey, T. H. (1987). *A history of psychology*. New Jersey: Prentice Hall.

Lewin, R. (1992). *Complexity: Life at the edge of chaos*. New York: Collier Books.

Mahoney, M. (1989). Scientific psychology and radical behaviorism: Important distinctions based on scientism and objectivism. *American Psychologist, 44*, 1372–1377.

Maslow, A. H. (1968). *Toward a psychology of being*. New York: D. Van Nostrand Company.

May, R. (1969). *Love and will*. New York: W. W. Norton & Co.

Robertson, R. (1995). Chaos theory and the relationship between psychology and science. In R. Robertson & A. Combs (Eds.), *Chaos theory in psychology and the life sciences* (pp. 3–15). Hillsdale, NJ: Lawrence Erlbaum Associates.

Rogers, C. R. (1951). *Client-centered therapy*. Boston MA: Houghton Mifflin.

Rogers, C. R. (1959). A theory of therapy, personality and interpersonal relationships, as developed in the Client-Centered framework. In S. Koch (Ed.), *Psychology: A study of science. Vol. 11. General systematic formulations, learning and special processes* (pp. 184–256). New York: McGraw-Hill.

Rogers, C. R. (1961). *On becoming a person*. Boston: Houghton Mifflin.
Urban, H. B. (1991). Humanist, phenomenological, and existential approaches. In M. Hersen, A. E. Kazdin, & A. S. Bellack (Eds.), *The clinical psychology handbook* (2nd ed.) (pp. 200–219). New York: Pergamon Press.
Waldrop, M. (1992). *Complexity: The emergence of science at the edge of order and chaos*. New York: Simon & Schuster.

Part Three

Chaos Theory Application in Clinical Research and Practice

In Part 3 of the book, we will look at applications of chaos and complexity theories to specific issues and areas in clinical work. The authors of these chapters have found nonlinear dynamics theories to have practical implications for their research and clinical work. Some of the "pragmatics" of chaos theory can now be explored by focusing on discrete areas of clinical practice. This is the "how to" portion of the book.

The editors wish to issue a caution, however, about moving too quickly into application of these theories. One of our concerns is the rush to go from science to technology. While we believe that chaos and complexity theories offer many useful ideas for clinicians, we don't want to "technologize" the theories by looking only at their application. It has been our experience that clinicians are often in too much of a hurry to find tools or techniques to use in therapy without having a sound theoretical foundation. Also, scientific understanding has often been used without consideration for the "bigger picture" of how new technologies will impact systems. Given chaos theory's emphasis on interdependence of elements in a system and the fact that even small change can have profound impact, we feel it is important to stay close to the ideas before developing techniques. Also, chaos theory is more a way of observing and understanding phenomena than a strategy to manipulate behavior. For that, we are grateful.

With these cautions in mind, we hope that this part of the book offers some sense of how to begin applying the theory in ways that assist clinicians in gaining new understandings. These chapters are written by pioneers in the field. Welcome along in this exploration of new territory.

Chapter 8

Dynamics of Substance Abuse: Implications of Chaos Theory for Clinical Research

Raymond C. Hawkins, II & Catherine A. Hawkins

In this chapter, the possible implications of chaos theory, or the study of dynamical systems, for understanding the etiology and treatment of substance abuse or dependence will be considered. Earlier models have focused on the individual's fluctuating drinking behavior (R.C. Hawkins, 1990, 1992), particularly the neurophysiological actions of alcohol (Ehlers, 1992). In contrast, this chapter argues that chaos theory can be usefully applied to the progressive oscillation of "wet" and "dry" states at both the levels of the individual and the ecological systems context. After outlining the conceptual model, clinical data will be presented which includes a six-year longitudinal time series of daily drinking by one client. It is a case that illustrates a quasi-periodic bifurcating behavior pattern in which shifts in the client's drinking are contextualized and made meaningful by corresponding evolutions in his feelings of shame, social rituals, and employment status.

LINEAR VS. NONLINEAR DYNAMICS

Most causal theories explaining the development of alcoholism and substance abuse have been linear. According to Masters (1991), there are two properties of linear systems: (1) the response is directly proportional to the inputs driving it, and (2) its response can be analyzed as the combination or sum of its separate input factors. For example, Figure 1 depicts a linear progression from a weak habit, or normal drinking, to a strong habit involving obsessive or troublesome use or abuse (Orford, 1985). Orford describes this progression in terms of a series of failed decisions leading to the escalation of use. According to this view, excessive substance use would be the result of a succession of decisions to drink or take drugs. The branching of this tree is linear, by Masters' (1991) definition, since

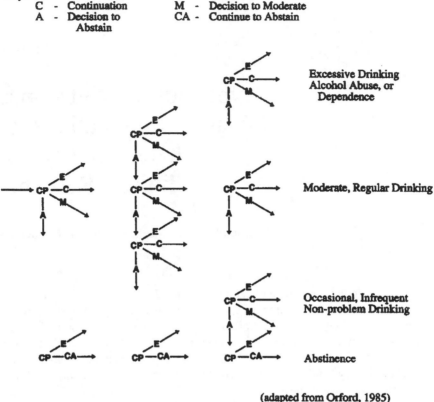

Key: CP - Choice Point   E - Escalation
     C - Continuation   M - Decision to Moderate
     A - Decision to   CA - Continue to Abstain
         Abstain

(adapted from Orford, 1985)

Figure 1   A linear model depicting substance use as a series of choice points (Reproduced with permission. From Orford's Excessive Appetites: A Psychological View of the Addictions. Copyright 1985 by John Wiley & Sons, Limited).

each step is proportional and each outcome is specifiable as the summation of the individual paths leading up to it.

This linear perspective has considerable utility, particularly when embedded in a stress-coping framework which includes multiple life contextual factors (R.C. Hawkins, 1992). It may be limited, however, in accounting for the complex and sudden oscillations of an individual's placement along the continuum of severity of substance abuse over time. Recently, H.A. Skinner (1989) has described nonlinearities in several of the stages of substance use, abuse, and recovery. Skinner has speculated that chaos theory may permit modeling of the relative influences of genetic factors ("initial conditions") and environmental perturbations resulting in a multidimensionality of types of substance abuse in a population. Citing Lorenz's (1963) metaphor of the "butterfly effect" (see Chapter 1), he has speculated that chaotic influences may dramatically affect whether a given individual will develop problems with alcohol or drugs, and also whether these problems will become chronic and degenerative.

To provide an illustration and focus for the application of chaos theory to substance abuse, we shall briefly outline what can be regarded as four problems with current linear models regarding the etiology and treatment of chemical dependency. It is the authors' contention that the current linear model does not adequately offer explanations for these four problems.

The first difficulty is that, despite the advances in behavior genetics and cognitive social learning theory, it remains very uncertain why an individual with a positive family history of alcohol abuse (FHA+) becomes a problem drinker or alcoholic.

Secondly, there is a problem reconciling the unidimensional disease concept of alcoholism with the contrasting view of cognitive social learning theory and social psychology (e.g., Peele, 1985). According to this latter perspective, substance use or abuse is multidimensional and primarily determined by psychosocial, cultural reinforcers. The unidimensional disease model, which is popular among chemical dependency counselors (J. Wallace, 1989), alternatively describes chronic alcoholism as a final common pathway or as a progressive and ultimately fatal disease characterized by social degeneration, alcohol dependence symptoms, and loss of control of drinking. Vaillant's (1983) longitudinal data suggest that the chronicity of problem drinking is an imperfect indicator of severity, since only 3 to 5% of white male alcoholics were found to exhibit this unidimensional pattern of chronic, progressive alcoholism.

A third problem is the difficulty of predicting drinking status at follow-up based on the person's response during treatment (Cronkite & Moos, 1980; Moos, 1985). What Moos and colleagues have discovered (and explained within a social ecological theoretical framework) is the importance of life contextual factors after treatment ends, such as the adequacy of familial and occupational supports for sobriety. These contextual factors are highly influential in affecting an individual's trajectory of recovery after treatment (R.C. Hawkins, 1992). Individuals with family support and stable jobs are less likely to display problem drinking at follow-up.

A fourth problem is that there does appear to be some clinical validity to the commonly alleged phenomenon of alcoholics quickly returning to abuse levels of drinking after taking the first drink following periods of abstinence. Related to this point is the observation of many substance abuse counselors that alcoholics will allege that they are not alcoholic because they can abstain from drinking for a month or two. After such dry periods, wherein abstinence is described as relatively easy, there can be a quite rapid return to excessive drinking.

CHAOS THEORY AND SUBSTANCE ABUSE

How can the concepts of chaos be helpful in addressing these four problems? While reading Gleick's (1987) book titled *Chaos: Making A New Science*, the authors were struck by the potential applicability of the modeling of the rhythm of a dripping faucet as an analog for the fluctuating trajectory of an individual's drinking behavior as a "chaotic attractor." The dripping faucet is a simple example of a system that can exhibit rapid shifts from predictable behavior to unpredictable behavior. The subtle variations from periodic rhythm do not require the careful mapping of a multiplicity of variables such as flow rate, fluid viscosity, or surface tension, but instead can be emulated by a relatively simple, single-variable, non-linear equation. Thus, in like fashion, it may not be necessary to measure all of the multiple life contextual factors to be able to estimate the fluctuating individual trajectory of substance use or abuse.

Why do many persons with a family background of alcoholism not develop substance abuse problems? A genetic component of alcoholism does not necessarily indicate the inevitability of alcoholism for a particular individual. Skinner (1989) applies the phenomenon of sensitive dependence on initial conditions, or the "butterfly effect," to describe how random or chaotic influences may potentially exert a dramatic effect on whether a given individual will develop problems related to drinking. The advantage of chaos theory is that very complicated behavior patterns may be simulated quite successfully using rather simple deterministic models which allow for nonlinear discontinuity effects to operate (Skinner, 1989).

Skinner's potential solution for the problem of whether alcohol dependence reflects a unitary vs. a multidimensional disorder involves a reference to Mandelbrot's (1977) notion of the effective dimension as a heuristic for understanding the dimensionality of alcohol dependence. He describes how an object such as a ball of thread or string can manifest a succession of different dimensional appearances depending on the object's relation to the observer. Thus, at a great distance, the ball of thread may appear as a point (zero-dimensional), but when the thread is seen at arm's length, it appears as a three-dimensional ball. As the ball is brought closer to the eye, it appears as a mass of one-dimensional threads. The effective dimensionality continues to shift or crossover down to the subatomic level, where the thread becomes once again zero-dimensional. Using this model, alcohol dependence can be viewed as both a unitary and a multidimensional disorder, according to the effective dimension:

> At a macro level of resolution, individuals can be ordered quite reliably along a global dimension that encompasses consequences from drinking, alcohol dependence symptoms, and excessive alcohol consumption patterns . . . It is likely that this global factor may be a major contributor to the widely held perception that 'alcoholism' is a unitary disease . . . At a finer level of resolution individuals with alcohol related problems can be distinguished on a number of specific dimensions . . . vital for differential diagnosis and treatment (Skinner, 1989, p. 354).

Fractals, the term coined by Mandelbrot (1977), are defined by self-similarity at different levels of resolution and by "fractional" dimensions (Devaney, 1990). Skinner contends that for chronic substance abusers (e.g., older white males with alcohol dependence), a single dominant dimension ($D = 1.2$) might characterize the effective dimensionality, while for young individuals with a sub-chronic history of substance use or abuse (e.g., a teenage drinker with one DUI) the effective dimensionality might be highly multidimensional (D = 8.4, for instance).

Brown (1985, 1987, 1991) has outlined a unidimensional trajectory for the development of alcoholism and the recovery process. It is similar in appearance to the well-known Jellinek curve (Jellinek, 1960). According to Brown's cognitive-constructivist viewpoint, which incorporates the 12 Steps of Alcoholics Anonymous (AA), the development of alcoholism is characterized by the drug alcohol, and possibly the alcoholic family system as a whole, becoming a central organizing principle with a resultant progressive narrowing of other personal and social experiences not involving drinking. This model postulates alternating contraction and expansion oscillations in a spiral or gyre trajectory, not only at the point of "hitting bottom," but also periodically during recovery. R.C. Hawkins (1992) has elaborated on the life contextual aspects of different points in this unidimensional curve.

Skinner's (1989) assertion of a dimensionality estimate of 1.2 for this unitary dimension implies a substantial decrease in the level of informational complexity of the system, consistent with Brown's view that hitting bottom involves a loss of control or a loss of options and flexibility for deployment of alternative forms of coping. This is not an example of healthy complexity, but rather of a loss of resilience. C.A. Hawkins (1992) has studied the relationship between the invasion of healthy family rituals by the abuse of the drug alcohol, and the manifestation of the subjective experience of shame in the offspring of alcoholic families. It is interesting to speculate that subjective experiences of shame vs. hope may accurately mark the phase transition between systems of varying effective dimensionality. This point will be illustrated in the clinical examples presented at the end of this chapter.

The remaining problem noted earlier involves the alcoholic individual's often clinically observed frequent return to abusive levels of drinking after taking the first drink. This high relapse-proneness may be contrasted with a paradoxical appearance of dry periods wherein abstinence is alleged to be easy. The usual scientific linear explanation brought to bear on this problem involves the specification of high risk situations or expectancies for relapse (Marlatt & Gordon, 1985). We propose that the notions of chaos, and in particular the period-doubling bifurcation orbit, may provide a more parsimonious heuristic for explaining or accounting for this difficulty.

In the period-doubling bifurcation orbit model, which can be reproduced by relatively simple iterations of a particular form of a single-variable quadratic equation (Devaney, 1990, p. 63), there is an initial bifurcation from a baseline unitary state at period two. At period four, there is another bifurcation, yielding four paths, and at period eight a third bifurcation occurs, yielding eight paths.

Consider the possibility that at period one the initial state reflects an individual's choice to have his/her first drink of alcohol. At period two, the subjective experience of drinking is differentiated perhaps into the first mild, pleasurable

Table 1   The Wet and Dry States for the Period Two and Period Three Phase-transitions

Wet states	Dry states
Period Two	
Enjoyable intoxication	Relaxation, sleepiness
Stimulating "high"	Positive expectation of
	next occasion to drink
Period Three	
Euphoria, "blackouts"	Craving
Power-seeking/energization	Anhedonia, alexithymia
Grandiosity/impulsivity	Shame (toxic), denial
"Numbing" (less self–awareness)	"Dry drunk" features:
	Hypersensitivity
	(control, compulsiveness,
	anger, externalization
	of blame, rigidity)

intoxication either as relaxation or as an enjoyable, stimulating "high." Simultaneously, at period two, the non-drinking state is altered from neutrality (the simple absence of the positive drinking state) to a positive feeling-toned expectation of pleasure upon redosing with alcohol (see Table 1). The period-doubling continues with subsequent bifurcations to four, eight, sixteen, thirty-two, etc., on to chaos. In this model, there are bands or "windows" where order appears to emerge out of chaos. Each band is period three (i.e., there are three states), called the "kernel" of chaos (Walter, 1994), because of a mathematically proven theory (see Devaney, 1990) that dynamical systems showing this period-three feature contain all the necessary information for progression to chaos.

We suggest that perhaps at period three, the beginning of chaos, Solomon's (1977) opponent process theory of addiction might be operative. Thus, as chemical dependency begins, the alcoholic's amount and frequency of alcohol intake has reached the point that an inhibitory opponent process ("B") has become activated (i.e., in opposition to an "A" process associated with the state of pleasure associated with drinking). The subjective experience of "B" would be an unpleasant state of craving which can be alleviated most readily by redosing on the desired substance, alcohol. Perhaps for the wet state (Table 1, left column) the period-three bifurcation would yield states of transitory euphoria (correlates of the "A" process), with alternative manifestations such as power seeking/energization, inflation/grandiosity/impulsivity and/or "numbing" (e.g., alcohol-induced decreases in self-awareness, as theorized by Hull [1981]).

Similarly, at period three, dry states (Table 1, right column) (correlates of the "B" process) might be characterized by negative states of craving, and by a spreading sense of anhedonia ("not feeling") or alexithymia ("not talking about feelings"), as described in shame-based theories of the purported adult children of alcoholism syndrome (C.A. Hawkins, 1996a, 1996b; C.A. Hawkins & R.C. Hawkins, 1995). Additional period-three states might include the shame-based denial and dry drunk characteristics associated with hypersensitivity (Twersky, 1990): control, compulsiveness, rigidity, anger, and externalization of blame, as shown in Table 1. These wet and dry states progressively oscillate, not only at the level of the individual drinker, but also at the level of the family system. The degenerative states at period three involve the disruption of daily family routines and celebratory rituals by the alcoholism (C.A. Hawkins, 1997).

More important, though, than our trying to describe and label the nature of the alteration of subjective experience (and any behavioral/neurochemical correlated events) corresponding to the paths at period three is that we note the essential contrast between the Orford (1985) linear, tree-branching model and the nonlinear, relational, analogic process reflected in the period-doubling bifurcations. In Figure 1 the progression from normal drinking to excessive drinking is a linear-branching one. A person's choices move him/her down only one branch at a time. In contrast, in the non-linear, period-doubling orbit model, the assumption is that the effect develops relationally: there is a simultaneous movement along all paths from the point of initial experience with the drug alcohol (period one), to beginning to experience positive reinforcing effects of alcohol intake (period two), to the definite appearance of addictive features (at period three). Once period three is reached, chaos ensues and distinctions between states (or paths) appear to become unpredictable and disorderly. For the alcoholic, it is not that the next drink necessarily produces a loss of control. As J. Wallace (1989, 1992) has pointed out, it is rather the unpredictability of the consequences of a return to drinking. This unpredictability would be consistent with chaos at or beyond period three.

This application of chaos theory implies an addictive process which is presumed to be progressive and irreversible once period three is reached. Thus, there is "no turning back" to pre-abuse levels or states of drinking and non-drinking. This model would also be predictive of the high relapse risk for return to substance abuse at any point in the recovery process. A corollary assumption would be cross-addiction: once period three has been reached for alcohol, this phase transition would be more likely reached for other addictive substances.

At the period-three windows there is an appearance of order emerging out of chaos. Then period-doubling recurs and the system returns to chaos. Perhaps, during these period windows, an alcoholic may experience a dry period and erroneously believe that he/she can engage in controlled drinking thereafter. Unfortunately, however, this control is illusory and the drinking (and social ecology) soon returns to abusive levels.

The value of chaos theory as applied to substance abuse in this fashion is that it describes in a rather simple, deterministic model the unfolding of an addictive process, wherein once the kernel of chaos (at period three) has been reached, the system may be permanently altered. Certainly, models such as this, as Skinner (1989) indicates, may be too simplistic. The real situation may be more complicated. Still, the major contention of this chapter is that nonlinearities or sudden oscillations in alcoholic behavior and subjective experience which appear to be complex can be modeled by fractal dimensions and single-variable mathematical equations with chaotic features.

Our preference is to add a bit more complexity to this basic deterministic process by hypothesizing multiple perturbational fields (e.g., stressors, personal coping resources, social ecological coping resources) surrounding each choice point (scc Figure 1) for the paths of substance use or abuse. Thus, there would be a magnification of influences which may exhibit chaotic features, as the individual or family system is undergoing phase transition. Gleick (1987) has stated that "the border between calm and catastrophe can be far more complex than anyone has dreamed" (p. 235). These fractal basin boundaries seem to describe the confluence of factors potentially operative upon the individual at the choice point. An individual's personal coping resources and his/her social ecology form the life context which may or may not be sufficient to buffer stresses (R.C. Hawkins, 1992). These influences may interact in a highly influential chance fashion on individual life trajectories (Bandura, 1982). In the case of "gamma" (chronic, progressive) alcoholism, personal and social ecological coping resources may be nearly depleted, thus leaving the individual more vulnerable to the period-doubling chaos process, called "hitting bottom" in the Jellinek curve, with the associated loss of healthy chaos (flexibility and resilience).

Theorizing a role for multivariate life contextual factors may provide an explanation for the recovery process. The earlier interpretation of the single-variable period-doubling orbit model as applied to alcoholism was that once the individual had reached period three, there could be no return to normal drinking and nondrinking states. Perhaps a "structural coupling" (Chubb, 1990, citing Maturana and Varela, 1987) happens in which two self-organizing systems—the alcoholic individual and the AA fellowship, for example—engage in a healing dialogue. In this case there would be a breaking free from the chaotic period-doubling process in the individual and his/her dysfunctional social system. Remember that humans are open systems, highly differentiated and integrated in nature. Thus, there could be many points for altering a basic addictive process, but these salutary influences would need to be sustained in order for the recovery process to continue. The high relapse-proneness suggested in the period-doubling orbit model would otherwise prevail.

The rapid relapse to excessive alcohol use predicted by the period-doubling chaos model would require active intervention not only to prevent a redosing on alcohol, but also to alter the dry drunk characteristics involving dysfunctional cognitions, attitudes, and beliefs controlling behavior, as well as shame effects which have covered over normal emotional responses. These cognitive-affective processes appear to involve the paradoxical combination of hypersensitivity to external stress and dampened emotional responsiveness (e.g., anhedonia and alexithymia). Twersky (1990) has clearly described these thinking distortions, which he calls "addictologia." We contend that the overarching marker of increasing addiction is cognitive-affective narrowing, which has been termed a defensive preference for simplicity by Vitousik and Hollon (1990). The process of recovery (e.g., the 12 Steps of Alcoholics Anonymous) represents one clear example of an external intervention (a "perturbation" in the constructivist framework of Maturana and Varela, 1987), which may provide the countervailing force against this degenerative, chaotic addictive process. Therefore, if we look at chaotic processes in chemical dependency at different levels of abstraction (e.g., according to the theory of logical types, Bateson, 1979), we can model complex interactions through coupling of simpler systems.

CASE STUDIES

This chapter has attempted to show how several difficulties of linear models of substance abuse can be clarified within the conceptual framework of chaos theory. These concepts will now be applied to describe nonlinearities in the individual trajectories of three male alcoholics, each of whom the first author worked with in outpatient group chemical dependency treatment as well as in individual psychotherapy for over five years. All three men are FHA+, and, viewed at the macro level, they display some of the negative consequences of the drug alcohol in their lives as hypothesized in the unidimensional disease model. These three patients' trajectories, however, are quite dissimilar and multidimensional: the first patient has displayed periodic excessive drinking in the form of lengthening and intensifying binges to the end point of "gamma" alcoholism (Jellinek, 1960). The second patient has displayed a combination pattern (Miller & Marlatt, 1984) in which binge episodes were superimposed on heavy daily drinking. He has been sober for the past four years through AA, and individual psychotherapy has focused on identifying and modifying various manifestations of dry drunk cognitive-affective phenomena. Finally, the third patient, also a binge drinker and FHA+, had episodic excessive drinking which could be described as a quasi-periodic bifurcating behavior pattern in which drinking episodes were becoming less frequent over a 6-year period of individual psychotherapy, perhaps suggesting the gradual emergence of order out of chaos. In all three cases there are ample indications of sudden discontinuities in the rate and amount of drinking, which may be construed as psychic "complexes" (in the Jungian sense), associated with life events involving significant social ecological changes. In all three cases, loss of a significant relationship was associated with alcohol consumption.

Figure 2 presents the average overall weekly alcohol intake of the third patient over the entire six year period of his therapy. He kept a daily record of alcohol intake, yielding over 2,000 data points. Analysis of these data by T. Masters (personal communication, 5–17–91) suggested a periodic cycle with the period slowly lengthening, a bifurcating behavior pattern which might be reproduced by a network of cascaded dynamical systems, where the output (trajectory) in one dynamical system modifies the control parameter(s) in another and so on. The shifts in drinking may be interpreted in relation to corresponding fluctuations in this social

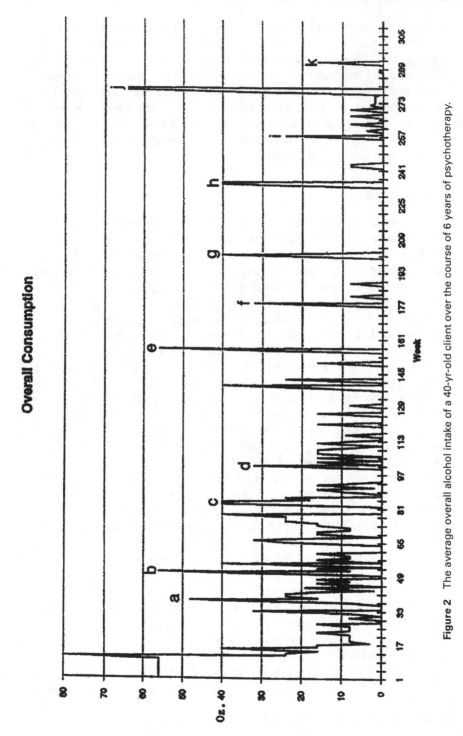

Figure 2   The average overall alcohol intake of a 40-yr-old client over the course of 6 years of psychotherapy.

Table 2   Self-reported Memories Associated with Increased Alcohol Consumption by the Client (Corresponding to Peaks "a" to "k" in Figure 2).

Peak	Memory
"a"	Sick with flu
"b"	Returned from out–of–town visit to see friends, lonely
"c"	At relative's funeral, thinks of parents' deaths
"d"	Frustrated after heavy rain washes out newly planted grass seed
"e"	Anxious thinking of going to Europe alone
"f"	Lonely before Thanksgiving; Female supervisor "hovers" over him "like mother"
"g"	Resentment over having to pay large tax bill
"h"	Depressed over the holidays
"i"	Went to club with friend who bought beer and gave him pot
"j"	Blackouts, awoke with gun on table, didn't know how it got there
"k"	Feeling "mentally inactive," bored, and ill

ecological context. Table 2 shows the subjective reports corresponding to these choice points where alcohol intake increased (shown in Figure 2), which suggests disproportionate, non-linear relationships. This client was a 40-year-old, single white male whose alcohol intake pattern over the 10 years preceding therapy was 1/2 to 1 pint of bourbon 3–4 times per week with weekly smoking of 1–2 joints of cannabis. Negative consequences of this pattern included health problems, increased social isolation (aggravating a sense of shame and inferiority stemming from a childhood disability), and social phobia (which limited his occupational level of functioning). He initiated treatment after his substance use increased following the death of his last surviving parent. Significant lapses involving drinking were often recalled in conjunction with a negative emotional and/or social event. An integrative cognitive-behavioral and Jungian approach seemed to be effective with this client, who found AA unsatisfactory. He essentially re-narrated his life experience by journaling both his difficulties and his social accomplishments throughout treatment. Therapy finally ended when the client obtained a well-paying job in a field which utilized his creative abilities and provided an affirming network with social rituals which diminished his shame and increased his self-efficacy.

THE LIFE-CONTEXTUAL CLINICAL MODEL

In conclusion, it is helpful to view these phenomena within the life contextual systems framework, which can incorporate Skinner's (1989) speculations based on chaos theory. This model is based on the work of Moos (1985), Brown (1985, 1987, 1991), Katakis (1989), and Orford (1985). This formulation is a cognitive-constructivist theory which facilitates understanding of the multiple pathways for the development of substance abuse and chemical dependency. At the macro level, there is the unhealthy chaos of the degenerative process of narrowing of alternative enjoyable experiences, as described in the Jellinek curve and by Brown (1985, 1987, 1991). Thus, the course of an individual's substance use or abuse can be plotted as an upwards or downwards fluctuating trajectory with choices to maintain, increase, or decrease use. These bifurcations may display chaotic features (e.g., period doubling involving changes in organismic states in both wet and dry phases).

Reformulating Orford's (1985) linear sequential model within the nonlinear, relational, analog, life contextual perspective may permit exploration of the influences of life stress events and of personal and social-ecological coping resources on an individual's choices at any given point in time. It is at these choice points that the individual will be most susceptible to the influences of chaotic processes, either in a healthy or unhealthy fashion.

REFERENCES

Bandura, A. (1982). The psychology of chance encounters and life paths. *American Psychologist, 37*, 747–755.

Bateson, G. (1979). *Mind and nature: A necessary unity.* New York: Dutton.

Brown, S. (1985). *Treating the alcoholic: A developmental model of recovery.* New York: John Wiley & Sons.

Brown, S. (1987). *Treating children of alcoholics: A developmental perspective.* New York: John Wiley & Sons.

Brown, S. (1991). Children of chemically dependent parents: Academic perspectives. In T. M. Rivinus (Ed.), *Children of chemically dependent parents: Academic, clinical, and public policy perspectives.* New York: Brunner/Mazel.

Chubb, H. (1990). Looking at systems as process. *Family Process, 29,* 169–176.

Cronkite, R., & Moos, R. H. (1980). The determinants of posttreatment functioning of alcoholic patients: A conceptual framework. *Journal of Consulting and Clinical Psychology, 48,* 305–316.

Devaney, R. L. (1990). *Chaos, fractals, and dynamics: Computer experiments in mathematics.* Menlo Park, CA: Addison-Wesley.

Ehlers, C. L. (1992). The new physics of chaos: Can it help us understand the effects of alcohol? *Alcohol Health & Research World, 16*(4), 267–272.

Gleick, J. (1987). *Chaos: Making a new science.* New York: Viking Press.

Hawkins, C. A. (1992). *Pathogenic family relations, adult children of alcoholics, and shame dynamics in alcoholics, depressives, and normal controls* (Doctoral dissertation, University of Texas, Graduate School of Social Work).

Hawkins, C. A. (1996a). Pathogenic and protective relations in alcoholic families (I): Development of the Ritual Invasion Scale. *Journal of Family Social Work, 1*(4), 39–49.

Hawkins, C. A. (1996b). Pathogenic and protective relations in alcoholic families (II): Ritual invasion, shame, ACOA traits, and problem drinking in adult offspring. *Journal of Family Social Work, 1*(4), 51–63.

Hawkins, C. A. (1997). Disruption of family rituals as a mediator of the relationship between parental drinking and adult adjustment in offspring. *Addictive Behaviors, 22*(2), 219–231.

Hawkins, C. A., & Hawkins, R. C., II. (1995). Development and validation of an Adult Children of Alcoholics Tool. *Research on Social Work Practice, 5*(3), 317–339.

Hawkins, R. C., II. (1990). Dynamics of substance abuse: Nonlinearities in individual trajectories. *Network: The Newsletter for Psychology Teachers at Two-Year Colleges, 8*(3), 9–10. Washington, DC: American Psychological Association.

Hawkins, R. C., II. (1992). Substance abuse and stress-coping resources: A life contextual clinical viewpoint. In B. C. Wallace (Ed.), *The chemically dependent: Phases of treatment and recovery.* New York: Brunner/Mazel.

Hull, J. G. (1981). A self-awareness model of the causes and effects of alcohol consumption. *Journal of Abnormal Psychology, 90*, 586–600.

Jellinek, E. M. (1960). *The disease concept of alcoholism.* New Haven, CT: College and University Press.

Katakis, C. D. (1989). Stages of psychotherapy: Progressive reconceptualizations as a self-organizing process. *Psychotherapy, 26*, 484–493.

Lorenz, E. H. (1963). Deterministic non-periodic flow. *Journal of Atmospheric Sciences, 20*, 130–141.

Mandelbrot, B. (1977). *The fractal geometry of nature.* New York: W. H. Freeman & Co.

Marlatt, G. A., & Gordon, J. R. (1985). *Relapse prevention: Maintenance strategies in the treatment of addictive behaviors.* New York: The Guilford Press.

Masters, T. (1991). *Computable chaos: A seminar on computable chaos* (Presented at Austin, TX, April 12–13th). Seattle, WA: Orion/Wellspring.

Maturana, H. R., & Varela, F. J. (1987). *The tree of knowledge.* Boston: New Science Library.

Miller, W. R., & Marlatt, G. A. (1984). *Manual for the Comprehensive Drinker Profile.* Odessa, FL: Psychological Assessment Resources, Inc.

Moos, R. H. (1985). Foreword. In S. Shiffman & T. A. Wills (Eds.), *Coping and substance use* (pp. xiii–xix). Orlando FL: Academic Press.

Orford, J. (1985). *Excessive appetites: A psychological view of the addictions.* New York: John Wiley & Sons.

Peele, S. (1985). *The meaning of addiction: Compulsive experience and addiction.* Lexington, MA: Lexington Books.

Skinner, H. A. (1989). Butterfly wings flapping: Do we need more 'chaos' in understanding addictions? *British Journal of Addiction, 84*, 353–356.

Solomon, R. L. (1977). An opponent-process theory of acquired motivation: IV. The affective dynamics of addiction. In J. D. Maser, & M. E. P. Seligman (Eds.), *Psychopathology: Experimental models* (pp. 66–103). New York: W. H. Freeman & Co.

Twersky, A. (1990). *Addictive thinking: Understanding self-deception.* San Francisco: Harper & Row.

Vaillant, G. E. (1983). *The natural history of alcoholism: Causes, patterns, and paths to recovery.* Cambridge, MA: Harvard University Press.

Vitousek, K. B., & Hollon, S. D. (1990). The investigation of schematic content and processing in eating disorders. *Cognitive Therapy & Research, 14*, 191–214.

Wallace, B. (Ed.). (1992). *The chemically dependent: Phases of treatment and recovery.* New York: Brunner/Mazel.

Wallace, J. (1989). *Writings: The alcoholism papers.* Newport, RI: Edgehill Publications.

Walter, K. (1994). *Tao of chaos: Merging of east and west.* Austin, TX: Kairos Center.

Chapter 9

Implications of Chaos Theory for the Prevention and Treatment of Child Abuse

Ray Quackenbush

In recent years there has been an explosion of interest in the treatment and prevention of child abuse. The popular media is full of reports of the battering, sexual molestation, and serious neglect of children, while self-help and recovery books are perennial best sellers. Each year, the professional journals print an ever increasing number of articles dealing with this vital subject; and yet, few graduate programs offer a specialization in this area. Many do not even include a course on child abuse in their curricula. The topic is certainly not ignored when training clinicians, but, as will be argued in this chapter, more complex and successful treatment and prevention methods require a more detailed approach than is generally offered. Chaos theory has an important contribution to make toward understanding child abuse. Indeed, chaos theory can contribute significantly to an understanding of how to prevent the recurrence of child abuse.

DYNAMICS OF CHAOS

At the onset, it is useful to review a few of the basic concepts in chaos theory which impact a discussion of the family dynamics of child abuse and the dynamics of the individual abuser. One of the most important, as noted in Chapter 1, is that of sensitive dependence on initial conditions. Complex systems can never be predicted in all of their myriad details even though they are mathematically deterministic (Kellert, 1993). To be able to precisely foresee all of the possible outcomes, one must be able to specify exactly the conditions from which one begins. In practice, it is never possible to specify the initial conditions of any system which would be clinically interesting, or for that matter any complex system, in sufficient detail to accurately predict all of the possible later behavior of the system.

A second important concept is bifurcation. As noted in Chapter 1, bifurcation occurs when the trajectory of a system reaches a point where it can take either of two possible routes. The system makes a "decision" about its future behavior when it follows one or the other route. The routes not taken, as well as those followed, remain as possibilities in the behavior of the system (Briggs & Peat, 1989). Through the process of bifurcation, the system can quickly reach a point where it is impossible for the observer to predict its behavior in any meaningful way. Bifurcation is the best understood route to chaos, but there are potentially many others which are not yet understood (Kellert, 1993). Bifurcation is very important in understanding child abuse.

In Chapter 1, the reader was introduced to one of the best known concepts in chaos theory, that of the strange attractor or, as many scientists know the term, chaotic attractor (Barton, 1994). Many human systems, both behavioral and biological, have been shown to exhibit strange attractors (Barton, 1994; Bütz, 1995; Post, 1992; Abraham, Abraham, Shaw, & Garfinkel, 1990; Briggs & Peat, 1989; Glass & Mackey, 1988). It is the movement of the system about a strange attractor which produces the apparent noise in the system—the data outliers which are so pesky for psychologists and others employing stochastic methods of data analysis (Peitgen, Jurgens, & Dietmar, 1992; Judd & McClelland, 1989; Briggs & Peat, 1989; Glass & Mackey, 1988). If the researcher is using statistical methods, these outlying points are treated in some way so that they will be obscured by the rest of the data. When this is done, important detail which can be critical to describing the behavior of the system is lost. Psychology, and the other social sciences, relies heavily on statistics. While this has proven to be a generally fruitful approach, it is not always adequate for dealing with complex systems (Gleick, 1987). In what follows, we will examine the complexity of child abuse using chaos theory to explore certain implications.

DYNAMICS OF CHILD ABUSE

Child abuse can be defined as any act or omission by a parent or other caretaker of a child which causes lasting harm or injury to the child either physically or psychologically. This includes physical abuse such as striking the child in a way that produces physical or psychological damage. It also includes things such as placing the child in scalding water. Sexual abuse in all of its many forms is also included. While this certainly includes incest, it would also include any age-inappropriate sexual stimulation of the child by another person. Also a part of the definition of child abuse is the neglect of any important need of the child by a parent or caretaker, such as not obtaining medical attention for the child which results in serious illness or other harm. It also means depriving the child of needed food or education to the point of causing lasting harm. Neglect has become a leading cause for intervention in families by child protective agencies in recent years.

While this definition of child abuse may seem overly detailed, or a statement of the obvious, many people do not recognize serious acts of abuse toward children. Also, this definition is flexible enough to be used in widely differing cultures. Declaring a particular act to be abusive can be ethnocentric. Some acts which are very damaging to children in one cultural context are not as serious in others. People from a broad cultural spectrum seem to be able to accept the essential idea that it is taboo to cause permanent harm to a child physically or psychologically, provided that they understand how the child is harmed by their act or omission. This understanding is often a critical element in stopping and preventing child abuse.

Child abuse occurs in a context which includes not only the individuals involved, but also other family members and the larger society. The interplay of biological and social systems is staggering in its complexity. It is important to examine the interaction of neurophysiological and hormonal systems in the abuser, to begin to understand the myriad of details involved in the dynamics of child abuse. Post (1992) has suggested a model which is useful in explaining the physiological processes of the emotional system of the child abuser. This model was developed to describe recurrent affective disorders, but much of it can be adapted to other cyclical emotional processes. Post presents both a behavioral-sensitization model and an electrophysiological-kindling model. He notes that the first episode of affective disorder is likely to be associated with major psychosocial stressors.

Instances of child abuse often are likewise associated with major psychosocial stressors. Post (1992) also notes that electrical and chemical stimulation and psychosocial stressors affect gene expression and thereby present a way in which acute events can have long-lasting effects on the subsequent reactivity of the individual. He points out that recent systematic studies have explicitly tested and confirmed the notion that there is a greater role for psychosocial stressors in the initial episode than in later episodes of emotional disorder. This may be the significant bifurcation point in which abusive behavior moves the system on a different pathway and becomes amplified over time.

Psychomotor stimulant-induced and stress-induced sensitization share many elements, and each can produce cross-sensitization to the other. This has an implication for child abuse, since stimulant drugs are sometimes a factor in the etiology of episodes of child abuse. Post goes on to explain that there is increasing recognition that activation of neurotransmitter pathways produces not only acute events associated with rapid alterations in neural firing and short-term neuronal adaptation, but also a series of events which have much longer lasting consequences for the individual. The process of neuronal transmission sets in motion intracellular changes at the level of gene transcription. One change he describes is the induction of a series of transcription factors which alter later gene expression by binding at DNA sites and inducting mRNAs for other substrates that may exert effects over long time periods of days to months. By virtue of their acute effects, these transcription factors may provide the basis for a spatiotemporal cascade of events that result in more enduring neurotransmitter, receptor, and peptide changes that might provide the biochemical and anatomical basis for long-term synaptic adaptations and memory that could last indefinitely. The neurological system thus retains a record of the bifurcations leading to a particular emotional state.

Post continues by noting that the type, magnitude, and frequency of repetition of the stressor may be critical to its long-term effects. Similarly, the quality of the stressor may affect particular neural systems based not only on the type and location of short-term biochemical changes but also on the type, location, mixture, and interaction of the transcription factors, with differential consequences for subsequent coding of long-term protein and peptide changes. Stressors involving losses and threats of loss in a social context may have very different cognitive, behavioral, and neurobiological consequences from stresses including the threat of bodily injury. Stress related to separation, loss, and impaired self esteem which are associated with the onset of depression, may provide a long-term vulnerability to subsequent recurrences and serve as a mechanism for the retriggering of episodes with lesser degrees of psychosocial stress. Sufficient repetitions of episodes and specific triggers may no longer be required to induce a full-blown symptom.

Post (1992) points out that it is also likely in some instances that long-term neurobiological responses to stress may be encoded not just in biochemical processes but also in microanatomical ones. This suggests that, depending on the stage of temporal evolution in the course of the alteration of the individual, not only might the neurochemical and microstructural synaptic mechanisms markedly differ, but the gross neuroanatomical substrates may be different as well. If this proves to be the case, it would support a reconceptualization of the neurobiology of affective disorder (and by extension, the propensity toward abusive behavior) as a sequentially evolving process rather than a static one.

Abraham, Abraham, Shaw, and Garfinkel (1990) have developed a model of the hypothalamic–pituitary–adrenocortical system which supports Post (1992). They have constructed differential equations which allow them to examine the effects on the trajectory of the system for various levels of stress and feedback. Situations of strong feedback result in a damped oscillatory, out-of-phase trajectory. The authors speculate that stronger feedback would result in bifurcation of the trajectory.

There are important implications for child abuse in the models of Post (1992) and Abraham, et al. (1990). First, the organism seems to undergo a series of changes at levels from the gross anatomical to the molecular as it becomes conditioned to respond emotionally to psychosocial stressors. Second, the emotional response to psychosocial stressors occurs at lower and lower levels of stress. Eventually, the organism may not require the stressor before emoting spontaneously. Third, at higher levels of stress, the response of the organism can take alternate forms, as suggested in chaos theory. The trajectory of the system has the possibility to bifurcate. Finally, the organism retains a memory within its neuroanatomy of the bifurcations taken by the system in reaching a particular emotional state in response to stress. The system begins to self-organize around the new behavior patterns. The organism retains the ability to return to prior emotional responses to specific stimuli, even after new responses have been developed.

As noted in Chapters 1, 6 and 10, families are persistent, self-organizing, self-renewing, autonomous, far-from-equilibrium, complex systems called "autopoietic structures" (Briggs & Peat, 1989). They have unique histories. Families tend to maintain their identities over long periods of time. They have definite boundaries which separate them from the rest of society. Certain structures within families can persist for many generations. These structures are examples of solitons—precise correlations of positive and negative feedback loops which are exactly counterposed so that behavior is maintained over extraordinarily long periods (Briggs & Peat, 1989), often for generations. Child abuse is an example of a soliton. It represents a complex, persistent counterposition of positive and negative feedback within the autopoietic structure of the family which can persist not only for many years within a single generation, but can be reproduced in successive generations.

In order to more fully understand the complex dance which occurs in abusive families, the reader is referred to the literature of family therapy, especially that of Bowenian systems theory (Friedman, 1991; Kerr, 1981). Briefy, within any family, the members move together in a sort of lock step. Each member of the system responds in a patterned way to the actions of the other members. The various actions of family members fit precisely together to maintain the structure of the family. The members of the family system are said to be phase locked. While each member of the family maintains integrity as a biological entity, members move in concert together. This can be easily demonstrated by video recording a family acting together for an hour and then playing the recording back without sound at an enhanced speed. The family members will be seen to move physically as if in a carefully choreographed dance.

Carl Whitaker is reported to have observed that there are no nuclear families, only two families of origin competing to reproduce themselves (D. Rohland, personal communication, 1989). People seem to pair with others who are able to fit the patterns of positive and negative feedback which were featured in the family systems in which they grew up. This is how the solitons which represent the various patterns of behavior that characterize the structure of the new family are maintained from one generation to the next. The actual process is very subtle and complex and takes place almost entirely out of the consciousness of the people involved. In other words, it is as if each one knows how to perform the steps of a single dance. Only those who know how to perform the same or a very similar dance will feel right as a dance partner.

Persons who come from families which either have child abuse or feature many of the dynamics which support child abuse are at high risk of paring with others who will support similar family dynamics. Both individuals seem to carry a record in some way of the bifurcations which lead to child abuse. Even if child abuse does not occur in later generations, the systemic record of bifurcations brings the family trajectory to the soliton of child abuse. It is not necessary for a person to come from a family which was abusive for him or her to pair with an abuser. If the dynamics of a family are similar enough to those with child abuse, the record of bifurcations will be similar enough to allow the person to fit with another whose family dynamics support child abuse and thereby reproduce the soliton of child abuse in the new family.

Clinically, acts of child abuse appear to be cyclical in their occurrence. There is an observable sequence of events which takes place on both family and individual levels, which repeats over and over. A typical sequence would include an interval during which the level of stress in the family and the individual abuser is lower, and there is less risk, or even no risk, of child abuse occurring. This is followed by a period during which the level of family stress increases, and the abuser begins to show some emotional response to the increased systemic stress. At some point, while the level of stress in the family remains elevated, the abuser responds by doing something which is harmful to a child. In some cases this may temporarily lower the systemic level of stress, in others it does not, or even raises the stress level for the system. As long as the stress continues at a level which produces an emotional reaction in the abuser, the incidence of child abuse continues. When the level of stress is eventually lowered, the abuser ceases to abuse and the cycle is back at the initial phase.

The key to understanding this process is the family level of stress. Family system theorists regard the dynamics of the family system as more powerful in determining behavior than the dynamics of the individual members of the family system. The factors which affect the level of stress in the family are often not well understood by the clinician or others involved in interventions around child abuse. If the clinician focuses only on the individual abuser or victim, then much of the systemic detail needed to formulate an effective intervention will be lost.

CYCLES OF ABUSE AND NEGLECT

To facilitate an understanding of this model of child abuse as a response to stress in the family and the individual abuser, a few examples are offered. In the case of physical abuse, a frequently seen example is that of a child who has come to the attention of the clinician or of the authorities as a result of having been injured in the course of being disciplined physically by a parent. Not uncommonly, the abuse is discovered when the child comes to school with bruises on the face or welts on the arms or legs. This may cause school personnel to make a report of suspected child abuse to the local child protective services agency, triggering an investigation and possibly some intervention in the family. The child's injuries are the result of events which began years before. Often one or both parents grew up in homes where it was accepted for parents to hit children, sometimes with belts or other weapons, as a routine form of discipline. This has produced both neurophysiological and behavioral patterns in the abuser which create a predisposition toward physical assault under certain circumstances. Likely, each member of the family has been experiencing increasing stresses from job, school, economic, or health circumstances. The family system is moving toward abuse and usually the abuser will not recognize the danger. Finally, the inevitable occurs: the child makes some demand on her parent when the parent is emotionally unable to cope. An explosion of rage occurs and the child is injured. For a while, the tension in the system is lessened.

Close examination of the circumstances surrounding the incident of abuse will often reveal the cycle of events in the family. The parent(s) or caretaker(s) of the child frequently were punished physically themselves as children. This has established a constellation of dynamics in the family which support the use of physical force as a means of controlling behavior. This constellation includes the neuroanatomical consequences in the abuser of the acts of abuse they suffered as a child. Over some interval of time, the level of stress in the family system has risen from what it was before abuse was likely. This may be a slow process or a rapid one. As the system progresses through various bifurcations in response to the increased stress, a bifurcation point is reached after which abuse can occur with little or no change in stress level. This point is usually not identifiable except in retrospect, if at all (Arthur, 1990). Once that point is reached, all that is needed for child abuse to occur is some trigger such as an ill-timed remark or action of defiance by a child in response to efforts by the overstressed parent to control his or her behavior. Once the abusive sequence has occurred, there may follow a period when both child and abuser avoid doing anything to precipitate a recurrence. There may also follow a period of prolonged abuse until something happens which lowers the overall systemic level of stress, such as the abuser becoming sedated by alcohol or drugs.

A scenario for sexual abuse would be similar. However, clinically, sexual abuse often has the characteristic of occurring during periods of elevated family stress lasting weeks, months, or even years, whereas physical abuse often occurs in cycles of hours to days. Clinical experience indicates that over two thirds of abusers have reported that their abuse of the victim took place during a period of prolonged, increased economic stress. Acts of sexual abuse seem to fall into two rather distinct patterns; they occur as isolated events which may recur after an interval of months or years, or else they occur as more frequent events, recurring in rapid succession. The prognosis for change in the abuser is much better in the former than the latter situation. Most of the sexual abusers in treatment have reported being sexually molested themselves as children. While there has been a greatly increased interest in the dynamics of sexual abuse in recent years, this area is not well understood. It is probable that in sexual abuse as well as physical abuse, there is a bifurcation point beyond which sexual abuse is likely to occur and which can be identified only in retrospect.

Neglect is an area of child abuse which has seemed to rise dramatically in recent years in response to the increase in the use of stimulant drugs. That is not to say that drugs such as alcohol and heroin do not increase the risk of abusive neglect of children—they do. Rather, it seems to be easier for many parents to maintain a minimal level of functioning on alcohol or heroin which does not result in a level of neglect which is as likely to come to the attention of the authorities as that seen with users of crack cocaine and smokeable methamphetamines. Neglect in extreme substance-abusing families follows a prolonged, and heart breaking cycle. The level of systemic stress in these families is often unbearably high, and includes elements such as serious chronic medical conditions, economic collapse, repeated failure to protect children from abuse (both physical and sexual) by visitors to the family, legal difficulties, and even starvation. Against a constant background of substance-induced stress, the family cycles through events of physical and sexual abuse while the vital needs of the children are not met. Often, well intentioned extended family members or even social welfare agencies attempt to intervene, but the family responds by withdrawing and continuing the cycle. Frequently, children from these families have babies at very young ages in a futile attempt to escape from the despair and hopelessness of the neglect cycle. This often serves only to reproduce the cycle again in a new generation.

CLINICAL IMPLICATIONS

So far, a general model of child abuse has been presented that draws on several elements of chaos theory. It is now time to look at what these ideas mean in terms of implications for the clinician in the prevention and treatment of child abuse. What should stand out clearly is the notion that child abuse involves a very complex set of dynamics which persist over generations unless something is done which effectively changes them. Child abuse seems likely to produce a series of alterations in the neurological system of the individual which affect responses to stress indefinitely. These changes form a permanent record of the bifurcations of the individual organism's emotional systems which are available to the individual for the rest of his or her life. For this reason, clinicians must never assume that the effects of child abuse have been "cured" or are so changed that the individual would never abuse a child in the future. This is not to say that victims of abuse are doomed to repeat the abuse on others. That is certainly not in agreement with clinical experience. What is meant is that since the system preserves the record of past behavioral alternatives in its neuroanatomy, and since this record is always available, it is always possible for the individual to return to past behavior given the presence of the right family dynamics. The clinician must work to make certain that such a situation is unlikely.

Likewise, the family will retain a record of the bifurcations which led to abuse in the past. Like the individual, the family system can always return to remembered past behavior if presented with similar enough circumstances. Child abuse is a far more complex and persistent problem than most people who work with it professionally realize. The tendency is to do something which seems to alter the aspect of child abuse which brought the matter to the clinician's attention in the first place and to ignore the rest of the individual and family dynamics involved. This is a serious mistake. As described by the paradigm of sensitive dependence on initial conditions (Chapter 1), the clinician can never know the conditions at any point in the family well enough to accurately predict future behavior where child abuse is concerned. Attempting to predict future behavior around child abuse is just like trying to precisely predict the closing high and low temperatures in San Francisco for a specific day ten years hence. Because the clinician is dealing with a very complex system, precise future predictions of behavior are impossible. The nature of chaos makes it so. That is the implication of both sensitive dependence on initial conditions and the bifurcation route to chaos in a system.

Of course, the clinician would like to be able to alter things so that future abuse is not possible. Because the record of past bifurcations remains, this is impossible. The system will always retain the ability to revert to previous behavior. What the clinician can do is to develop a thorough understanding of the risk factors involved in child abuse in general and especially for the particular family with which one is dealing. This understanding can then be used to guide work which will allow the clinician to assist the individuals involved in developing alternate behaviors and alternate emotional responses. This process generally takes more time and involves more work by the clinician and the clients than traditional approaches to treating child abuse. It has the advantage of more effectively preventing relapse within the family system.

It is essential that this work be done. The system not only retains the record of past bifurcations, and hence the ability to revert to past behavior, but one can never be certain when a bifurcation point has been reached which will lead to child abuse until after the fact. Detailed risk assessment and detailed planning for relapse prevention are the essential steps in prevention and treatment of child abuse. They are often overlooked with serious consequences.

Too often, clinicians and other child abuse professionals, such as juvenile judges, do not understand the implications of chaos theory for child abuse, with the result that they attempt to produce only part of the changes in the system needed to insure that there is no future child abuse in the family. A common mistake that is made is to assume that if one partner in a relationship has been abusive to a child, the other partner needs to focus on leaving that partner to protect the child. Merely removing the abuser from the family leaves all of the other dynamics in place. Very little has changed and there is a high probability that the remaining parent or caretaker will replace one abusing partner with another. A much safer and more comprehensive approach is for the clinician to do whatever is needed to make a thorough inventory of the dynamics—both individual and familial—which led to the incident of abuse. This is then used to guide the clinical work so that one by one, every important risk factor is uncovered and the client is helped to develop alternate behaviors and emotional responses. The client also must be taught to recognize what behaviors or emotional states are dangerous for him or her because they can lead to an incident of child abuse. These behaviors and emotional states must be avoided by the client. If the client starts down the route these represent, he or she must recognize he/she is on dangerous ground and immediately take corrective measures.

This is a tall order for both clients and clinicians, but it is not impossible. It has in fact been successfully accomplished by thousands, if not millions, of individuals already in preventing the relapse of child abuse and in preventing the relapse of substance abuse. The approach is actually borrowed from substance abuse relapse prevention (Gorski, 1990; Marlatt & Gordon, 1985). The situation for child abuse is, however, much more complicated than that for substance abuse. In substance abuse relapse prevention, not using alcohol or drugs is enough to say that relapse has been successfully prevented. In child abuse, not using alcohol or drugs may be only one important element in the equation.

Successful treatment of child abuse involves not only helping the victim to "heal" the psychic wounds of his or her abuse, but also helping the family adopt a new way of living and of looking at their lives. This involves work from several perspectives. In extreme cases, it may involve the intervention and cooperation of child protective agencies and the courts to produce sufficient leverage to begin to change the underlying family structure.

No matter what setting one works in, it is necessary to meet clients where they are in order to begin the clinical process. This seems like common sense, but many clinicians are not prepared by experience or training to work with the extremely powerful material which is the daily fare of therapy around child abuse. Too often, therapists shy away from the strong emotions and horrible images they must work with clinically to meet clients on their own ground and join with them in the search for a better way of living. People who become psychologists, social workers, and mental health professionals often do so for strong personal reasons. These reasons may involve some experience of child abuse in their own lives. When the clinical work touches the record of past bifurcations in the clinician's own memory, powerful feelings which may not have been resolved, can be stimulated. It is important that those working clinically with child abuse do so in the context of a team where they can confer as much as needed with other professionals and get adequate supervision and support. It is also vital that they have the courage to face their own issues squarely and obtain whatever help is needed in working them through. If the clinician does not take these precautions, he or she risks a path which can not only damage the client, it can seriously harm the clinician as well. Where one will meet these dragons from one's past is as unpredictable as anything else concerning child abuse, but it is to be expected and should be taken seriously.

Comprehensive clinical work with child abuse often involves multi-impact therapy. That is, the client receives the services of professionals working from several perspectives. The family requires family therapy. The individual members may require both individual and group therapy. It is difficult to deal with perpetrators initially in any setting other than a specialized therapy group for abusers. This addresses both the frightened victim part of their psyche as well as the aggressive abuser part. It is sometimes the only way to get past the denial which surrounds abuse.

Usually, but not always, child abuse is associated with substance abuse. It is vital that the clinician recognize when substance abuse plays a role in the family. There may be no active substance abuse when the client presents for treatment of child abuse. The clinician must make a detailed inquiry to assess if there was substance abuse in previous generations. Then it is necessary to understand the dynamics which currently exist as a result of the substance abuse and how they affect the child abuse dynamics. Construction of a genogram is a valuable technique to assess past family patterns and their impact on the present situation. Use of substances is so accepted in society that many people will not recognize how their use affects their lives and many therapists will not recognize it either. Alcohol and drugs are the lubricant that allows a family system to slide along the route to child abuse. The clinician must make the effort needed to understand exactly what the dynamics around substances are for a family and how these interact with the rest of the family dynamics in child abuse. When a member of the family— adult or child—is found to have a relationship with chemicals which contributes to child abuse, changing that relationship is the first priority for stopping the child abuse. Child abuse creates powerful reasons for adults and children to use alcohol and drugs to cope. If substance use is identified as a risk factor in a family, then so long as anyone in the family uses, the family is at risk of relapse for child abuse.

CONCLUSIONS

How long does it take to do the detective work, to arrest the dynamics of substance abuse and child abuse, to identify all of the risk factors which support the abuse of children in a family, and finally to put in place alternate ways of behaving and responding emotionally while at the same time recognizing and avoiding identified risky behaviors? A long time. Often the clinician will not be able to work with all of the family members as required in such a comprehensive approach. It is important to make the effort anyway. A less comprehensive approach is doomed to defeat by the nature of complex systems. The work does not have to be all done at once. It may take some people a long time, years perhaps, to integrate the new behaviors and knowledge into their lives. Children are able to work on issues from child abuse only in so far as their developmental level permits. The same issue may need to be returned to again and again as the child matures and develops. Some issues in child abuse prevention and treatment are still beyond the ability of psychotherapy and chemotherapy to deal with effectively. Some people are more damaged than others. Some family systems are more abuse-prone than others. Recovery from child abuse can take a lifetime, or, in rare instances, it can take a few months. For many, it is a process of taking two steps forward and one step back until they reach a bifurcation point where the system transitions to a much less problematic level.

From working with child abuse, the author has developed a very deep reverence for the complexity of families and for their resilience in the face of change. Someone who undertakes to do clinical work with child abuse will never cease to be surprised by the unexpected turns such therapy takes. The same dynamic processes which allow a soliton of child abuse to develop and continue are the very ones which will eventually cause it to dissipate. The clinician's task is largely to understand and use those dynamical processes so well that the family moves to a new level where old dynamics support new behavior. Weaknesses are turned into strengths and the dynamics of abuse become the dynamics of nurturance. It is possible to develop a profound sense of wonder and respect for the clients one meets in this venture.

REFERENCES

Abraham, F. D., Abraham, R. H., Shaw, C. D., & Garfinkel, A. (1990). *A visual introduction to dynamical systems theory for psychology*. Santa Cruz, CA: Aerial Press, Inc.

Arthur, W. B. (1990). Positive feedbacks in the economy. *Scientific American, 269*(2), 92–99.

Barton, J. (1994). Chaos, self-organization and psychology. *American Psychologist, 49*(1), 5–14.

Briggs, J., & Peat, F. D. (1989). *Turbulent mirror*. New York: Harper & Row.

Bütz, M. R. (1995, January). Chaos theory, philosophically old, scientifically new. *Counseling and Values, 39*(1), 84–98.

Friedman, E. H. (1991). Bowen's theory and therapy. In A. S. Gurman & D. P. Kniskern (Eds.), *Handbook of family therapy, vol. II*. New York: Brunner/Mazel.

Glass, L., & Mackey, M. C. (1988). *From clocks to chaos: The rhythms of life*. Princeton, NJ: Princeton University Press.

Gleick, J. (1987). *Chaos: Making a new science*. New York: Penguin Books.

Gorski, T. T. (1990). The Cenaps model of relapse prevention: Basic principles and procedures. *Journal of Psychoactive Drugs, 22*, 125–133.

Judd, C. M., & McClelland, G. H. (1989). *Data analysis: A model-comparison approach*. New York: Harcourt Brace Jovanovich.

Kellert, S. H. (1993). *In the wake of chaos*. Chicago: University of Chicago Press.

Kerr, M. E. (1981). Family systems theory and therapy. In A. S. Gurman & D. P. Kniskern (Eds.), *Handbook of family therapy, vol. I*. New York: Brunner/Mazel.

Marlatt, G. A., & Gordon, J. R. (Eds.) (1985). *Relapse prevention: Maintenance strategies in the treatment of addictive behaviors*. New York: The Guilford Press.

Peitgen, H. O., Jergens, H., & Dietmar, S. (1992). *Chaos and fractals: New frontiers of science*. New York: Springer-Verlag.

Post, R. M. (1992). Transduction of psychosocial stress into the neurobiology of recurrent affective disorders. *American Journal of Psychiatry, 149*(8), 999–1010.

Chapter 10

Dynamical Family Systems and Therapeutic Intervention

Barbara Hudgens

Chaos theory has been described as "the broadest of all the great scientific discoveries of the 20th century" (Robertson, 1995, p. 12). This scientific approach to explaining complex, nonlinear dynamical systems, or sets of interacting variables that meet certain specified conditions (Abraham, 1995), seems to naturally apply to social systems, and has certainly provided an umbrella under which vast numbers of psychological theories can comfortably reside. The recent application of chaos theory to counseling has permitted psychotherapists to treat clients from an eclectic approach while still utilizing a theoretical framework. Chaos theory has also provided an excellent mechanism for more adequately understanding the relationship between the client and the therapist, as well as analyzing the interactions of couples and families. The methods and interventions emanating from the perspective of chaos theory effectively address many issues frequently associated with family systems, especially dysfunctional families struggling with difficulties associated with alcohol and other addictive behaviors (Chapter 8), physical and sexual abuse (Chapter 9), poverty, and so forth. Further applications of the theory that relate to family dynamics will be discussed in this chapter.

FRACTALS AND PSYCHOTHERAPY

When most clients enter a therapy session, they are motivated by a crisis of some sort, frequently associated with overwhelming anxiety. Thoughts may seem fragmented. The client may have difficulty discerning the existence of choices or may feel incapable of selecting from existing, perceived choices. It is not uncommon for thoughts to be jumbled and confused.

Such apparent unpredictability and lack of coherence may give the appearance that there is little or no connection among various events or relationships in a person's life. Fahey (1994) explains how chaos theory envisions the world as dynamic and systemic webs of relationships and processes. As part of that view, the concept of fractals can be helpful in understanding the impact of family relationships and past experiences on behavior and affect.

Fractals become important because, in certain cases, it is extremely difficult or impossible to understand the magnitude of psychological distress a client is experiencing without having an understanding of his family history. Without such information, patterns that are critical for effective treatment may be missed. Gleick (1987) states that "in the mind's eye, a fractal is a way of seeing infinity" (p. 98). Wolinsky (1994) describes fractals as being "fractions of dimensions, made clearer by moving our awareness in rather than out" (p. 53).

By examining and analyzing the reiterating patterns that emerge in the tapestry of the client's life, the therapist can note how apparently minor occurrences have unpredictable but significant consequences, and how the impact of strange attractors (Chapter 1) can lead to bifurcations, or choices, resulting in change. Clients can choose to work through the chaos, which often intensifies with therapy as one lets down defenses and examines underlying issues, or they can choose to avoid facing the uncertainty that comes with discovering new options. Clients who drop out of therapy prematurely are in jeopardy of recreating the chaos of childhood throughout adulthood because they function so comfortably within the predictable patterns of apparently unpredictable lives. For those who stay with the process of therapy, self-perpetuating patterns begin to emerge and to be understood.

A useful metaphor for understanding the process of therapy is that a client enters the counseling setting with a box containing a 1,000-piece jigsaw puzzle. The individual tosses the contents into the center of the floor stating that he or she can't make sense of the mess. A good therapist sees the situation not as overwhelming, but as a challenge, setting out to sort the pieces into color, shape, and line, looking for small sections that make sense of the basic pattern. As sections of the overall design become apparent, the bigger picture gradually begins to emerge. Some clients are quicker to identify patterns or the significance of these parts to the whole. The therapist's job is to provide cues or suggestions about how to fit together these pieces. Significantly more clients experience success when taught a process for recognizing how to assemble small patterns than those given specific "answers." The information processing concept of scaffolded instruction allows therapists to ask key questions leading the client successively closer to the place where understanding occurs. First, however, the therapist must begin with the basics of emotional and trust issues that clients bring into early sessions.

In an alcoholic family where sexual abuse occurs, outsiders may see either total chaos and dysfunction or they may perceive the unidentified abuser as a pillar of the community. But the child growing up in the family eventually learns to predict the sequence of events that follow the opening of a whiskey bottle or mom going to the grocery store alone. Others, unfamiliar with the dynamics, may not believe the child's story even if he or she should have reason to believe there was any usefulness in trying to explain it to someone. Children growing up in such environments often become extremely perceptive, even hypervigilant, about identifying and anticipating predictable patterns of behavior in those around them. At the same time, they often grow up with distrust of their own interpretations, and even of their sanity. Life appears as total chaos.

The therapist can be instrumental in validating a client's perceptions, in helping to order the apparent randomness of a chaotic life, and in empowering an individual to work through the chaos toward making significant changes. This process often entails not only having the client explore thoughts and feelings, but also in learning to analyze the global picture, understanding the recurring patterns and the impact of childhood experiences on present relationships.

A MODEL FOR CHAOS AND THE DYSFUNCTIONAL FAMILY

Self-similarity and Repeating Loops

Sulis (1995) states that a system must be dissipative for attractors to exist. The idea that a central fixed point "attracts" energy from outer regions easily fits the example of a dysfunctional family in which the central figure, generally a dominant parent (Pd), controls the energy of each family member, keeping each spinning in his or her own orbit of confusion and isolation. A useful image is that of a performer in a circus who keeps numerous plates spinning atop sticks held by various parts of the entertainer's body. The Pd keeps other family members spinning through their random, chaotic patterns of behavior. By the Pd maintaining emotional isolation, there is little chance of group energy coalescing to overpower that of the central character. Chaos theory teaches us, however, that there exists a "delicate balance between the forces of stability and the forces of instability" (Gleick, 1987, p. 309).

Families, as social systems, represent the association of a group of autonomous entities with boundaries, internal structures, and self-perpetuating behaviors. There is energy at the edges of the boundaries, thus creating instability. In a dysfunctional family, the enmeshment that occurs dissipates the boundaries. Thus, the arbitrary identities that exist for individuals within the group create chaos, but maintain the unity of the group. The energy of the Pd is so strong that, concomitant with the disorder from any abuse that is occurring, the family is closely bound to that energy source. In other words, chaos and order occur together.

Gleick (1987) defines the repeating loops of strange attractors as "a system that repeats itself at regular intervals forever in continuous long-term behavior" and self-similarity as "symmetry across scale ... [which] implies recursion, pattern within pattern" (p. 103). These concepts correspond to phenomena frequently associated with alcoholic families. Family dynamics and behaviors in the alcoholic family tend to persist trans-generationally, even skipping generations. The pattern may even be evident in the families of children of alcoholics where no alcohol is ever consumed. Even if the child of an alcoholic does not succumb to the disease, it is also quite common for these individuals to find they are friends

with, or intimately associated with, other children of alcoholics, even when neither knows of the others' background and neither abuses any substances.

Black (1981) explains the self-similarity that is common among adult children of alcoholics. Over half of all alcoholics had at least one alcoholic parent.
Even those who manage to avoid becoming alcoholics are more likely to marry
an alcoholic, or to carry into adulthood emotional and/or psychological patterns
that may cause problems. Black states that adult children of alcoholics experience
difficulties associated with rigidity and control, difficulty identifying and expressing feelings, dependency issues, lack of empowerment over choices in their lives,
guilt, fear, depression, and intimacy issues that may impact personal and professional relationships.

Another way to understand the repetitive behavioral patterns that emerge
is that the brain has ways of ordering information so that input impacts output.
Therefore, if a child inputs chaos, or the randomness that comes with dysfunction
and enmeshment, the brain becomes comfortable with and proficient in dealing
with those patterns. The brain continues to search for similar patterns to experience in the future, although the patterns may not even be immediately realized
by the person experiencing the repeated situations. Therefore, fractals become
important in that it is difficult or impossible to understand the magnitude of any
specific incident without a view of the repetitive pattern imbedded in the family
history.

Case Example

Another area where self-similarity and repeating loops are readily understood is
in the system that facilitates repeated victimization from sexual abuse. A case
study will explain the complex, random ordering of iterative patterns.

Over several months, Mary described to her therapist the memories and flash-
backs of childhood sexual abuse she had experienced. She was abused by her father when she was younger than five, and possibly by an uncle. Mary speculates
that both her father and uncle may have been sexually abused by their father as
children, and she had recently learned that siblings and cousins were also abused.
The father began by gentle enticement, calling the toddler "angel," giving her
positive attention along with the sexually abusive behavior. As the child matured
and objected, he progressed to intimidation and threats. After several suicide attempts, when it became obvious that the client no longer cared whether she died,
threats were made toward the younger sister. In order to protect her sister, Mary
endured the increasingly violent attacks by dissociating, flying into the clouds of
a religious picture on her wall to sit among the angels.

Other memories of victimization included being urinated on by a neighbor
boy while her father watched and encouraged him, followed by another instance
when the boy forced his younger sister to abuse Mary. The client recalled seeing
the terror in the young girl's eyes and feeling more concern for her than for herself.
The boy had learned his threatening, abusive behavior from Mary's father. Mary

had learned to feel more responsible for the needs of others than for her own needs.

Mary's story shows the self-perpetuating patterns of victimization and abuse as clearly as a snowflake shows its self-replicating pattern when viewed under extreme magnification. Mary's case exemplifies a model for how sexual abuse can become prevalent in certain families and communities. The younger boy learning to abuse and dominate his younger sister is a fractal image of Mary's father abusing her.

BIFURCATIONS RESULTING FROM STRANGE ATTRACTORS

Goerner (1995a) views the concept of nonlinear interdependence as responsible for such essential elements as patterns and self-organization. Nonlinear systems are versatile and can produce either positive (amplifying) or negative (dampening) feedback (Goerner, 1995b). Tschacher (1995) reminds us that all attractors have stability, although there is less stability at or near bifurcation points, and that any attractor can be either positive or negative. At bifurcation points (or crises), perturbation of the system opens up new possibilities of action at a higher level of functioning than has occurred previously (Sundararajan, 1995).

As an individual or members of a family begin to attain stronger ego boundaries through therapy, maturity, or exposure to new experiences, the dysfunctional family system is in increasing jeopardy of transformation from its historic patterns. An individual may self-organize, using new information as a way to gain enough energy to break away from the system. By learning that friends' parents act differently toward their children, by reading or watching movies about people in similar situations, or by changing self-awareness through any number of experiences, a child may begin to perceive new options and undergo a transformation in his or her self-organization.

To stop the pain felt by a child in an abusive home, strange attractors become important in our theory of chaos since they are mechanisms to minimize the constancy of the pain. There are many such random attractors. Losing oneself in school or sports is a commonly accepted healthy escape. There are examples of girls who appear to have everything, portraying the "perfect" student and beauty queen during the day while enduring sexual abuse by their fathers at night, merely waiting for the day when college becomes their escape. Running away, "escaping" into the safety of a psychiatric hospital, developing psychiatric disorders, abusing substances, marrying the first boyfriend, or suicide may all be perceived as a way out and form a point in the strange attractor that pulls the girl's behavior.

The highly controlling nature of the dominant family figure seeks to minimize complexity in the family system. Goerner (1995a) explains how increasing levels of complexity contribute to a buildup of energy that creates a force which may be resisted. If the pressure of the energy is strong enough to overcome the resistance, a crisis occurs through restructuring of the previous pattern. It is when a strange

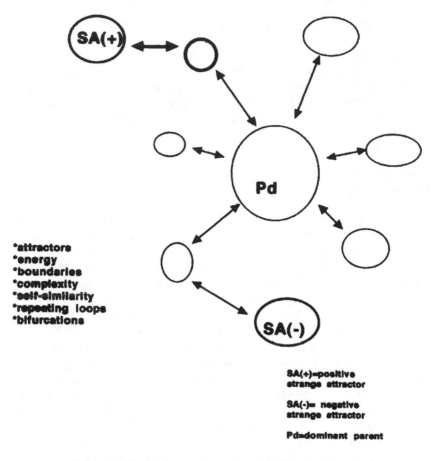

*attractors
*energy
*boundaries
*complexity
*self-similarity
*repeating loops
*bifurcations

SA(+)=positive
strange attractor

SA(-)= negative
strange attractor

Pd=dominant parent

Figure 1   Chaos Theory: Dynamics of dysfunctional family.

attractor from outside comes unexpectedly into the picture that a bifurcation point occurs. This new strange attractor pulls energy toward it.

Figure 1 illustrates how a child from the family is either drawn toward the initial attractor (Pd) or toward the outside attractor described above. If the decision is toward the new attractor (e.g., a boyfriend), there may be intensified chaos as change occurs. The Pd, in an effort to maintain control and the sense of safety that comes from power, may resist the outside energy that seeks to change the existing family structure. That is, no boyfriend may be good enough, college may be discouraged, or a multitude of economic or health crises may serve to keep the young adult child living in the home. If the bifurcation is successful and the new choice is a positive one, then the randomness may settle into comforting patterns. That is, the child may make a new life in which he or she can become a survivor rather than a victim. Conversely, if the choice is similar to the initial attractor (Pd), then self-similarity or repetitive behaviors may occur (e.g., the child marries an alcoholic, or becomes an alcoholic, or an abused child becomes an abuser). The new strange attractor point can be either positive or negative in its impact on the child's life.

Another way that a dominant parent might try to maintain enmeshment is by discouraging individualism. Individualism and independence increase the complexity in a social system, thus rigidity by the dominant parent is an attempt to maintain control of the energy in the system. Rebellion can lead to a breakup of the enmeshed family so the authoritarian figure feels the need to subdue independence in order to preserve group cohesion. Essentially, the controller (alcoholic or abusive parent) must keep each individual as submissive as possible, emotionally isolated, and feeling responsible for the distress that exists within the family. Externalizing emotion, especially anger, leads to the rebellion that must be discouraged.

The price for being submissive is internalizing of anger by suppression or denial. This act helps the child to avoid the anger and abuse of the adult as much as possible, but it also sets the child up for self-abuse because the anger must be acted on in some way. Thus, the abuse of drugs and alcohol or the self abuse that is so common with adult children of alcoholics is easily understood.

CHAOS AS OPPORTUNITY FOR CHANGE

Very often, individuals who have been abused have great difficulty with boundaries. People who have had their physical, emotional, or sexual boundaries ignored or violated, who have been taught that they have no right to create their own identities, need help setting and restoring those boundaries. For some, this may mean trusting their feelings for the first time, and then overcoming the fear and shame of expressing those feelings to others. The resistance that may come when the individual initially takes a stand will be experienced as chaos. But the crisis that is created is a bifurcation point, an opportunity to do something differently in order to get different results. If we never go beyond our existing comfort zone, we never grow.

As the client becomes more secure and continues to work on individual issues, he or she will eventually notice that a new, higher level of understanding has been reached. Moving away from an abusive situation may provide the strength and clarity of vision to take a person to a higher level of insight. Clients may suddenly look at their abusive fathers and realize that the powerful, frightening figure of their childhood has become a grizzled, old man who no longer merits fear. Alternately, such initial insights may require the guidance of the therapist in asking probing questions designed to help the client identify repetitive behavioral patterns.

Even a small change in the predictable pattern can make changes in the reactions of family members. Thus, the first phase of growth in the model is two-dimensional, pushing the circle of familiarity to new boundaries, followed by

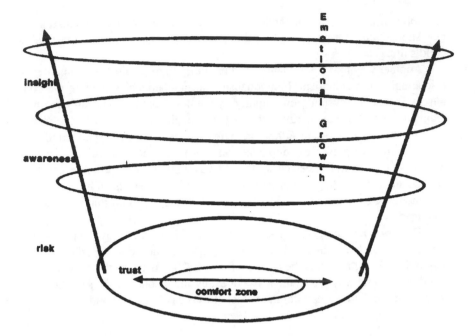

Figure 2 Increasing complexity of emotional growth as client moves past comfort zone in two-dimensional space and toward successive levels of growth in three-dimensional space.

three-dimensional phase space. The diagram in Figure 2 visually represents the process of individual change, as well as systemic change.

Such changes in behavior can begin in small ways. For example, a client might be encouraged to work on self-esteem or to model "I" messages to family members. If needed, the client can be guided toward discovering the patterns that lead to bifurcations in thinking that can result in changes of behavior. The following dialogue suggests how a therapist might approach the situation:

> Therapist: You've described how you feel depressed when your husband puts you down. Who else has put you down in the past?
> Client: I don't know.
> Therapist: Think hard. You talked about someone the other day who used to call you names and call you stupid.
> Client: My father!
> Therapist: And how did you feel then?
> Client: Angry . . . sad and depressed.
> Therapist: How did you deal with that situation?
> Client: I ran away and got married.
> Therapist: What is happening in your marriage now?
> Client: Well, I'm thinking of divorcing him.
> Therapist: Do you see a pattern?

Client: Yes, I escape . . .
Therapist: Are you content with that pattern?
Client: I guess I can't run away my whole life. Maybe I could do it differently . . .
maybe I could tell my husband to stop putting me down.

As additional insights occur, complexity increases as new levels of awareness and understanding develop. Each successive level provides the client or family with new behavioral and emotional alternatives as the interactional process
changes. Overcoming fears such as disclosure or confrontation opens the door for
improved communication which is the basis for a strong family system. A healthy
communication framework allows flexibility for choices about whether an individual wishes to share feelings or particular information with family members or
not, depending on the situation. The individuality of group members is not lost by
rigid conformity to restrictive group norms that leave little room for change.

Healthy families allow for the ongoing changes that are a part of life. Natural
events such as birth, death, marriage, graduation, job changes, aging, or the myriad of unexpected crises that are a part of living require modifications in the family
structure and pattern of interactions. Healthy families adapt to these changes with
little disruption to the unit, whereas dysfunctional families tend to struggle and resist. When the flow of energy is smooth, as in a healthy family, small disturbances
die out. In contrast, a dysfunctional family attempts to deal with the small, natural
changes rigidly, thus stopping the natural flow, blocking and building up energy
to the point of turbulence (e.g., arguments), growing to catastrophic proportions,
resulting in bifurcations.

RECOGNIZING PATTERNS OF DYSFUNCTION

Chaos theory has provided a useful vehicle for viewing the turbulence and apparent randomness of behavior that results in dysfunction and abuse (Chapter 9).
When a system is observed long enough and in sufficient detail, existing patterns
become evident. When therapists understand the major emotional and behavioral
reactions to crises, sessions can be geared toward helping clients discover the reiterative patterns they display, and come to terms with the underlying issues that
drive behaviors and emotions.

The initial session is the most important in terms of gathering vital information and setting the tone for future therapeutic interactions. The goal of the first
session is to get a general view of the presenting problem, including what specifically caused the client to seek counseling at the current time. The client is asked
to paint a picture of the significant individuals who make up his or her everyday
life. What are their relationships like? How does the client perceive each person in
terms of support? Can she trust and depend on various family members? To whom
can she turn in times of crisis? Who is in her support system and how vital is the
system? Also, what are the current issues the client has with various significant
others?

The next step is to get a picture of the client's family structure while he/she was a child. The goal is to construct a family tree for both childhood and the present. Within the family tree, which relationships are positive or negative? Where do alliances exist? What are the strengths and weaknesses of each relationship? What were the issues in the family when the client was a child?

The work moves from the general to the specific as rapport increases over subsequent sessions. The family history is the basis for seeing the fractal nature of the patterns which are associated with dysfunctional families that impact present relationships. It is uncanny how frequently the issues and quality of interactions with certain family members of childhood, coupled with learned emotional and behavioral reactions, play out in mirror images in later relationships. Without the family history, however, there is no mirror to reflect the past.

When the client describes his or her parents, inquiries are made about problems with alcohol and drugs. "When you think of your father, what are the strongest emotions you feel? What about your mother?" Questions about physical, emotional, and sexual abuse are raised. All of these questions are asked in a matter-of-fact way without asking for details in the initial session. The details come later. The first session is focused on getting a general background, starting out in a wide circle of non-intrusive general information-gathering, circling ever closer to intimate, potential secrets that may never have been shared. The tone for future sessions is set. If the therapist cautiously avoids painful topics, the client is given permission to avoid those topics too. The tacit message given using this model is that all secrets are safe to come out and nothing is forbidden. An even more important message is that the therapist does not have to be protected from the truths, the shame, and the guilt that a client may have carried for years.

The tone of non-judgemental acceptance in gathering information is basic to the trust that emerges and allows the therapist to work with clients. As in the "law of thirds," probably a third of clients will respond to this (or any approach), a third will stay until the therapist gets too close to the issues, and a third will drop out after one or two sessions. For those who stick with the process, this approach has contributed to exposing issues that, several clients reported, their previous therapists never discovered.

THERAPIST AS "STRANGE ATTRACTOR"

Therapists function as "strange attractors." They permeate a client's boundaries in a positive way through respecting the individual's right to say no, instead of in a negative way that ignores personal boundaries and shows a lack of respect for the person's rights. The therapist's energy then combines with the energy of the client to propel that person toward identifying issues, setting goals, discovering problem-solving options, and working on problem resolution. The client is always in control. Effective communication patterns are modeled, the therapist acts as an advocate when necessary, and provides feedback and support. Confrontation is used, as needed, only after significant trust has been established, and then in a gentle way, often using humor. This approach respects that people who grew up in of dysfunctional families tend to be hypersensitive to perceived criticism, blame, and judgment.

Certain issues tend to emerge. Anger and rage are common themes that act as red flags to issues such as abuse. Anger may be turned either outward in the form of sexual acting out, delinquent behavior, or aggressiveness, or turned inward as in self-destructive behaviors such as substance abuse or suicide attempts. Clients should be helped to understand that anger was a natural reaction to the events of their lives and that they manifested their anger in a way that seemed the safest to them at the time. For example, a boy who, as a child, lived with an all-powerful and dangerous abuser who reacted violently to the child's anger, made a wise choice to turn his anger inward, suppressing it. Another child may have found that aggressiveness or other outward displays of anger kept others at bay. Unfortunately, many of the useful choices made for survival earlier, in the context of childhood, become dysfunctional later, in the context of adulthood, or when interacting with a different set of people.

On the negative side, turned inward, anger becomes a cancer that eats at one's insides. Turned outward, it can be thought of as mud flung indiscriminately at innocent people who, in turn, become angry at being treated that way and retaliate, resulting in a mud-slinging match that serves no purpose. A more positive manifestation is to direct the anger at the person or persons who deserve it. If face-to-face communication is too threatening, letters (that may or may not ever be sent), journaling, talking to an empty chair, visual imagery, or other techniques may serve as a vehicle for catharsis. Finally, anger may be used as a vehicle for positive change. That is, clients can use anger as a motivator by developing an attitude of "I'll show you" and overcoming the limitations of the abusive messages. This choice can propel them forward toward worthy goals.

There are several areas where the energy of the therapist can be used to aid the client in moving from victim to survivor status. Therapists can facilitate developing a sense of personal power, building self-esteem by pointing out strengths and skills, assuring physical and emotional safety, validating the right to whatever emotion a client experiences, and recognizing the interdependence of people in viable relationships. The increasing complexity of a client's personal resource system eventually allows recovery from insecurity and dispels the tendency to distrust one's own judgement.

CONCLUSIONS

By helping clients to understand that behaviors and reactions that are causing difficulties in interpersonal relationships or intrapersonally were probably adaptive and necessary for survival in the past, but are maladaptive for present and future happiness, the client-therapist team can then explore alternatives to that behavior. This process can take time. It is not unusual for two to three years to be required to pass through the stages from first identifying the problems to eventually reconciling the debilitating effects of broken trust, anger, shame, guilt, and worthlessness that underlie a childhood spent in an abusive or dysfunctional family.

By supporting this emotional-perceptual awareness, the therapist operates as a facilitator to take the randomness and disorder out of the emotional chaos in which the client exists. It is the therapist's job to monitor whether the client is experiencing the emotion necessary for working through the chaos, to push harder if work isn't occurring, and to slow down, be supportive, and help a client better understand what is occurring should she become overwhelmed. The journey is embarked on together, and the therapist sets the tone. But it is the client who determines the route and the timing of the venture. In therapy, as in life, there is no superhighway leading straight from one point to another, but neither is the scenic route of chaos totally random.

REFERENCES

Abraham, F. D. (1995). Introduction to dynamics: A basic language; a basic metamodeling strategy. In F. D. Abraham & A. R. Gilgen (Eds.), *Chaos theory in psychology*. Westport, CT: Praeger.

Black, C. (1981). *It will never happen to me*. Denver, CO: M.A.C.

Fahey, C. P. (1994). Religious life: Coming or going (Doctoral dissertation, St. Louis University). *Dissertation Abstracts International, 55*(01), 107A.

Gleick, J. (1987). *Chaos: Making a new science*. New York: Viking Press.

Goerner, S. J. (1995a). Chaos and deep ecology. In F. D. Abraham & A. R. Gilgen (Eds.), *Chaos theory in psychology*. Westport, CT: Praeger.

Goerner, S. J. (1995b). Chaos, evolution, and deep ecology. In R. Robertson & A. Combs (Eds.), *Chaos theory in psychology and the life sciences*. Hillsdale, NJ: Lawrence Erlbaum Associates.

Robertson, R. (1995). Chaos theory and the relationship between psychology and science. In R. Robertson & A. Combs (Eds.), *Chaos theory in psychology and the life sciences*. Hillsdale, NJ: Lawrence Erlbaum Associates.

Sulis, W. (1995, August). *Toward a formal theory of collective intelligence*. Paper presented at the meeting of the Society for Chaos Theory in Psychology and the Life Sciences, Garden City, NJ.

Sundararjan, L. (1995, August). *Myth as strange attractor: Levi-Straus and chaos theory*. Paper presented at the meeting of the Society for Chaos Theory in Psychology and the Life Sciences, Garden City, NJ.

Tschacher, W. (1995, August). *Order and complexity in psychotherapy: An empirical approach*. Paper presented at the meeting of the Society for Chaos Theory in Psychology and the Life Sciences, Garden City, NJ.

Wollinsky, S. H. (1994). *The tao of chaos*. CT: Bramble Books.

Chapter 11

The "Lost World" of Psychopharmacology: A Return to Psychology's "Jurassic Park"

Linda Chamberlain & Michael R. Bütz

The recent surge of interest by clinical psychologists in obtaining prescription privileges may not be a benign endeavor. This chapter will examine the potential hazards we are now facing with the movement to further "medicalize" the treatment of behavioral and emotional disorders. Using some of the tenets of chaos theory that were popularized in the novel and movie *Jurassic Park* (Crichton, 1990), and now further explored in *The Lost World* (Crichton, 1995), we will discuss possible consequences of not only psychologists prescribing psychotropic medications, but the ramifications of the idea of psychopharmacology itself.

> "I wish to propose complex animals become extinct, not because of a change in their physical adaptation to their environment, but because of their behaviors. I would suggest that the latest thinking in chaos theory, or nonlinear dynamics, provides tantalizing hints to how this happens. It suggests to us that the behavior of complex animals can change very rapidly and not always for the better. It suggests that behavior can cease to be responsive to the environment and instead lead to decline and death. It suggests that animals may stop adapting." Ian Malcolm in Crichton's *The Lost World* (1995).

Could it be possible that the over-reliance on psychopharmacological treatment of emotional and psychological problems might interfere with humans' adaptability? Is psychology's attempt to undertake prescription privileges a potential disaster, as some have alluded (Baron, 1991; Bütz, 1994; Chamberlain, 1994; DeNelsky, 1991; Karon, 1993; Kingsbury, 1992; Kramer, 1993; May & Belsky, 1992; Saeman, 1992; Sanua, 1990, 1994a, 1994b)? Two ideas in chaos theory, sensitive dependence on initial conditions (the "butterfly effect") and self-organization theory will be used in assessing this possibility. The larger implications for our society in pursuing the linear, medical model of treatment for emotional distress, likewise represents a set of important issues for our discussion.

Jurassic Park (1990) is novelist Michael Crichton's analysis of the chaos that ensues when scientists assume they can introduce new elements into a biological system and exert control over the behavior of these elements (in this case, dinosaurs). The story offers an exquisite warning about the inherent complexity of natural systems and the unpredictability regarding how these systems will react to the introduction of novel components, patterns, or objects. Other scientists have also attempted to warn us about the impossibility of complete control or prediction in natural systems (Briggs & Peat, 1984, 1989; Gleick, 1987). Certainly, some of the environmental problems that we currently face are the result of the pursuit of scientific technology (e.g., the development of vehicles that rely on burning fossil fuels) without an understanding of the interdependence of elements in the environment (e.g., the discharge of pollutants that are destructive to the atmosphere).

> "Scientists are actually preoccupied with accomplishment. They never stop to ask if they should do something." Ian Malcolm in Crichton's *Jurassic Park* (1990).

Psychopharmacology is a linear model based on the self-ascribed ability to predict and control human behavior through the use of drugs. The field itself originated in the 1950s with the reclassification of major tranquilizers as psychotropic medications. Now, with the advent of more sophisticated pharmacological agents, typified by the selective serotonin reuptake inhibitors (SSRIs) such as Prozac, Zoloft, and Paxil, we may be entering a pharmacological "Jurassic Park." Can we as yet understand the impact that the use of these and other medications will have as they become more widely available and distributed? During the 1950s, little was known about the long-term use of powerful drugs like Thorazine. With time, we came to find that its continued use causes the awful problem recognized as tardive dyskinesia, an uncontrolled movement disorder. More importantly, is the increased use of medications a model that psychologists and other health professionals wish to pursue?

In his novels, Crichton draws on the concept of sensitive dependence on initial conditions to dramatize the limits of linear thinking. Scientists who are experienced in dealing with mechanistic systems cannot simply apply the same theories to natural, biological systems and expect to exert the same types of controls or have the predictability that is seen in quasi-closed, mechanical systems. We have found it to hold true even in studies on chaos theory (Rapp, 1995) that biological systems are more difficult to model than other systems. Sensitive dependence on initial conditions, or the "butterfly effect," defines the incredible sensitivity that exists in natural systems and the ease with which the behavior of interconnected systems can be influenced by the most minute factors (as described in Chapter 1).

In *Jurassic Park*, several variables, including a tiny, overlooked factor in the dinosaur's reproductive capacities, combined and interacted with the environment to create a problem of monstrous proportions. More recently, Crichton's "lost world" hypothesis reminds us that a certain level of complexity needs to exist for there to be a truly functional ecology. Description of this type of mix is found in the newer theories on complexity being spear-headed at the Santa Fe Institute (Horgan, 1995; Ruthen, 1993; Corcoran, 1992; Kauffman, 1995). What Crichton's characters in *The Lost World* found was that the environment artificially created by the scientists at Jurassic Park did not mimic a true ecology. Instead, it was a predator-rich environment with inherent flaws, since the scientists did not factor in the effects of tiny variables in their attempts at creation. We find that both at "Jurassic Park" and in "The Lost World," the effects were clearly disastrous, and fell short of a true ecology. Perhaps there is also the development of a false ecology, a tampering with the most powerful force in the universe—evolution.

There are a multiplicity of variables that are encompassed in psychopharmacological treatment: drug interactions, side effects of medications, toxic qualities, and addictive potentials, for example. Some of the problems presented by psychopharmacological treatment include:

1. A biological organism's ability to self-organize as a reaction to biological interventions;
2. Historic misuses and abuses of psychopharmacological methods;
3. Motivation for the increase in psychopharmacological treatment; and
4. The potential for large-scale social impact if the pursuit of medical treatments is not questioned and monitored.

Each of these problems will be addressed using some of the paradigms suggested by the models of chaos and complexity. Many of the concerns that emerge when using the lens of non-linear dynamics to explore these questions are philosophical in nature. Anticipating the effects of an increased use of pharmacological agents to treat emotional disorders is largely theoretical. These are questions of whether or not science and medicine *should* do something, not whether it can. As already stressed, specific prediction of the behavior of complex systems is unachievable, and abundant in the literature on these new theories. The lesson of *Jurassic Park*, however, is that failure to address these philosophical, "what if" questions when dealing with natural systems can have profound consequences.

SELF-ORGANIZATION IN ORGANIC SYSTEMS

The first concern raised by chaos and complexity theories focuses squarely on the ability of natural systems to self-organize. This question, and these new theories about biological systems, have their roots in General Systems Theory. According to von Bertalanffy's (1968) model, there are two basic states in an organic system: steady and transformative. In a steady state, the organism and its environment maintain fairly stable patterns of inter-relating. There is a balance or equilibrium that is established—a symmetry, as it is referred to in complexity theory. Although this state is confused with homeostasis (a mechanical concept from cybernetics, as further described in Chapter 13), it is not a period of rest or stability. Rather, it is an interactive pattern that accumulates data and promotes the maintenance and development of the organism and system during a period of limited fluctuation. The second, transformative state, occurs when a system is perturbed to behave outside of the parameters typical of its steady state. When some novel factor is introduced to the system, adaptation or transformation must occur in order for the organism to respond. The transformative state is a passageway to a more adaptive steady state in which the organism and environment develop a different relationship and achieve a new level of balance.

Prigogine (1980) focused on the adaptive capacities that occur at far-from-equilibrium states in organic systems. The pattern describes that at one time, a system exhibits a steady state that is adaptive for the current situation or relationship with the environment. Then, something comes along, perturbs the system, and it is knocked off balance, or bifurcates. In a natural system that is undergoing transformation, there can be a "bifurcation cascade" where stability is lost or very transient. For example, in persons suffering from immune deficiencies, one infection often compromises their system (a bifurcation from a healthy, steady state) and, if the person is exposed to additional infectious agents, they may be unable to return to a stable state, and experience a bifurcation cascade of medical problems.

Chaos may ensue when systems move further from equilibrium during bifurcation cascades. Within that chaos, however, an underlying order can exist which is not apparent. Prigogine points out that the system will not necessarily fly apart into disarray. Though this is possible, what is more likely to occur is that coherent systems (Bütz, 1996) will move to a higher, more adaptive level or capacity as a result. From this new level, a more adaptive steady state can develop. This new steady state self-organizes out of chaos. This emphasizes that chaotic periods are not necessarily something to be avoided; they may be the period out of which more adaptive and complex capacities emerge. Given that possibility, it is important to question the rush to increasingly rely on pharmacological agents to treat emotional and psychological dilemmas.

One of the key assumptions in psychopharmacological treatment is that these agents will return the person to a previous level of functioning or steady state—not to a new adaptive level through the transformative processes of chaos and complexity. Clinicians might do well to contemplate the therapeutic implications. If pharmacological agents are used to stop bifurcation cascades and restrict chaotic or complex processes, could they also interfere with the possibility for people to self-organize more adaptive behaviors? Pharmacological agents are invasive drugs that appear to keep people in non-adaptive steady states, and may actually rob individuals of the potential to adopt more functional ways of coping with or relating to changes in their circumstances on both a local and global level. Are these medications, in fact, sometimes intervening in processes that need to occur in order for some people suffering from anxiety and depression to attain a more satisfactory level of adaptation?

A HISTORY OF PSYCHOPHARMACOLOGICAL INTERVENTIONS

Several voices have called attention to the history of biological interventions as a means of social and political control (Rodgers, 1992; Breggin, 1991; Szaz, 1970; Foucault, 1965). Many previously-utilized types of biologically-based "therapies," such as hydrotherapy, insulin shock, and lobotomies, have been abandoned. At one time, all of these methods were thought "viable" due to one common factor—lack of knowledge.

For example, frontal lobotomies were vigorously pursued as a treatment method earlier in the 1950s. One problem that practitioners and proponents failed to recognize during lobotomy's "heyday" was that this procedure destroyed several of the most "human" aspects of functioning which were largely housed in the frontal lobe. "It was later recognized that many patients, although relieved of severe agitation, also suffered from severe personality deficits" (Andreasen, 1984, p. 120). An oversimplified, linear model of psychological problems led to inappropriate treatment and profound consequences for some sufferers of mental problems.

Although biological methods, including pharmacological agents, were developed with good intentions, each has proven dangerous in its own way. Social scientists and students of human behavior would do well to admit that our science is still operating largely out of an incomplete understanding of the etiology and dynamics of mental and emotional problems. Certainly, it is time to acknowledge that humans are not machines that operate by mechanistic rules. Humans are biological organisms with irreversible processes that move them between steady and transformative states. Within these transformative states, bifurcations can move people through chaos into more adaptive states. Biological interventions are based on a linear model that essentially assumes people function as machines that can be "fixed" by returning them to a previous level of adaptation.

MOTIVATIONS FOR THE INCREASED USE OF PSYCHOPHARMACOLOGY

With the advent of managed care, mental health professionals are being encouraged, if not coerced, to provide quick results with their clients. If a clinician has only ten sessions to assist someone, relief must be apparent in a very limited time. Relief is not necessarily change. The pharmaceutical, insurance, and medical establishments make a substantial income from the increased use of pharmacological agents. Psychotherapy is becoming increasingly solution-focused, perhaps even solution-forced. Pharmacological agents clearly serve a role in reducing the demand for psychotherapy. The reduction of disquieting, uncomfortable symptoms helps to reduce the need for an examination of factors that contributed to the onset and maintenance of those experiences. If a client's sensation of feeling depressed is relieved, why should she then undertake the pursuit of a greater understanding of how her relationships, patterns of behavior, view of the world, or other factors contributed to the depressed state? Why make substantive, difficult changes when one can experience relief? Why not take a so-called "magic pill?"

The biological argument is that depression, anxiety, and almost every other psychological problem are neurochemically based, and thereby, are best treated by neurochemical agents. The assumption is that neurochemical imbalances are the cause of these disorders. This linear model denies the interactive, contextual, and environmentally-based factors that both influence and are influenced by neurochemistry. The psychobiologists seem disinterested in the question, "Why has this neurochemical change occurred in this person at this time?" As Breggin (1991) warns, "We have no idea, for example, how the brain makes a thought or an emotion. It seems foolhardy to imagine that blocking one of the brain's biochemical functions would somehow improve the brain and mind" (p. 35). Moreover, if this is truly the case, then why is it that recent studies have shown psychotherapy alone to be more effective than pharmacological treatment alone or a combination of psychotherapy and drug treatment?

THE POTENTIAL FOR SOCIAL CONSEQUENCES

The burgeoning use of psychoactive medications is more than a personal issue, it is a social issue. Instead of making more and more referrals for psychopharmacological relief from minor symptoms of depression or anxiety, perhaps psychotherapists should begin to ask why there is such a prevalence of these experiences in society. If medicine can begin to engineer a class of "happy people," just as the biologists in *Jurassic Park* engineered dinosaurs, what happens to the dissatisfaction, self-examination, and anger needed to engender social change? Is making people "happy" the goal of the mental health profession?

In *Jurassic Park*, Ian Malcolm comments that "increasingly, the mathematics will demand the courage to face its implications" (p. 365). Medical science based on empirical models has promised humanity deliverance from pain, illness, boredom, fear, loneliness, and many other dilemmas of being human. People have become increasingly dependent on mechanistic science to provide solutions that are essentially homeostatic: they do not require individuals to make substantive changes in their lives, relationships, or environment. Psychologist Lawrence Le-Shan writes in *The Dilemma of Psychology* (1990) that: "Since this is a culture that sees science as the way to solve problems and the relevant science (psychology) was clearly helpless to do so, an increasing pessimism and hopelessness has spread through all Western society" (p. 158). Medical science is clearly demonstrating inherent limitations in its ability to provide salvation in the face of viruses such as HIV, destructive addictions, increasing violence, and the social realities of poverty and discrimination that exacerbate medical and emotional problems. Still, researchers have known for decades that the so-called unscientific enterprise of psychotherapy substantially reduces medical utilization (Cummings & Vandenbos, 1981).

Psychopharmacology may offer this contemporary culture of denial the last opportunity to avoid confronting our human dilemmas and the destruction we have wrought on each other and the environment. As Kramer notes (1993, p. 37), "we are edging toward ... the 'medicalization of personality.'" It is difficult to consider philosophical questions when faced with the quick and generally positive changes in mood and outlook that many clients experience when taking these newer medications. Are clinicians willing to define their role as encouragers of change without transformation? Is it the goal of psychotherapy to make people comfortable at the banquet table when they are surrounded by people who are starving?

CONCLUSIONS

If psychotherapists are to avoid the consequences of *Jurassic Park* or *The Lost World*, they must pause at this point to ask important questions. What is psychotherapy's role in society? What consequences could be incurred if clinicians increasingly were to focus on pharmacological "solutions" to human distress? How comfortable are therapists with modifying personality? What are the assumptions and forces behind the increased use of psychopharmacological agents?

As outlined in this chapter, some ideas encapsulated in the theories of chaos and complexity question whether or not psychopharmacological treatment should be promoted as a "solution." The dynamics of sensitive dependence on initial conditions and self-organization in biological systems raise important questions about reliance on the linear models of treatment epitomized by psychopharmacology. The direction the field of mental health takes over the next several years could produce profound consequences. As Ian Malcolm warned, clinicians would do well to stop and ask "why?"

REFERENCES

Andreason, N. C. (1984). *The broken brain: the biological revolution in psychiatry.* New York: Harper & Row.

Baron, J. (1991). Prescription privileges: psychologists taking responsibility for themselves. *Psychotherapy in Private Practice, 9*(3), 1–6.

Breggin, P. (1991). *Toxic psychiatry.* New York: St. Martin.

Briggs, J., & Peat, F. D. (1984). *Looking glass universe: The emerging science of wholeness.* New York: Simon & Schuster.

Briggs, J., & Peat, F. D. (1989). *Turbulent mirror.* New York: Harper & Row.

Bütz, M. R. (1994). Psychopharmacology: Psychology's Jurassic Park? *Psychotherapy, 31*(4), 692–699.

Bütz, M. R. (1996). *The theories of chaos and complexity, implications for psychological theory and therapy.* Washington, DC: Taylor & Francis.

Chamberlain, L. (1994, Fall). Further adventures in psychology's Jurassic Park? *Psychotherapy Bulletin, 29*(3), 47–50.

Corcoran, E. (1992). The edge of chaos. *Scientific American, 267*(4), 17–22.

Crichton, M. (1990). *Jurassic Park.* New York: Bantam Books.

Crichton, M. (1995). *The lost world.* New York: Bantam Books.

Cummings, N. A., & VandenBos, G. R. (1981). The twenty years Kaiser-Permanente experience with psychotherapy and medical utilization: implications for national health policy and national health insurance. *Health Policy Quarterly, 1*(2), 159–175.

DeNelsky, G. Y. (1991). Prescription privileges for psychologists: the case against. *Professional Psychology: Research and Practice, 22*(3), 188–193.

Foucault, M. (1965). *Madness and civilization, a history of insanity in the age of reason.* New York: Vintage.

Gleick, J. (1987). *Chaos: Making a new science.* New York: Viking-Penguin.

Horgan, J. (1995). From complexity to perplexity. *Scientific American, 272*(6), 104–109.

Karon, B. P. (1993, August). Psychotherapy: The appropriate treatment for schizophrenia. In P. A. Keller (Ed.), *Paradigms for treatment of serious and persistent mental illness.* Symposium given at the American Psychological Association National Convention: Toronto, Ontario, Canada.

Kauffman, S. (1995). *At home in the universe.* New York: Oxford University Press.

Kingsbury, S. J. (1992). Some effects of prescribing privileges. *American Psychologist, 47*, 426–427.

Kramer, P. D. (1993). *Listening to Prozac.* New York: Penguin.

LeShan, L. (1990). *The dilemma of psychology.* New York: Dutton.

May, W. T., & Belsky, J. (1992). Response to "prescription privileges: Psychology's next frontier?" or the siren call: should psychologists medicate? *American Psychologist, 47*, 427.

Prigogine, I. (1980). *From being to becoming—time and complexity in the physical sciences.* San Francisco: W. H. Freeman & Sons.

Rapp, P. E. (1995). Is there evidence for chaos in the human central nervous system? In R. Robertson & A. Combs (Eds.), *Chaos theory in psychology and the life sciences*, 89–100, Hillsdale, NJ: Lawrence Erlbaum Associates.

Rodgers, J. E. (1992). *Psychosurgery: Damaging the brain to save the mind.* New York: Harper Collins.

Ruthen, R. (1993, January). Adapting to complexity. *Scientific American*, 130–140.

Saeman, H. (1992). What price prescription privileges? *Psychotherapy in Private Practice, 11*(1), 9–13.

Sanua, V. D. (1990). The etiology of schizophrenia as perceived by psychiatrists in Europe and the United States. *Current Psychology: Research & Reviews, 9*(4), 355–371.

Sanua, V. D. (1994a). Quo Vadis APA?: Inroads of the medical model. *Journal of Humanistic Psychology.*

Sanua, V. D. (1994b, March). *Prescription privileges versus psychologist's authority: Psychologists do better without drugs.* Paper presented at the Mid-Winter Convention of the American Psychological Association, Phoenix, AZ.

Szaz, T. S. (1970). *Ideology and insanity: Essays on the psychiatric dehumanization of man.* New York: Anchor.

von Bertalanffy, L. (1968). *General system theory: Foundations, development, applications.* New York: Braziller.

Chapter 12

Creative Consciousness Process

Fred Graywolf Swinney

The human experience, and the matters with which most psychotherapists deal, do not readily conform to the predictable mechanistic laws of Newtonian science and Cartesian philosophy which have provided the basic paradigm underlying contemporary medical and psychological sciences. In truth, we are complex organisms that seem to be as much ruled by serendipity and chaos as by order. In fact, it is most often the compulsive and rigid structures and behaviors displayed in the individual, group, or family's interactions that define dysfunction and evoke pain. To better understand and help change these complex systems requires understanding and comfort with the models of reality suggested by the new sciences: relativity, quantum physics, and most appropriately, chaos theory. This major paradigm shift suggests a long overdue examination of our current healing practices in light of the changes in our fundamental views about natural process and of how reality is formed and structured according to the new sciences.

The Creative Consciousness Process therapy described in this chapter explores that shift. It is a practice and philosophy of therapy best understood in the context of the new sciences and the modified views of natural process implicit in them. It also seems a natural extension of many schools of psychological theory and practice, and at the same time, as suggested and illustrated in such books as Capra's (1975) *Tao of Physics*, and Zukav's (1979) *Dancing Wu Li Masters*, it is consistent with a broad range of spiritual/mystical philosophies and healing practices. These include shamanism, the ancient Aesculapian dream-healing practices, and the range of Eastern psychologies and philosophies. The philosophy and theory of the Creative Consciousness Process, however, arose not out of logical inquiry into how chaos theory fits into psychology, nor out of a spiritual quest but rather from the gropings of "one initially trained in the hard sciences of physics and chemistry–turned psychotherapist–turned shaman" to somehow describe a healing process that he had "serendipitied" into, in a way that faithfully described it.

THE BEGINNINGS

One morning in 1984 in a therapy group, the therapist was using the Gestalt process in working with a dream (Perls, Hefferline, & Goodman, 1951; Perls, 1969, 1973). Rather than following the usual Gestalt practice of exploring the relationships and conflicts between symbols or parts of the dream, the client and therapist ventured more deeply into the experience of one of the dream's symbols, into the heart of the dream itself, and found a healing state of consciousness that was profound in its impact and implications. As with the belief from the ancient Greek Aesculapian dream-healing myth, where the healing god Asklepios worked his healing magic from within the dream, this healing state was buried deep in the dream far beyond its manifest form and any interpretation or surface manipulation.

In the dream, the client, strapped to a platform, was being drawn feet first into a wheel of rapidly rotating razor edged knives. The therapist had been exploring shamanic philosophy and practice for several years because of a discontent with the limits of psychological science and practice. This time, rather than having her become the knives and begin a dialogue, as might normally have been done using the usual Gestalt approach, it was suggested that she let herself be pulled into the whirling blades instead. The purpose was having her face directly, in the dream, what she most feared. In truth, it was also a moment of strong intuition and curiosity.

She reported being slashed and cut into tiny bits with blood and flesh splattering and scattering to all directions, but strangely, the predominant sense she experienced and reported was the sensation of the icy coldness of the blades. She was encouraged to pursue it, to give in to that sense-image of icy coldness. As she did, she soon became a layer of ice, frigid, rigid, and very hard and cold. This was the therapeutic issue that had brought her to seek therapy: She was a very hard, very cold, and a very frigid woman.

From previous sessions, it was known that her condition stemmed from early and continued sexual molestation by several older brothers. In two years of therapy, although she had achieved insight as to the origins of her problem and had even made several breakthroughs, she had not reached a place of deep healing with which either party was satisfied. Nor, in truth, did it seem likely that would happen. The shared experience of incompleteness was typical and was the reason for the therapist's interest in other healing practices.

"Stay with it," she was urged. "Go even deeper into this sense of cold—become it." As she did, and was encouraged to go even further, she reported first a sensation of falling into bottomless, dark, absolute-zero cold, then entering and becoming the water beneath the ice and feeling warmer as she did so. She reported, in this state, a deeply felt sense of flowing, flexibility, and wave-like boundaries. Her rigid body eased into deep relaxation and softness. She was encouraged to remain in this state for as long as she needed. When she eventually came back from that state of consciousness, she was a different woman—flexible, flowing, and a softer self. Her deeper self shone through and in time her behavior and self image began to change. This new sense of self was deep and stable and continued to evolve. The work itself had been like other guided-imagery work, but was also somehow different in a way that couldn't yet be defined.

The more this experience was explored, the more remarkable the process seemed; physical as well as emotional and mental diseases yielded to new and profound senses of self and relationship with the outer world. The changes that took place were most often deep and continued to evolve long after the journeys ended. The search for understanding eventually led to chaos theory which seemed a natural fit. In conjunction with quantum and relativistic notions, here was a model that helped to explain the Creative Consciousness Process. Although much of it is presented as metaphorical, the relationships being suggested between chaos, creativity, new science, spirituality, and therapeutic effects may be more than just a metaphor. These relationships may reveal the mystery of the connections of consciousness, chaos, and creativity in the natural healing process.

Freud (1923) called the deep and hidden aspects of consciousness the id, and saw therein our drives and instincts. These, and subconsciously stored primal memory experiences, gave rise to the behaviors and defense mechanisms which largely define personality, behavior, sense of self, and ego. He saw the id as a chaotic and confusing primal aspect of our organism, barely controlled by the superego. By acting out, it would defy the constraints of acceptable social behavior. He attempted to understand and to shed light and reason on this chaotic morass of seething primal energies and instinctual drives through such indirect psychoanalytic techniques as free association, dream interpretation, and transference management. Exposed to the light of awareness, he believed that these basic forces that drove people could and would change.

Since then, aside from the staunch behavioral psychologies, most therapies and therapists have operated with the essential aspects of this concept as axiomatic, and have developed increasingly more precise, sophisticated, and apt ways and practices of finding, understanding, and/or attempting to release these trapped energy systems and memories. In that sense, the Creative Consciousness Process follows in this tradition and adds the dimension of the shaman's consciousness journey as a means of entering into this self-scape of primal consciousness patterns. The changes, however, take place at a basic level of sensory perception and organization rather than at the more surface levels of emotional or intellectual processes, and based on observations and reports from journeyors, the process seems to involve re-patterning of the neural pathways and structures that shape the ways we sense ourselves and the environment. This level, the zone between what our senses register and how we perceive them, and how we experience the self and world around us, is filled with primal structures or patterns of self image, and is where our personal reality is shaped.

CREATIVE CONSCIOUSNESS PROCESS THERAPY

The Creative Consciousness Process involves guided consciousness journeys in which the therapist guides the client's full awareness into direct, rather than indirect, experiences of the chaotic self-scape of the id. The journey is a multisensory imagery process. It involves the therapist entering co-consciousness (intuitive) states and interactions with the client and guiding him to the basic trapped sensory-energy patterns or consciousness states that underlie the manifested disease symptoms . . . then beyond into the chaotic or unbound consciousness in which the primal sensory existential image transforms. In one sense, it draws from the consciousness journey of the shaman who enters the underworld (id) to return with the lost soul or spirit. At the same time it reflects aspects of Milton Erickson's (Erickson, Rossi, & Rossi, 1976) concept and process of co-consciousness work which he defined as shared consciousness states that give the therapist intuitive insights about the client's state and journey. LeShan (1966) also identified this principle in his understanding of the healing process. In fact, the crux of his process calls for the therapist to meditate, to let go of the ego self, and enter into a sense of oneness with the client. The feeling of being accompanied on these quests is very important to the client, particularly at points in the journey where fear would normally turn him or her back.

White water rapids manifest chaos, and the white water river guide has much in common with the creative consciousness guide. Flowing consciousness is our river of life, and the frozen states that are our diseases are the rocks that create the rapids, chaos, and dangers in it, and challenge our soul on its journey. A good guide is trustworthy and inspires trust from those she guides. She is knowledgeable in the guide's principles and understands the hydraulic principles of flowing systems (creative consciousness processes). She has good rowing skills, and uses all that in service of her senses and intuition. There is fear on the river; sometimes in the guide, no matter how many times she has run the rapids, and always fear in her clients. But the guide must move them beyond it, use it to alter consciousness, and sharpen the senses and intuition. Her clients will learn by her example as she takes them through their own fears of the churning, whirling chaos to the calm and peaceful depths beyond them. On the river, the guide spots dangerous rapids well ahead and sometimes stops to scout them but eventually commits herself and those she is guiding to go into them. In its technique, the Creative Consciousness Process borrows heavily from Gestalt's psycho-drama by inviting the guided one to become and explore more and more deeply, elements of his or her self structure. Dreams are a starting point and this focus seems to induce awake dream experience. Even when other doorways are used, at some point the inner experience becomes more real than outer reality, as in a dream. The doorway may be a dream, or a symptom, or perhaps a drum journey or some other creative process that has evoked imagery or sensations. The imagery comes from the client, however, not from the guide. Dreams are preferred because in that state, the ego is least-actively involved in forming the imagery.

Dreams are considered manifestations of chaos and creativity coming into awareness. A dream is essentially a river of consciousness, its origins unformed or chaotic, but taking on its characteristic form as it flows by the obstructions and structures deep in the psyche, to incorporate their likenesses in its symbols. The final shape of the dream's symbols and interactions come from the ego, influenced by recent experiences, but its roots are the same structures that shape the self and its "dis-eases." Imagination is the raft that carries one down the river. The client is invited to imagine becoming one of the symbols or an element of the dis-ease experience.

From the client's reporting of this initial experience, the guide senses within, some symbol or aspect of it that will lead to the next deeper level. Emphasis is shifted to the more sensory nature of the experiences until the client is weaned away from the strictly visual, emotional, or intellectual images with which he or she usually starts. The underlying sensory pattern that describes the dis-ease is identified within the progressively deeper experiences, until its more elemental or primal form is reached. Within that experience is yet one more doorway that leads into chaotic, undifferentiated, or creative consciousness, and it is there that the transformation occurs.

From within this chaotic or undifferentiated consciousness, a new primal image spontaneously appears, a state of ease rather than disease which provides a new foundation for the self. Like the Phoenix, the old pattern of self is drawn into the flames of dissolution to arise as a new being. After time, with this new sense of being, the guide begins a re-entry process to help the client realize this new sense of being in his or her life. The new image, in subtle and/or overt ways, restructures the client's personality from personal mythological levels and belief systems to behaviors, emotional, and intellectual responses. It also seems to affect physical structures. For example, clients have reported changes in body chemistry, muscle tension, immune system function, food preference, or the functioning of various organs.

It is a therapy of being and becoming, not one of doing. The client is always invited to experience his symbols; seldom, if ever to manipulate or do anything with them. Interpretation is to be avoided; it is not to be used as a means of guiding the journey. It is the creative aspect of the client that is being called on in this process, and so it is the client's imagination and creative process that is nurtured, not the guide's. The guide is in service to this principle. The healing transformations can only come from and happen within the client. The guide keeps out of the way. He uses his own creative process to experience from his perspective what the client is experiencing in order to sense the consciousness dynamics and keep the client moving.

THE SIX ZONES OF CONSCIOUSNESS DYNAMICS

A number of models or consciousness maps, and principles of consciousness dynamics, are used to check where the client is in the process and to help maneuver. Creative consciousness journeys do not, however, always conform to a particular structure, model, or principle. Dealing with chaotic and complex systems is like that—unpredictable; it is the nature of creativity. The model that is being presented incorporates the six zones of consciousness dynamics which are generally found to be helpful in journeys and which most readily tie chaos theory to the healing process.

Zone 1: Behaviors and Symptoms

How people behave and interact in any situation follows certain behavioral patterns or strategies. For example, there are game and script patterns that Berne (1961) identified as pathologies in Transactional Analysis Therapy. In these patterns are the essence of the more fundamental primal disease structures at their most superficial or obvious manifestations. There is often a striking similarity in a person's game-script patterns and their physical symptoms. For example, a person whose life style and coping strategy is to meet every situation and challenge with a compulsive drive and anger, who takes on all responsibility and plays harried, whose life is one of high pressure (type A or achievement-oriented personality) is likely to have high blood pressure and other related symptoms. The manifest physical and psychological symptoms are certainly related and are a statement concerning the ecology of the entire organism. In them is the shape of the more profound state of dis-ease that underlies all the symptoms. In chaos theory, it is pattern, not event that is significant. With such a client, the guide may sense pressure, fear, control, and speediness.

In dreams, this behavior zone is found on the surface level—the symbols and actions as they are presented in the dream and its recall. In the example, the high pressure client dreams of being trapped in a long and massive black train speeding down a long straight track, and flashing by all the stations and water tanks on the way without slowing or stopping for them. To the guide, this imagery reinforces the initial senses of the client's lifestyle and disease symptoms. Rather than trying to deal with it at this level, the guide notes these sensory elements as components of the deeper core pattern to which they will journey. This is only the entrance to deeper-level patterns that overlay the healing chaos.

Zone 2: Thinking–Feeling–Mental

How we behave is largely shaped by how we think and feel about what is happening in our environment. This means "feel" in the emotional sense as well as in the opinion sense. This zone lies beneath the surface, and consists of thoughts and emotions locked in patterns that shape our behaviors, but are themselves merely reflecting even deeper patterns of energy and sensing. In this aspect, the creative consciousness journey reflects the experience of delving deep into the structure of a fractal image wherein each layer repeats the basic structure of the levels above and below it. Probing the structure of dreams or personality in this way is probing the nature of complexity and chaos itself.

This is the level at which the cognitive-emotive therapies such as Transactional Analysis (Berre, 1961), Rational Emotive Therapy (Ellis, 1962), Gestalt (Perls et al., 1951; Perls, 1969, 1973), and many of the humanistic therapies operate and look to effect change. Rather than worry about whether thoughts cause emotions or visa versa, we experience the activity in this zone of consciousness dynamics more as a dance; thoughts and emotions mutually interacting in a swirling absorbing pattern that eventually engulfs the entire organism and shapes the outer self. The imagery in this zone invokes and reflects a wide range of emotions and thoughts; in fact, it is that aspect of the imagery that identifies this zone. To the guide, it is the pattern of the dance that is important, not the dancers. It is the pattern of the dance that reflects the deeper core disease structure. The guide seeks to sense the music, the melody, and rhythm that shape and drive the dance.

For example, with the achievement-oriented personality and her dream, she describes that she is a large and heavy train confined to a single track pushed on faster and faster by an inevitable momentum that hurls her past the oasis of refreshment and the stations that define her purpose. She feels the emptiness and seeks the succor but she cannot stop. She is terrified lest some curve, even a gentle one, lies ahead, and that at her speed, she will be hurled from the track into a totally destructive wreck. The guide seeks the senses presented in this image but does not get trapped in the dance of the fears and thoughts associated with it. The sensations of heaviness, emptiness, irresistible momentum and speed, and the awareness of the wreckage and destruction resonate with what will open the door to the next level.

Zone 3: Belief Systems

How we think and feel about what is happening in our lives and how we react is generally shaped by our belief system. In some ways, this zone too, is full of thoughts and emotions, and is the home of our values. More than that, it is a zone of deeply felt senses, sometimes only peripherally present in our awareness, but sometimes more solid and unyielding or shocking. It holds the deep sense of what is possible and what is not, of what is right and what is wrong, of good and evil, of what is and what just can't or shouldn't be.

We are all strongly entrenched in our belief system. Any attempts to get someone to change at this level is usually met with much resistance. Justifiably so, for this is the level and these are the structures that define what we can manipulate and how to do it to ensure our survival. Beyond our belief system lies the unknown.

The imagery at this level reflects that principle. It is very intense and conspires to keep us within the boundaries of safety ... of the known. It is full of monsters, devils, and dire warnings that would force us to turn back when we venture too close to the edge. The senses scream imminent death and dismemberment, dissolution, uncrossable chasms, bottomless pits. The ego thrusts our worst fears into our face, presents obstacles that would discourage the most hardy and brave from going on. This type of imagery defines this zone. But, as in the archetypal journey of the hero, the monsters must be faced and engaged, and the fear used and transcended.

Zone 4: Personal Mythology

Our beliefs are shaped by and rest on even deeper patterns of consciousness structure and dynamics. This zone is an archaic and archetypal level, and the consciousness structures which fill it were adopted and integrated very early in life to best explain our experiences. It is deeply sensory, sometimes involving senses that seem to go considerably beyond normal sensing. This is a zone in which the personal and transpersonal begin to merge. It is archetypal in that it generally reflects on a sensory level the pattern of some archetypal story, myth, or protagonist. According to Berne (1961), it is encountered superficially as the favorite fairy tale, story, or hero that reflects the script pattern. Feinstein and Krippner (1988) have identified it as the Personal Mythology that shapes one's life. In general, these personal myths, and the sensory patterns that they incorporate and manifest, seem to have a deep sense of inevitability, perhaps even a feeling that there is no other possible path.

It could be argued that this is really just an aspect of the belief system zone, defining the same limits and boundaries. But this zone is indeed deeper and more elemental. In this zone, the concepts and polarities of right–wrong, good–evil are not in evidence. Here, the sense is more of the inevitable. There is less fear— that seems to have yielded to that same sense of inevitability. There is almost a calm acceptance of the sensory imagery experienced at this level, perhaps even a supreme sense of helplessness and acceptance of one's fate. What emotions may be evoked are very basic and are more sense than emotion. In it are the inevitability and archetypal patterns of a Greek tragedy, comedy, or myth. In this sense it includes conviction and intention, and hence leads to action and the drama of life. In it is the doorway to the next level.

"It's awful!" cries the client, her body beginning to shake. "I'm being thrown off the track and I can feel myself flying through the air. I know I'll hit the ground soon and I'll be destroyed.

"It's like a sense of . . . inevitability . . . helplessness and a heaviness that is pulling down," she reports.

Zone 5: The Edge of Creation

The next consciousness zone, the edge of creation, is the zone of consciousness dynamics where we literally create our reality. It is the zone of the primal existential images that hold in their structures the essences of our dis-eases, where these images take the raw energies of our senses and shape them into perceptions of self and the universe. On one side of this space are the psychic and physical structures of self and our reality, and on the other, the infinite creative potential of unstructured chaos—the unbound interacting energy fields that trigger our senses and perceptions.

It is in this zone that we find the elusive mind–body connection, the primal sensory images which are not of the mind or the physiology alone, but in essence, both. As in quantum physics, which deals with the idea that light somehow is both a particle (quanta or matter) and a wave (energy), so too, do these images display properties of both body and mind. They are bridges between what the body senses and how that is organized into perception of self and outer world. Through these structures, the mind patterns the body and all its functions, and the body in turn patterns the mind and all its functions.

These primal sensory images incorporate the patterns of surface symptoms in a vortex of trapped sensory memories. The momentum of this vortex holds the pattern virtually intact, and pulls in even more energy from current experiences, which adds psychic mass that further increases the momentum. It is only dissolution into the chaos, the universal solvent of the alchemist, that can create a transformation.

The imagery is distinctive in several ways. In passing through this layer, one moves beyond even the primal emotional and sensing imagery into a selfscape of archetypal strange attractors that define the limits and structure of the forms that come out of the primal chaos. Present at all levels of universal organization the "Archetypal Strange Attractors" that are experienced at this level draw structure from chaotic, unbounded, or undifferentiated consciousness and also provide the openings that take the dis-eased awareness into the chaos where they disintegrate. It is from this that new structures emerge. The guide knows that they must be entered into, but not lightly. Entering brings death and dissolution to a part of the self.

"It's closing in on me suffocating me and now I feel myself falling into it. It's like the sensation of speed but almost more like floating now," the client reports.

Zone 6: Chaotic Consciousness or the Cauldrons of Creation

The dis-eased structure carried into the chaotic consciousness is transformed. The imagery and sense of self and reality that emerge always bring the organism to a state of dynamic balance transformed from the dis-eased state. The guide and the nature of the journey itself probably become part of the new strange attractor that helps shape the new self now emerging from the unbound chaotic consciousness. Since the original dis-eased state is based in fear and pain, and the journey is one of courage and facing fear and pain, the new structure incorporates this new self sense. Other elements of the strange attractor that defines the new sense of self are the healthy elements of the client's coping skills. It is only the specific dis-eased structure that is taken into the dissolution; the rest remains.

There seems to be an underlying principle of evolution that might help explain the process. Evolution seems to work on the principle that an organism does well in its survival until it encounters changes in the environment that ensure its demise unless it changes. This is an evolutionary crisis, and as the old species dies out and goes into dissolution or chaos, a new and better adapted one takes its place. This is an apt description of the natural healing processes and what happens to the consciousness structures.

In this state or zone, the neural firings and pathways that defined the old sensory structures slip into random or chaotic firing mode, and in that chaos the equivalent of a quantum shift into the new structure takes place. This feeling of "shift" is one of the most commonly reported sensations of the experience at this level.

The imagery in this state reflects chaos. It may, for example, be a monochromatic color, and include the complete absence of any type of image. This may represent the subjective experience of an absence of specific sensory neural firing patterns. A shift is felt and then a new sense of self gradually emerges. Sometimes the imagery reflects a plethora and confusion of energy—for example, a field of flashing and shifting points of colors of all possible and imaginable hues that eventually resolves into a new sensory image of self.

"I have the sense of being the core of the earth," she states with wonder in her voice. "I am the center, the core of the earth and I feel very liquidy and flowing. I am the lava that creates the earth," she says very quietly.

RE-ENTRY

The end of a journey is really the beginning or the opening into a new way of experiencing life. The internal change has already taken place. It happened in the felt-imagery. The journeyer's outer world will begin to change also. She will experience differences in her behaviors and reactions. She will have a different sense of her body, and her physical symptoms may begin to disappear or change. These changes happen for the most part without any endeavor on her part. Much of it could be very subtle and noticed only in retrospect through their absence, particularly if they were not symptoms she had focused on or were perhaps ones that she had adapted to so completely that they were no longer in her awareness. The process mirrors other natural healing processes such as the changes that accompany nutritional work or naturopathic or homeopathic treatments.

In ongoing therapy, we have noticed a cumulative effect from one journey to the next. It seems that subsequent dreams and journeys build on both the imagery and healing states encountered in previous journeys. These previous gains are discussed and tied into current journeys.

CONCLUSIONS

During the time we have been using this process, the list of ailments and symptoms relieved includes both physical and mental problems. That is actually less important, however, than the changes in self image and empowerment attained, because this ensures continuing ease and health rather than just the solving of a problem. Most clients report facing life and new challenges with more courage and creativity. They feel freed from their old coping patterns, and act rather than react.

The Creative Consciousness Process, the journey, and the underlying consciousness states which are eventually reached, conform in all essentials to the dynamics of chaotic systems as described by Chaos theory. The journey itself resembles a fractal image. As one amplifies a small part, one finds the essence of its form repeated at deeper and deeper levels. The journey also reflects the dynamics of chaotic systems in that bifurcations characterize the unfolding journey, with the flow of imaginative imagery shifting and taking unexpected new twists in unpredictable ways. The healing or transformative, unstructured consciousness-energy beyond the bound consciousness also reflects these dynamics; new structures, experiences and images arise from within to replace the painful and diseased images. The butterfly effect, whereby small changes in the initial conditions may have a large impact on the system's development, is also descriptive of the process and its effects.

The new structures or primal, existential self images that manifest during these journeys are profoundly healing. They provide balance and deeply felt sensory repatterning: an internally, deeply sensed freedom for one who was trapped, peace for one who was agitated, wholeness for one who was scattered. The new sense of being reflects the nature of the journey-experience itself, and the guide's influence, in the forming of the new self image. In this sense, the therapist is a part of the strange attractor that influences this newly emergent existential self image. Over a period of time this new image reshapes the personality and behavioral patterns to reflect the balance and the creative process that evoked it.

It is a journey into the essence of creative spirit for our re-creation. Chaos is the birthplace of creativity; it is the the essence of no-thingness which allows expression of all things, and therein lies our freedom, health, and inspiration.

RECOMMENDED READING

Barnett, L. (1948). *The universe and Dr. Einstein*. New York: Time Incorporated.

Berne, E. (1964). *Games people play*. New York: Ballantine Books.

Berne, E. (1961). *Transactional analysis in psychotherapy*. New York: Grove Press, Inc.

Calvin, W., & Ojemann, G. (1980). *Inside the brain*. New York: Mentor.

Capra, F. (1975). *The tao of physics*. New York: Bantam Books.

Ellis, A. (1962). Reason and emotion in psychotherapy. New York: Lyle Stuart.

Erickson, M., Rossi, E. L., & Rossi, S. I. (1976). *Hypnotic realities*. New York: Irvington Publishers.

Fagan, J., & Shepherd, I. L. (1970). *Gestalt therapy now*. New York: Harper Colophon Books.

Feinstein, D., & Krippner, S. (1988). *Personal mythology*. Los Angeles: Jeremy P. Tarcher, Inc.

Freud, S. (1923). *The ego and the id., standard edition 19*. London: The Hogarth Press.

Friedman, M., & Rosenman, R. H. (1974). *Type A behavior and your heart*. Greenwich, CT: Fawcett Publications, Inc.

Gregg, P. M. (1989). *An Ericksonian approach to dream work*. Paper presented to the 6th International Conference of the Association for the Study of Dreams, London, England.

Harner, M. (1980). *The way of the shaman*. New York: Bantam Books.

Krippner, S., & Welch, P. (1992). *Spiritual dimensions of healing*. New York: Irvington Publishers, Inc.

LeShan, L. (1966). *The medium, the mystic and the physicist*. New York: Ballantine Books.

McAuliffe, K. (1990). *Get smart: Controlling chaos*. New York: Omni Publications International Ltd.

Perls, F., Hefferline, R. E., & Goodman, P. (1951). *Gestalt therapy*. New York: Dell Publishing Co. Inc.

Perls, F. (1969). *Gestalt therapy verbatim*. New York: Bantam Books.

Perls, F. (1973). *The Gestalt approach and eye witness to therapy.* Palo Alto, CA: Science & Behavior Books.

Restak, R. M. (1979). *The brain, the last frontier.* New York: Warner Books.

Simonton, C. (1982). *Getting well again.* New York: Bantam.

Steiner, C. M. (1974). *Scripts people play.* New York: Bantam Books.

Storm, H. (1972). *Seven arrows.* New York: Ballantine Books.

Storm, H. (1981). *Song of heyoehkah.* San Francisco: Harper and Row.

Ullman, M., & Krippner, S. (1989). Dream telepathy. Jefferson, NC: McFarland & Co.

Villoldo, A., & Krippner, S. (1987). *Healing states.* New York: Simon & Schuster.

Watts, A. (1970). *Nature, man and woman.* New York: Vintage Books.

Watts, A. (1975). *Tao: The watercourse way.* New York: Pantheon.

Wilber, K. (1984). *Quantum questions.* Boston & London: Shambhala.

Wollheim, R. (1971). *Sigmund Freud.* New York: Viking Press.

Zukav, G. (1979). *Dancing wu li masters.* New York: Bantam Books.

Chapter 13

Chaos, Complexity, and Psychophysiology

Stephen E. Francis

Historically, we have drawn on the scientific and technological models of the day either metaphorically or directly as explanatory devices. For the first part of this century, the switchboard operator analogy was used to explain brain function and processing. In the past twenty-five years, cognitive scientists have looked to computer models to explain cognition. As these models are also proving limited and inadequate, there is an imperative to find models that can account for a broader spectrum of reality.

The force behind this movement is the science of nonlinear dynamics, originated by Henri Poincaré at the turn of the century and brought to fruition with the advent of high-powered computers. These nonlinear theories have fallen under the term chaos theory, and more recently, complexity theory.

The purpose of this chapter is to illustrate that the concept of homeostasis, which has endured for most of this century, does not capture all aspects of humans as living organisms. Beyond that, it has been over applied. Homeostasis and equilibrium-based models such as cybernetics have not captured the learning, growth, and transformation that occur in living systems. As an alternative, dynamical, nonlinear living systems theory is proposed as a conceptualization of the human condition. This alternative includes both chaos theory and complexity theory.

This chapter will examine clinical stress-management practices with these new theories in mind, suggesting all the while that homeostasis be replaced by the notion of coherence. Coherence is that subtle process which exists within living systems that enables them to maintain their form. It is hoped that stress, human perception, and the processing of stress will one day no longer be limited by linear models and outdated biological concepts, but instead be replaced by descriptions that emphasize coherence and nonlinearity.

CONSIDERING HOMEOSTASIS

Homeostasis was a concept coined by Walter B. Cannon (1932), a biologist. A significant contribution to the biological sciences was the differentiation of living systems and non-living systems. This advance in thinking set the stage for theorists to move away from mechanistic concepts when looking at the processes of living systems. Unfortunately, it took most of this century for biologists and physiologists to begin to move away from mechanistic and reductionistic thinking. In the interim, several problems emerged from these lingering, mechanistic approaches. First, this sort of reductionism does not allow one to understand the working interactions of the different components of a system or a process. Second, complex systems, such as biological systems, have too many parts to disassemble such that a reductionistic analysis proves difficult if not impossible. Cannon (1932) was also influenced by an organism's internal matrix, or what was termed the internal milieu. In developing his concept of homeostasis, Cannon felt that the organism is invested in maintaining a balanced state of its internal milieu. The maintenance of this balance he termed homeostasis.

In physiology and psychology this concept is pervasive. If we examine the following definitions from the field of psychophysiology, we can see the staying power of the concept of homeostasis. Seyle (1976), in his pioneering work on stress, *The Stress of Life*, considers homeostasis to be the power to maintain constancy, or what he calls organic stability. Similarly, Green and Green (1977) state that:

> "It [homeostasis] refers to the tendency of an organism to compensate for disturbance, to maintain stability." "... includes the ability of the organism to adapt to its surroundings" and "... is an active tendency to restore equilibrium, to maintain steady states in the face of constant change" (p. 173).

Girdano and Everly (1979) define homeostasis as "the state of the body in which there exists a stable equilibrium of internal functions" (p. 58). They further add that there is a need for a healthy balance in the mental and physical processing of the organism. They feel that too much change can disrupt the homeostasis. Olton and Noonberg (1986) give the following definition: "A homeostatic mechanism maintains the same state, a point of equilibrium" (p. 17). A common example of homeostasis is the interaction of a thermostat and a furnace. The thermostat detects discrepancies, and signals the furnace to either ignite and warm the room or stay dormant and allow the room to cool. It maintains the system near a predetermined set-point.

In living systems, homeostasis serves as a form of negative feedback to aid an organism in maintaining normal healthy functioning. Essentially, negative feedback describes when the organism or a particular aspect or organ within the organism encounters too much stimulation. The feedback mechanisms of the organism will be activated to aid in the prevention of over-stimulation. As a result, the organism will engage in some processes to maintain balance.

More recently, Green and Shellenberger (1991) define homeostasis as the body's ability to maintain a steady state or to maintain the same state. They attempt to distinguish between homeostasis and healthy homeostasis. They feel that the self-correcting and self-regulating aspects of healthy homeostasis result from the interactions of feedback and homeostatic mechanisms. They assert that healthy homeostasis is the conscious choice made by an individual to help maintain the body's homeostasis by not exposing oneself to an unhealthy and toxic lifestyle.

There is a notion that when a system is continuously exposed to adverse conditions, the system will reset its homeostatic mechanisms such that it will maintain a balance around the new set of circumstances (Green & Shellenberger, 1991; Green & Green, 1977; Lovelock, 1979; Pool, 1998; Rapp, 1995). For example, high blood pressure can result from the kidneys being continuously required to provide more of the body's acid base metabolic needs, and to do this they increase the blood pressure. Other aspects of the circulatory system will respond to this new homeostatic "set-point," and unless an intervention is made either pharmacologically or through some other form such as biofeedback, the body will continue at this set-point and possibly even increase it if conditions worsen. This example suggests that the only direction in which growth and adaptation can be accounted for in these conceptualizations of homeostasis is a negative one.

From the perspective of chaos theory, the maintenance of the same state within a system will quickly lead to the death of that system. Goldstein (1995) proposed that the concept of equilibrium be returned to its position as only a determinate condition, and can only be viewed as one phase in the dynamics of a larger non-equilibrium system. Equilibrium is primarily an aspect of closed or mechanical systems. What will become evident is that homeostasis is inadequate to account for the dynamics of open systems.

THE IDEA OF OPEN AND CLOSED SYSTEMS

To understand the argument for a reconceptualization of stress in psychophysiology, it is helpful to first understand the distinctions between open and closed systems. In a closed system there is no interaction with the outside environment. They are, in effect, isolated systems. This is primarily the province of thermodynamics. In the words of Sheldrake (1981):

"According to the second law of thermodynamics, spontaneous processes within a closed system tend towards a state of equilibrium; as they do so, initial differences in temperature, pressure, etc. between different parts of the system tend to disappear. In technical language, the entropy of a closed macroscopic system either stays the same or increases" (p. 62).

Closed systems are mechanical systems, though scientists in today's world would be hard pressed to describe a fully closed system.

Jantsch (1980) makes the distinction between open and closed systems by stating that: "systems without exchange with their environment are called isolated. An exchange with the environment can be maintained by the system itself only when its internal state is in non-equilibrium; otherwise the process would die down" (p. 32).

Two key features of open systems are that they need to import energy from the outside environment and that they use energy as a function of maintaining order. An open system maintains its order by existing in a far-from-equilibrium state (Prigogine, 1980). When an open system is observed, the system is globally stable, but locally there may be large fluctuations.

It is also important to understand how feedback systems differ between open and closed systems. In a closed system, feedback is used to maintain stability or equilibrium. Disruptions and destabilizations occur and the feedback system within the closed system informs the system of the imbalance and deploys the necessary steps to regain equilibrium. In an open system, however, the feedback can be utilized for the maintenance of order, but it also accounts for the learning and evolution of complexity within the system.

WIENER'S CYBERNETICS

It is difficult, if not impossible, to speak about machines and humans as sharing similar features. Humans are different from machines, despite the very mechanistic agenda pursued by transformation. Machines, on the other hand, can only perform certain functions. Even the most sophisticated computers can only perform what they are programed to do. It makes sense that we want machines to be predictable and reliable. A car is not capable of going through a transformation. It might go through a decline, and it might get a tune-up. But a car does not come back from a long cross-country journey and feel changed the way the driver might. We can say that the car can self-regulate, but only to maintain some sort of equilibrium, possibly to avoid overheating.

While a cybernetic system is based on "information," an open system model is based on the dynamic interaction of its parts (von Bertalanffy, 1968). An interactive system that is capable of learning does not maintain homeostasis or equilibrium on whatever level the learning occurred. Learning would naturally imply a transformation. In natural systems, feedback accounts for more than just the maintenance of homeostasis or equilibrium of physiological function. Feedback is a crucial link to the idea that organisms learn new behaviors, and ultimately experience some sort of transformation from the learning process. It is unfortunate that in clinical psychophysiology, the language of cybernetics and homeostasis has limited the conceptualization of the human as capable of transformation. The language of mechanical systems limits a discussion of the human physiological system. The focus has been entirely on maintaining or regaining the set-point or homeostasis. This conceptualization is unfortunately limiting. A broader view for clinical psychophysiology must be pursued.

ADVANTAGES TO THE CHAOS MODEL IN PSYCHOPHYSIOLOGY

As outlined in Chapter 1, chaos theory had its origins at the beginning of this century with nonlinear equations and subsequent developments ensued with the work of meteorologist Edward Lorenz (1963). Chaos theory, by the methods inherent in its approach to a problem, is able to characterize a system as a whole. The reductionistic view of science, for the last several hundred years, has proved inadequate in characterizing physiological processes in humans. The various organs and systems of the body have been studied in isolation. Only in the past fifteen to twenty years has a field like psychoneuroimmunology allowed us to realize a richer communication that exists between the mind, the nervous system, and the immune system (Schleifer, Keller, & Stein, 1985; Ader, 1981; Barthrop, Lazarus, Luckhurst, Kiloh, & Penny, 1978). With this sort of advance, we can see an advantage to approaching the human organism as a whole.

A second advantage to chaos theory is that it allows one to study complex living systems and not lose that complexity through reductionistic methods. Traditionally, science, in its attempts to understand phenomena, has simplified processes thereby eliminating key features. In the early days of cardiovascular research, respiration was considered to be a nuisance variable because breathing rate would affect the heart rate (Fried, 1987; Grossman, 1983). Eventually it was discovered that the respiration rate and the heart rate covaried together and needed to be understood in their natural relationship (Angelone & Coulter, 1964).

To capture the complexity of an interactive system, chaos theory seeks to find a few key determinants of the system. A metaphor might be useful here. If we think of a jazz band that is beginning to improvise on a composition, there are certain constraints on their playing. These determinants would be the musical key in which they are playing, and the time signature. Within these minor constraints, the improvisation could become completely unrecognizable compared to the original composition. A chaotic system might initially look random from the outside, but there is an underlying order to the behavior of the system. The methods of chaos theory seek to ascertain those key determinants that give rise to the system's complex order.

The final point to consider is what is known as the sensitivity to initial conditions (as described in Chapter 1). This is at the heart of nonlinearity. It occurs when something that is assumed to be relatively minor influences large systemic changes. In considering these points, we have the idea that human physiology is more complex than either cybernetics or homeostasis has been able to account for.

CHAOS IN PHYSIOLOGICAL SYSTEMS

At this point, the question must be asked: Why chaos, and what are the advantages to having chaos in the nervous system? It appears that the application of nonlinear mathematical models of physiological systems provides a more accurate picture of physiological processes. However, there is some debate about whether chaos represents a diseased state (Glass & Mackey, 1988) or whether the presence of low level chaotic variability provides a degree of healthy flexibility within the organism (Goldberger, 1990; Skarda and Freeman, 1987).

There is ample data to support the concept of chaotic dynamics being a healthy feature of the human nervous system. Goldberger (1990) concluded that in cardiac fibrillation, "periodicity" exists. It had previously been proposed that the healthy human heart exhibits stability and the diseased heart exhibits chaos. Goldberger contests this position showing that there are subtle irregularities in the inter-beat interval of the heart which allow the heart to adapt flexibly to the demands of the environment. Golberger's research demonstrated that the loss of chaotic variability within the heart's dynamics is a movement away from a healthy state, and sudden cardiac deaths could be predicted based on the heart-rate variability becoming highly stable and regular.

Skarda and Freeman (1987) also found a similar feature in the EEG. There existed a low-level chaotic variability almost as a background signal that allowed the organism to adapt rapidly to novel stimuli in the environment. According to Skarda and Freeman:

> "Brains rely on mechanisms not found in other models; we propose four such mechanisms that may be necessary to solve problems critical to the efficient functioning and survival of any system that has to behave adaptively in an environment subject to unpredictable and often violent fluctuations." and "Chaos constitutes the basic form of collective neural activity for all perceptual processes and functions as a controlled source of noise, as a means to ensure continual access to previously learned sensory patterns, and as the means for learning new sensory patterns" (p. 161).

In a very elegant study, Freeman (1991) showed that the chaos inherent in the brain allowed for new information to be learned easily and that it influenced previously learned information. His study demonstrated that new information presented to his subjects (rats) changed the organization of previously stored information. This delivers a strong blow to the notions that information, once learned, stays fixed in the brain. This also illustrates the dynamics of self-organization. The nervous system is able to self-organize itself as new information continues to inform it.

It seems that the language of chaos theory could allow us to speak about transformation. Once we leave the realm of physiology, however, and move to speaking about psychological systems, the level of complexity and the degrees of freedom grow to the point of creating considerable difficulty. Within the realm of clinical psychology, Barton (1994) feels that chaos theory could be "intuitively appealing, yet so analytically difficult" (p. 10). He emphasizes that we should consider the characteristics and dynamics of a self-organizing system rather than the mathematics. Current scientific trends often influence the metaphors of the social sciences. It seems that chaos theory, even without its mathematical rigor, can offer a powerful metaphor for psychology. Rather than one more conceptualization within a mechanistic framework, chaos theory truly offers a paradigmatic shift by moving the emphasis away from reductionism and placing it on process (Combs, 1995).

There is a series of studies that could provide direction for those wishing to understand more about the chaotic dynamics of psychophysiological systems. Historically, psychophysiology has represented the interface of mind and body. In a very elaborately designed study, Redington and Reidbord (1992) have tried to capture the shifting dynamics of the cardiac system. They looked at the inter-beat intervals of the heart rate of a psychotherapy patient during a psychotherapy session. Measuring the spaces between the inter-beat intervals and graphing them, they found several distinct trajectories. Each trajectory could be associated with a particular experience for the patient during the session. The trajectories grew in complexity, thus capturing more complex mood states of the patient. Finally, during a moment of insight for the patient, the trajectory went unpredictably into chaos. Redington and Reidbord concluded from this that there exists a flexibility in the cardiovascular system that is reflective of states of being. It is interesting to note that one's mental state can be reflected in one's physiology. The elegance and rigor of the design of their study far exceeds the capabilities of most clinicians. Therefore, it seems fair that we find a more suitable means for psychologists to speak about flexibility, growth, and transformation.

COMPLEXITY THEORY AND THE EDGE OF CHAOS

If chaos theory does not adequately capture this interpretation of living systems, what are our alternatives? One candidate that is emerging is complexity theory. Like chaos theory, it is a new approach to science that is attempting to unify the life sciences by emphasizing the inherent striving for diversity and complexity that makes up living systems. What is it that makes a system strive for complexity? At this point, it seems too early to tell, but it does seem that complexity within a system seems to safeguard the organism/environment relationship. The most important point to emphasize is that we are no longer speaking about "isolated systems." With complexity theory, we are interested in how the organism and the environment interact as a whole.

What distinguishes complexity theory from chaos theory? Several key differentiations include the fact that complex systems have more variables and more choices of behaviors than do chaotic ones (Corcoran, 1992). As stated, chaotic systems appear to be lawless, but actually have a few key determinants that govern their behavior. Because chaotic systems have fewer variables, they tend to converge to a smaller number of attractors (Corcoran, 1992). Jantsch (1980) adds that:

"complexity marks an open evolution which reveals ever new dimensions of novelty and exchange with the environment. It is not adaptation to a given environment that signals a unified overall evolution, but the co-evolution of system and environment at all levels, the co-evolution of micro- and macrocosms" (p. 75).

Another key distinction between chaos theory and complexity is that within the model of chaos theory, self-organizing behavior happens when the system is emerging out of chaos. Within complexity theory, self-organization happens at an earlier stage in the system's transformation—usually at the edge of chaos.

Several key proponents of complexity theory concede that there is not yet a generally accepted comprehensive definition (Kauffman, 1991). However, several important questions have been raised within the field. For instance, why do orderly systems become completely disorganized over time? A second question raised is how do disordered systems spontaneously "crystallize" into a higher degree of order? Finally, the question that seems most germane to the present discussion, "why does innovation seem to thrive at the boundary separating order from disorder?" According to Kauffman (quoted in Ruthen, 1993): "It turns out that in a wide variety of coupled systems the highest mean fitness is at the phase transition between order and chaos" (p. 140).

STRESS RESEARCH: APPLICATIONS OF CHAOS AND COMPLEXITY THEORY

In stress management, are there examples of persons existing at the edge of chaos—in complex regimes? If so, what are the characteristics of such regimes? Some of the most promising work is that of Kobasa and her colleagues (Kobasa, Maddi, & Courington, 1981; Kobasa, Maddi, & Kahn, 1982; Kobasa, Maddi, & Puccetti, 1982). Although they use the term "stress resistance," a problematic term, they focus on a key question: In the face of change and potential adversity, why do some people stay healthy and others get sick? Moreover, what are the key personality variables that distinguish these two groups? Instead of focusing on only those persons who became sick—a customary practice in the history of a psychology and medicine—Kobasa wanted to evaluate and understand those persons who stayed well. This emphasis away from pathology and toward what is healthy and exceptional has its roots in humanistic psychology (Maslow, 1968).

Those people who stayed well were described as "hardy." Hardiness was characterized by three key features. The first was challenge. For the people who stayed well, they perceived the changes going on in their lives as challenges rather than threats. As the environment they were in became complex and unpredictable, they developed a more efficient mode of engaging with the complexity rather than feeling threatened by it.

> "The challenge disposition is expressed as the belief that change rather than stability is normal in life and that the anticipation of changes are interesting incentives to growth rather than threats to security" (p. 170, Kobassa, Maddi, & Kahn, 1982).

A second characteristic that was identified was that of commitment. One group of executives that Kobasa and her colleagues studied were involved in the divestiture of AT&T during the early 1980s. She found that those executives who exhibited hardiness had a commitment to the company and were willing to see the divestiture through to its completion. Commitment includes the ability to stick with a plan or a vision in spite of increasing complexity in the environment.

The final characteristic of the hardy personality is control. Persons exhibiting hardiness believed that they at least had partial control of the events around them. In an earlier study, Kobasa (1979, cited in Kobasa, Maddi, & Puccetti, 1982) divided a group of business executives into high stress–low illness and high stress–high illness. She found that her measure of hardiness clearly differentiated the two groups. None of the demographic variables such as socioeconomic class differentiated the two groups.

The conclusion from this research is that the hardy personality style encouraged transformative coping (Kobasa, Maddi, & Courington, 1981). In their words:

"Hardy persons have considerable curiosity and tend to find their experiences interesting and meaningful. Further, they believe they can be influential through what they imagine, say, and do. At the same time, they expect change to be the norm, and regard it as an important stimulus to development. These various beliefs and tendencies are very useful in coping with stressful events" (p. 1981).

While original, Kobasa's research is reminiscent of another researcher working during the same time period—Antonovsky (1979). Antonovsky's research culminated in what he termed the sense of coherence. Like Kobasa, he endorsed an emphasis on health instead of pathology—what he referred to as the salutogenic approach. He defined coherence as follows:

"A global orientation that expresses the extent to which one has a pervasive, enduring though dynamic feeling of confidence that one's internal and external environment are predictable and that there is a high probability that things will work out as well as can reasonably be expected" (p. 123).

He emphasizes that this definition should not be confused with the notion of "I am in control." He also feels that the use of the word "dynamic" in the definition allows for an individual to cope with more than minor fluctuations. Antonovsky also differentiated his concept of coherence from the notion of locus of control. He felt that locus of control either is perceived internally for an individual or that an individual perceives events as being externally controlled. In his concept of coherence, a flow of internal and external is allowed for and the emphasis is placed on recognizing a predictable world in which the individual can maintain some coherence in spite of adversity.

How does a sense of coherence come to be? Antonovsky describes coherence through the development of what he calls General Resistance Resources (GRR). He feels that the GRRs are what an individual uses to combat or avoid stress. Like Kobasa, he employs the term "resistance." The intention is implicit that stress is negative and should be avoided. From their perspective, health is maintained through strong resistances. Interestingly, both Antonovsky and Kobasa are describing a more flexible and complex model in their notions of coherence and hardiness. Unfortunately, coming from an implicit steady state model, they both conceptualize the maintenance of health in terms of stress resistance.The concept of a resistance resource is rooted in a steady state model. It is posited that as long as stressors are resisted, then the system can maintain equilibrium.

New models of science have delineated the limitations of steady state theories in depicting living systems. To create a more inclusive model, a dynamical systems perspective could add to both Antonovsky's and Kobasa's models—for instance, if resistance were replaced with metabolism as in a general metabolism resource. It becomes imaginable that stress may be used as energy, and thereby brought into the system (voluntarily or involuntarily). One's sense of coherence enables one to break down and assimilate the stress, allowing stress to augment one's growth and transformation.

In a similar vein, Peat (1992) discusses his conceptualization of coherence which is heavily influenced by his background in physics. He states:

"Imagine an analogous process within the body, in which the circulation of a subtle correlating energy, i.e. a form of active information or meaning, could act to coordinate all the different processes within the organism. In this way, the metabolic processes of the body could be focused and would give rise to the circulation and amplification of energy far beyond its normal range" (p. 18).

Further he adds:

"The physicist H. Froehlich (personal communication) has proposed that collective states are entirely characteristic of all living systems and that *coherent* [italics added] correlations act to coordinate flows of energy and matter within cells. One could even speculate that correlates of non-local processes are also of key importance within the brain" (p. 18).

Is it possible that concepts like stress resistance or resistance resources might fall away if we were to consider the edge of chaos, or chaos, as inherently transformative states? This is not some semantic "splitting of hairs." Up to the edge of chaos it's possible that the resistance resources can still exist, sort of like the canoeist who paddles backstrokes to keep from heading into white water without some course in mind. Our canoeist has had time to plot some course through the whitewater, which is similar to complexity. The course is not too placid, nor too turbulent. But if our canoeist entered the white water without any plan whatsoever, his experience would be something akin to chaos. Likewise, it would become imperative for new behaviors or ways of perceiving and being in the world to emerge, quickly in this case, given the simultaneity of many changes or challenges all at once.

What features in the personality allow flexibility for new expressions to emerge? It requires a tremendous amount of energy to initially sustain new behaviors at this level. It requires a set of resources that are beyond the scope of resistances which previously have been employed in the service of maintaining stability. Up to this point we have been romanticizing transformation as occurring primarily in a positive direction. It is also possible that an individual can develop new behaviors in response to chaos that are less adaptive (Crichton, 1995).

DEVELOPING A NONLINEAR MODEL OF PSYCHOPHYSIOLOGY

So what would a more dynamic conceptualization of psychology, especially with regard to stress management look like? Several features would have to be highlighted and developed. They would include "non-linearity" and flexibility as part of our concepts of health (Francis, 1995). The best definition of nonlinearity is that sometimes one plus one equals two hundred. Nonlinearity seems to be a core concept of living systems. An important question to ask is, "what are the factor(s) responsible for triggering a system to stay at or cross the edge of chaos?" The urgency for psychology and psychophysiology to look more closely at the implications of chaos and complexity theory is that these fields are concerned with living systems.

The problems within these fields are inherently nonlinear, and to ignore nonlinearity is to ignore huge facets of our field. For instance, it has been noted that in the treatment of chronic pain, there is a wide variety of responses across patients for the same treatment. For example, the late Dr. Edgar Wilson, during his struggle with amyotrophic lateral sclerosis, or Lou Gehrig's disease, was receiving a sponge bath. During the experience, he was struck with such feelings of love that he regained a desire to live. Subsequently he survived for almost another year. This is but one example of unpredictable, discontinuous, and spontaneous transformation. Can we replicate sponge baths across patients and expect the same results? Of course not. Can we isolate the specific effects of the sponge bath apart from all other therapies? Of course not. Placebos fall into a similar category. The mix of factors both within the individual and in the environment create a climate for unique, and at times, unpredictable effects. This unpredictability is due to nonlinearity. We could not have predicted the effects of Dr. Wilson's sponge bath, nor that it would occur at that moment. But a seemingly small event such as the bath stirred him in such a way that he was able to self-organize at a higher level.

In many discussions on the regulation of health, there is an implicit emphasis on linearity. From this perspective we are told to keep the mind/body system within certain parameters, and health is maintained. This would be an example of maintaining the system's equilibrium or homeostasis. It is, therefore, believed that perturbations that move a system too far from its center will likely cause disease. In spite of a shifting paradigm in health from a fiercely biomedical to a biopsychosocial model the linear models of equilibrium still hold sway. The teleological explanatory power of equilibrium as "that towards which a system tends," is as prevalent today as it was when Galileo moved it to such a place of prominence (Goldstein, 1995).

At the same time that the equilibrium concept is applied to body/mind health, countless stories are being told about the depths of darkness that are reached before healing happens. This is not to mention the stories of profound healings, or the mystical states described by artists, writers, and saints through the ages. Ideas of this sort bring to mind notions of coherence. The experiences of symmetry and coherence provide a sense of organization. It is assumed that such experiences allow one to self-organize and thereby increase in complexity. These are what could be called far-from-equilibrium experiences, and from these experiences, healing followed. Incorporating chaos and complexity as metaphors could help us create a more unified model of psychology that just might account for the diverse realms of human experience and transformation.

It has been suggested (Francis, 1995) that even such processes as interoception can initiate healing processes. This becomes possible when we view healing from a non-linear perspective such that small additions or changes can create profound shifts in the system. Further, great fluctuations within a system are not always indicative of a threat to the system's well-being. This conceptualization emphasizes a much different notion of health than that of the equilibrium-based models. This is not to say that one must move far from equilibrium to achieve health, but it does suggest a more dynamic formulation of health that allows for more extreme experiences to be considered part of health's repertoire and not pathologized or feared. These nonlinear ideas also align with the recent trend that does not define health only in terms of the absence of disease, but takes a broader definition that views dying in a healthy manner as well.

THE PATHOLOGY OF HOMEOSTASIS

Habit, or behavioral homeostasis, can occur at many different levels of organization: neural, vascular, psychological, sociocultural. Are these states, as was suggested earlier, irreducible? The stress response, as a habitual expression in the presence of stress, organizes the person on multiple levels creating stress-related disorders or stress-related disorganization. This is when illness becomes the attractor (Francis, 1995) and the seriousness of the disorder is the slope of the attractor, metaphorically speaking. This habit, or attractor region, becomes the consistent style of expression in the face of challenging or adverse stimuli. Biofeedback and stress-management techniques work to replace this habit with what has heretofore been characterized as normal homeostatic functioning. In removing the maladaptive habit or style of coping with stress, the individual undergoing biofeedback or stress-management training is now gaining flexibility—a choice which allows him/her not to respond habitually. The flexibility can begin at the level where training is taking place (e.g., neurally, neuromuscularly, or neurovascularly for instance) and can generalize to other levels of being (organization) such as psychologically. In some cases it seems to happen in reverse, or even, on all levels at once. Regardless, this notion of flexibility is not expressed in the writings of those who speak of a return to homeostasis.

Flexibility is discussed indirectly in the bioenergetic perspective of Lowen (1975), Reich (1951), and Hanna (1987). Hanna talks about a soma, an intelligently sensing being. This implies an integration of body and mind. This soma can tolerate challenges and adversity (excursions across the edge of chaos) because it has developed a non-rigid style of responding to internal and external demands. It does not have the acquired habits of responding that generate stress-related disorders. As a result of its flexibility, this soma is able to take on greater demands—learning and self-organizing at a higher level of development. Hence, a soma is capable of transformations of bodymind.

A rigid soma is also expressing an aspect of dysponesis or "faulty or misplaced effort" (Whatmore & Kohli, 1979). Through biofeedback and stress-management training, an individual is able to reduce the "misplaced effort" and possibly respond with more flexibility. This goes beyond the previously proposed models of homeostasis and cybernetics common in stress-management theories. Moving from such notions as static and isolated systems, a consideration of steady states (von Bertalanffy, 1968) enables us to entertain a wider array of possible dimensions of health. These new ideas conceptualize human physiological capacities as transformative.

The shift from steady state models to a dynamical systems perspective endorsing the concepts of chaos and complexity will cause "chaos" in the field of psychology, and particularly stress management, which has developed its techniques based on the notions of homeostasis. However, it is hoped that a case has been made for moving away from the homeostatic model and toward a more open systems model that accounts for the nonlinearity seen in human behavior.

REFERENCES

Ader, R. (1981). *Psychoneuroimmunology*. Orlando, FL: Academic Press.

Angelone, A., & Coulter, N. A. (1964). Respiratory sinus arrhythmia: A frequency dependent phenomenon. *Journal of Applied Physiology, 19,* 479–482.

Antonovsky, A. (1979). *Health, stress and coping*. San Francisco: Jossey-Bass.

Barthrop, R. W., Lazarus, L., Luckhurst, E., Kiloh, L. G., & Penny, R. (1978). Depressed lymphocyte function after bereavement. *Lancet, 1,* 834–839.

Barton, S. (1994). Chaos, self-organization and psychology. *American Psychologist, 49*(1), 5–14.

Canon, W. B. (1932). *The wisdom of the body*. New York: W.W. Norton & Co.

Combs, A. (1995). Psychology, chaos, and the process nature of consciousness. In F. D. Abraham & A. R. Gilgen (Eds.), *Chaos theory in psychology*. Westport, CT: Greenwood Publishing.

Corcoran, E. (1992). The edge of chaos. *Scientific American, 267*(4), 17–22.

Crichton, M. (1995). *The lost world*. New York: Alfred A. Knopf.

Francis, S. E. (1995). Chaotic phenomena in psychophysiological self-regulation. In R. Robertson & A. Combs (Eds.), *Chaos theory in psychology and the life sciences* (pp. 253–265). Hillsdale, NJ: Lawrence Erlbaum Associates.

Freeman, W. (1991). The physiology of perception. *Scientific American, 264,* 78–85.

Freid, R. (1987). *The hyperventilation syndrome*. Baltimore: Johns Hopkins.

Girdano, D. A., & Everly, G. S. (1979). *Controlling stress and tension*. Englewood Cliffs, NJ: Prentice-Hall.

Glass, L., & Mackey, M. C. (1988). *From clocks to chaos: The rhythms of life*. Princeton, NJ: Princeton University Press.

Goldberger, A. L. (1990). Nonlinear dynamics, fractals and chaos: Applications to cardiac electrophysiology. *Annals of Biomedical Engineering, 18*, 195–198.

Goldstein, J. (1995). Unbalancing psychoanalytic theory: Moving beyond the equilibrium model of Freud's thought. In R. Robertson & A. Combs (Eds.), *Chaos theory in psychology and the life sciences*. Hillsdale, NJ: Lawrence Erlbaum Associates.

Green, E., & Green, A. (1977). *Beyond biofeedback*. New York: Dell.

Green, J., & Shellenberger, R. (1991). *The dynamics of health and wellness*. New York: Holt, Rinehart & Winston.

Grossman, P. (1983). Respiration, stress and cardiovascular function. *Psychophysiology, 20*(3), 284–300.

Hanna, T. (1987). *Somatics*. New York: Addison-Wesley.

Jantsch, E. (1980). *The self-organizing universe, scientific and human implications of the emerging paradigm of evolution*. New York: Pergamon Press.

Kauffman, S. A. (1991). Antichaos and adaptation. *Scientific American, 265*(2), 78–84.

Kobasa, S. C., Maddi, S. R., & Courington, S. (1981). Personality and constitution as mediators in the stress-illness relationship. *Journal of Health and Social Behavior, 22*, 368–378.

Kobasa, S. C., Maddi, S. R., & Kahn, S. (1982). Hardiness and health. *Journal of Personality and Social Psychology, 42*(1), 168–177.

Kobasa, S. C., Maddi, S. R., & Puccetti, M. C. (1982). Personality and exercise as buffers in the stress-illness relationship. *Journal of Behavioral Medicine, 5*(4), 391–404.

Lorenz, E. N. (1963). Deterministic nonperiodic flow. *Journal of Atmospheric Sciences, 20*, 130–141.

Lovelock, J. (1979). *Gaia: A new look at life on earth*. Oxford: Oxford University Press.

Lowen, A. (1975). *Bioenergetics*. New York: Penguin.

Maslow, A. (1968). *Toward a psychology of being*. New York: Van Nostrand Reinhold.

Olton, D. S., & Noonberg, A. R. (1980). *Biofeedback: clinical applications in behavioral medicine*. Englewood Cliffs, NJ: Prentice-Hall.

Peat, F. D. (1993). Towards a process theory of healing: energy, activity and global form. *Subtle Energies, 3*(2), 1–25.

Pool, R. (1990). Is it healthy to be chaotic? *Science, 243*, 604–607.

Prigogine, I. (1980). *From being to becoming—time and complexity in the physical sciences*. San Francisco: W. H. Freeman & Sons.

Rapp, P. E. (1995). Is there evidence for chaos in the human central nervous system? In R. Robertson & A. Combs (Eds.), *Chaos theory in psychology and the life sciences* (pp. 89–100). Hillsdale, NJ: Lawrence Erlbaum Associates.

Redington, D. J., & Reidbord, S. P. (1992). Chaotic dynamics in autonomic nervous system activity of a patient during a psychotherapy session. *Biological Psychiatry, 31*, 993–1007.

Reich, W. (1951). *Selected writings*. New York: Farrar, Straus & Giroux.

Ruthen, R. (1993). Adapting to complexity. *Scientific American (January)*, 130–140.

Schleifer, S. J., Keller, S. E., & Stein, M. (1985). Central nervous system mechanisms and immunity: Implications for tumor responses. In S. M. Levy (Ed.), *Behavior and cancer*. San Francisco, CA: Jossey-Bass.

Seyle, H. (1976). *The stress of life*. New York: McGraw-Hill.

Sheldrake, R. (1981). *A new science of life*. Los Angeles, CA: J. P. Tarcher.

Skarda, A., & Freeman, W. J. (1987). How brains make chaos into order to make sense of the word. *Behavioral and Brain Sciences, 10*, 161–195.

von Bertalanffy, L. (1968). *General system theory, foundations, development, applications*. New York: Braziller.

Whatmore, G. B., & Kohli, D. R. (1979). Dysponesis: A neurophysiological factor in functional disorders. In E. Peper, S. Ancoli, & M. Quinn (Eds.), *Mind/body integration*. New York: Plenum.
Wiener, N. (1961). *Cybernetics, or control and communication in the animal and the machine* (2nd ed.). New York: John Wiley & Sons.

Chapter 14

Organizational Chaos: Penetrating the Depths of the Orgmind

Laurie A. Fitzgerald

Albert Einstein once observed in words to the effect that "no problem can be solved from the same consciousness that created it." While this truism certainly includes the myriad difficulties endured by human organizations, we have not been deterred in our dogged pursuit of "quick fixes" stemming from the very same way of thinking that got us into trouble in the first place. Wouldn't you think those raised in the proud tradition of "scientific management" would heed the counsel of one who is perhaps the most brilliant scientific mind of the 20th century? Yet, managers who are confronted with his sage counsel tend to respond by affecting a look of perplexity as if to say, "Surely, you can't be talking to me."

It's not just managers but the entire Western world that seems determined to keep pounding away at the same old problems by using the same old mind-set they have employed since the opening rounds of the Industrial Revolution: and this in spite of rapidly mounting evidence of the futility of their quest. Once, long ago, neither the content of the *orgmind* (the collective mind of the enterprise) nor the quality and depth of organizational thought really mattered too much: Change rolled out smoothly and continuously at a manageable pace; the competition was a known, and relatively friendly, quantity; and the marketplace was local and often captive. However, on this eve of a new millennium, these most propitious circumstances are no more. Change is rapidly approaching warp speed, its discontinuity and lurching nature apparent. New and unexpected competitors abruptly materialize out of nowhere to wrest away huge chunks of the market; and businesses that have dallied while the world globalized find themselves on long and painful slides into oblivion. Today, what and how we think about the organization and the circumstances it faces matters a great deal (Argyris, 1993).

THE PARADOX OF IRRATIONAL RATIONALITY

Why, then, are we prone to behave in such an irrational, dysfunctional, obsessive-compulsive, and inevitably self-destructive way? Any freshman in the school of psychology could correctly diagnose this pervasive pattern of managerial behavior as symptomatic of a full-blown neurosis. But then, the practicing deranged probably wouldn't pay much attention to the sentiments of a "shrink" anyway. After all, they're "scientific managers," proud of their finely-honed rationality and dearth of emotion. You won't catch them messing around with any of that "touchy-feely, new age, higher consciousness" stuff. Why the very idea of introspecting, that is, venturing inward even momentarily to contemplate one's thoughts, is anathema to these tough-minded, thick-skinned, no-nonsense executives.

If "scientific" managers are inclined to dismiss the counsel of behavioral scientists; if they reject as well the wisdom of eminent quantum physicists, then whose advice might they heed? Perhaps they would attend to the admonitions of one of their own, some captain of industry; a seasoned business executive willing to "tell it like it is." Well, maybe not. That very thing was tried back in '86 when Konosuke Matsushita, founder of Matsushita Electric, one of the most highly regarded and successful electronics firms to ever grace the Japanese business landscape, was invited to address a distinguished gathering of his Western counterparts at a conference on the future of business:

We are going to win and the Industrial West is going to lose. There's not much you can do about it. The reasons for your failure are within yourselves. Your firms are built on the Taylor model. Even worse, so are your heads.

Unfortunately, Matsushita's less than diplomatic remarks were simply too much for the proud nobility of the Western business empire to bear. To this day, few who were in attendance can recall much of anything following the man's initial stinging volley. It is a tragedy indeed that the pearl of wisdom the VIPs desperately needed to hear was lost in the balance: When (and if) the West fails—a fate that appears more and more likely with each passing moment—we will have only ourselves to blame. The Asian elder was correct in pointing out that it is the notions we carry around in our heads that will ultimately cause our undoing. The collective mindset of Western management is anchored in a set of assumptions we are wont to vigorously defend—deep-seated beliefs about our organizations, our work, and ourselves—that will seal our fate.

Not unlike the young hero from the children's fable The Emperor's New Clothes, Matsushita has stated what is painfully obvious: Except for the grungy and tattered mental model that serves as our psychological underwear, Western management stands naked before the world of commerce and industry it has dominated for hundreds of years. Embarrassing as the exposure of our deeply entrenched mindset may be, the Asian's observation is essentially correct: Our minds are clothed in the apparel of one Frederick Winslow Taylor, a turn of the 19th century industrial engineer hailed today as the "Father of Scientific Manage-

---

Scientific Management: Taylor's Doctrine

1   Specialize for control. Reduce work to its smallest and simplest elements.

2   Establish precise policies and procedures so that work is performed in the same way every time. Closely monitor workers to ensure full compliance.

3   Reserve all responsibility, decision-making, discretion, and authority for occupants of the hierarchy's upper tier.

4   Match each worker to specific, pre-determined requirements of the job slot assigned.

5   Eliminate redundancies by requiring that all tasks be performed only by those to whom they have been assigned.

Figure 1

ment." Taylor's gift to the world of business at the apex of the Industrial Revolution was a management credo that is still practiced with gusto to this very day.

Although Taylor's principles have been softened around the edges as a result of the movement to humanize the workplace that began in the 1950s, his fundamental tenets remain solidly in place. For all intents and purposes, the dogma of scientific management remains the foundation upon which our managerial heads are built. Lamentably, we have failed to notice that our mental substructure has been cracking, crumbling, and corroding for nearly a century—collapse is imminent. "How can this be so?" you ask. "After all, isn't the Western approach to management the envy of the modern world? Doesn't our long history of industrial dominance and business success count for anything?" The unhappy answers appear to be: because it is, not any more, and not much.

THE SCIENTIFIC REVOLUTION: PART II

Classical physics, or more accurately classical "mechanics," a nearly four hundred year-old view of the world founded in the Cartesian notion of a "clockwork universe," was Taylor's science of choice. But what he and his managerial disciples did not know, was that during the first three decades of the 20th century, the science thus codified into his management canon was superceded: A wholly "new" science had emerged. Even so, the machine metaphor left an impression on the Western world so profound that the classical view had come to be accepted as the immutable truth.

Its central claim was that the universe was likened to a gigantic mechanical contraption constructed of solid matter, the metaphorical equivalent of cogs and wheels. The world machine was not only governed by the "laws" of mechanics, but subject to the absolute control of its human operators. One can imagine how easy it was for Taylor, an engineer by training, to make the leap of abstraction from the "clockwork universe" to the "clockwork enterprise."

PLIGHT OF THE NEWTONIAN JUNKIES

Today, when someone claims to be a practitioner of "scientific management," they are referring to the science of the Enlightenment and its primary architect, Isaac Newton. Furthermore, they are confessing to regarding the universe and in particular, that special corner of the universe known as the enterprise, as if it were but a passive, inanimate instrument of production. To top it all off, they are admitting to an obdurate addiction to *certainty, constancy,* and *control.* The modern managers craving for the "3-Cs" of the classical worldview is no less than a manifestation of addiction: What else can explain the often fierce and frenzied reaction of the managerial junkie when his or her habit of being "in charge" is threatened?

And nothing of late has proven more threatening to the corporate addict than news that the "old" science has been transcended by a new and exponentially improved view of reality. Subsumed under its broad umbrella is a multiplicity of premises, concepts, theories, tenets, axioms, principles, methodologies and tools that have emanated from the astounding scientific discoveries of the 20th century—particularly the first three decades when science for the first time was successful in peering into the sub-atomic soul of the universe. What they saw there shook the entire scientific establishment to its roots, subsequently shattering the prevailing mechanistic, deterministic, and reductionist conceptual legacy of Newtonian physics. Although one would think that word of discoveries of this magnitude would quickly find its way to the lay-public, it has not until very recent times.

One reason for the failure to translate the phenomenal findings of modern science into managerial practice has been the uneasy reluctance of scientists to broadcast what they had learned outside their own community. Many were apprehensive about the prospect of being dismissed as raving maniacs ... a fear that was not altogether unfounded. After all, as long as the classical worldview remained intact, any new conceptualization of reality (especially one as startling as that which would become known by the shocking term "Chaos") to emerge from the confines of the scientific laboratory would remain impossible to grasp and quite natural to reject. Even Einstein himself, a physicist trained in the Newtonian tradition, lamenting his career choice, imagined how much easier life might have been had he chosen to be a bricklayer.

Nevertheless, a more significant explanation of the tragic disconnect was that turn-of-the-century management had already become hooked on the opiates of certainty, constancy, and control—key ingredients in Taylor's concoction. To this day, the collective addiction of managers has them acting in ways that ensure the stagnation and decay of the organizations they're supposed to be managing. So blinded are they by the Master-of-the-Universe self-image they have come to hold, that few recognize Chaos as a vastly superior way to both see and act in the world of enterprise.

CHAOS: SYNTHESIS OF SCIENCE FOR THE NEXT MILLENNIUM

In 1977, a consortium of doctoral candidates studying at the University of California at Santa Cruz discovered that they shared a deep and abiding fascination with the mysterious dynamics of non-linear systems.[1] Together they formulated what is known officially as the "Theory of Complex, Dynamical, Non-Linear Systems." Underpinned by the solid foundation of scientific knowledge established earlier in the century, this conceptualization of reality would soon come to be known by the somewhat misleading appellation "chaos" by the scientific mavericks who referred to themselves as the "Chaos Cabal." By surmounting the traditional boundaries separating various scientific disciplines, the Cabal was able to tap the vast reservoir of knowledge in the formulation of a powerful theory of the universe.

Their interdisciplinary research proceeded from the basis of a singular governing principle: Chaos and order are not opposites from which to choose as they have been portrayed by classical science. Instead they are two inseparable, intertwining, and interpenetrating aspects of the same reality. In fact, the unbreakable relationship between chaos and order is implied in a term coined only recently by Dee Hock, founder and former CEO of Visa Card International which he refers to with fatherly pride as a "chaordic" system.

A NEW AGE IN THE MAKING

Presumably, the reader can appreciate the extraordinary shift in perspective the concept of interpenetration mandates. From the Newtonian point of view, chaos and order are not only discrete, but one is "good" and the other "bad" (can you guess which is which?). One can understand the desire to dichotomize the two by considering the intellectual climate of what historians refer to as the "Dark Ages," a period in which the Church held sway as the absolute and final authority on the interpretation of human experience (Wilber, 1993). It defined existence as an eternal battle waged between two mutually exclusive forces: Good—the will of God, and Bad—the work of the devil.

Since only the clergy were thought to know the difference, the Church soon amassed enormous power and influence over the minds of the faithful in its role of advisor. It is no surprise then that even as Europe emerged from the darkness, the prime mover and shaker of the Enlightenment managed to carry the dichotomous thinking into his work. Isaac Newton was both a pious man devoted to the teachings of the Church, and a scientist equally dedicated to the pursuit of truth. He succeeded in managing the psychological balancing act called for by his dual-persona by incorporating the orthodox view of good (*a.k.a.* order) and evil (*a.k.a.*

---

[1]Closed, linear systems—central plank of Newtonian mechanics—turn out to be the exception (and a rare one at that) rather than the rule throughout Nature. That is precisely why Chaos is so extraordinary: It explains virtually every system we know of while its predecessor can be applied to but a sliver of reality.

chaos) directly into his physics of reality. As a result, the historical mission of science—in fact of society as a whole—was cast in the cement of the human psyche: Our ultimate objective became to "correctly" choose between order and chaos in all aspects of our lives. Only by imposing order and vigorously resisting any sign of turbulence or flux, could we enjoy the "eternal" reward of domination over Nature. Now, more than three hundred years later, the Enlightenment mission of science remains firmly clutched by "scientific" managers throughout the Western world. Although the scientific establishment still concentrates on phenomena of the natural world, management's ambitions for mastery are directed at well-bounded, and what they believe to be self-contained, enterprise.

Our unwavering conviction that strategies of control and dominance will produce the precise, predictable, and orderly outcomes we crave, and our persistent attempts to permanently eradicate chaos from our organizational lives, is nothing less than mind-boggling, especially in the face of our abysmal record of failure. The conventional wisdom promulgated in every modern business textbook urges us to play the management game in an orderly and consistent manner; every modern management guru extolls us to take charge, assert control, assume our rightful place in the system's driver's seat; and we listen and respond.

WHOLE AGAIN

Perhaps the greatest benefit that the "new" science called Chaos has rendered is that it has begun to knit back together the tattered edges of what the classical mindset has torn apart. By examining the enterprise through its lens, the magical intertwining of chaos and order can be seen. What's more, the organization as the complex, dynamical, "living" system it is, becomes readily apparent. Chaos gives us a powerful way to envision the enterprise as an integrated whole, reducible not into "parts," but to a few fundamental properties. These core characteristics contain within a code of "law" that governs the behavior of the system, and are thus able to inform the action we take in it. Even so, it must be realized that chaos is not something one does *to* an organization, but instead a way to think about and be in the system.

THE CHAOS QUINTET

There are five primary properties of the whole now embraced by chaos enthusiasts. Every "chaordic" system ranging from the visible universe to the lowly amoeba colony, and consequently including the enterprise, is characterized by the properties of *Consciousness, Connectivity, Indeterminacy, Dissipation* and *Emergence*. Given the restrictions on space, aside from brief statements of principles for the latter four in the graphic on the next page, we will concentrate on the first property—the causal reality of *consciousness*.

LEARNING DISABLED

One of the most incapacitating effects of the Cartesian image of reality—the one that sees the universe as a "clockwork"—is its legitimization of the human sense

The Principle of Consciousness

Mind, not matter, comprises the fundamental groundstate and essential force of the Universe.

The Principle of Connectivity

The universe is one—an unbroken, unbreakable pattern of relationships between elements whose meaning is derived solely and entirely from their connection to the whole.

The Principle of Indeterminacy

The universe is so dynamically complex that any link between cause and effect is obscured, rendering the future from the next moment on, unknowable.

The Principle of Dissipation

The universe is a "dissipative" structure: a temporary condensation of energy into patterns, subject to the perpetual process of "falling apart" and then "falling back together" again, each time in a wholly new configuration.

The Principle of Emergence

The inexorable thrust of the universe is toward infinitely ascending levels of coherence and complexity.

Figure 2 The Chaos Quintet

of alienation so pervasive in modern society. Peter Senge (1990), author of the bestseller *The Fifth Discipline: Art & Practice of the Learning Organization*, describes two "learning disabilities" that foster an altogether negative impact of our prolonged estrangement from Nature and each other: Together, the beliefs that "I am my position" and "the enemy is out there" continue to divide and will ultimately conquer the very essence of humanity: our responsibility for the consequences of our actions.

The mechanistic worldview with which we in the West have become enraptured portrays a universe consisting of multitudes of independent, material elements arranged in a working system governed by laws of simple causation, that produces predictable, well-defined, and above-all, controllable outcomes. As we have learned to see ourselves as operators of, and therefore distinct from, the universal machinery, whenever anything goes wrong with our production plans as it inevitably does, we look outside ourselves for the cause. Furthermore, we believe we can find and isolate the cause "out there," implement a technical intervention, and produce a precise "fix" to our problems. According to the principle of consciousness, however, the cause, and therefore (as cartoon character Pogo so profoundly opined) the real enemy, is none other than our very selves.

Several tacit assumptions forming the bedrock of the worldview of classical physics are particularly relevant to the property of consciousness. For example, we have come to believe (1) that an objective world made up of various clumps of matter exists and operates apart from and independent of the human observer,

(2) that the picture of this world we produce through the application of our five senses is essentially accurate and complete, and (3) that we play out our lives as a series of events along an absolute line of time—self-contained experiences each caused by the preceding occurrence, and in turn precipitating what happens next.

Due to the deep entrenchment of these premises in our thinking, the realization that neither our universe nor our organization fits the glass slipper of classical physics anymore is likely to upset the most stoic among us. Even the most unflappable scientists will experience distress and anxiety upon discovering the fundamental role of their own minds in evoking the very reality they once believed could be observed objectively. Chaos and its foundational principle of consciousness has in effect shattered the footwear of Newtonian/Cartesian science beyond repair.

Consciousness disillusions us of the popular fiction that humans can observe their world objectively and without effect. Consciousness debunks the logic behind the stubborn belief that our sensory impressions of the world are one and the same as that world. And the reality of consciousness disabuses us of the erroneous idea that we are somehow separate from, and therefore not responsible for, what "happens to us" in our lives. In short, chaos mandates a spectacular revision of the outmoded classical conceptualization of the universe, and likewise demands that we figure out a way to more fully engage our seriously underutilized minds in the creation of a the reality that we truly desire.

It was Einstein himself who laid the unshakeable groundwork underlying chaos. The most significant discovery of the 20th century, captured in the elegant equation $E = mc^2$, has effectively altered the course of the history of the world even though the average person would hardly notice. Nevertheless, the Master Physicist proved beyond doubt the *equivalence* of energy and matter. Decades later, chaos would take Einstein's discovery a quantum leap forward by demonstrating the fundamental source of all energy/matter in consciousness. The implications of this realization are mind-boggling indeed.

We now know that the universe is not the clumps of irreducible hard "stuff" bouncing around aimlessly in three-dimensional space and obeying fixed, mechanical laws we have conceived it to be since the Age of the Enlightenment. Heisenberg, one of Einstein's best known proteges, would later formulate a precise mathematical equation calling into question the central plank in the foundation of Newtonian physics. An approximate interpretation of the "Uncertainty Principle" attests to the fact that matter does not exist *with certainty* at definite places. Nor do events occur *with certainty* at definite times. Our universe is better understood as a vast pulsating sea of "non-stuff" inherent in which is *the potential to exist*.

"And so," you ask, "how is it that I can see, hear, taste, touch and smell all these things if they are not real? This 'non-stuff' sounds like a bunch of 'nonsense' to me." But consider this before dismissing this startling revelation: By asking the question the way you do, you admit that the "stuff" of the universe is experienced with your sensory apparati, all five of which have been shown to be mental operations. Therefore, it follows that world is known through the mind. And the fact is, there is no other way.

The view Einstein, Heisenberg, and a growing legion of other equally credible scientists continue to try to get across is this: Not only is reality experienced with mind, but it appears to be "real-ized" with the same. Think of it this way: If the universe is really the vast sea of non-substantial potential it has been shown to be, then consciousness must be involved *causally* in order for reality to appear solid to the touch, visible to the eye, audible to the ear, and so on. Although the notion of hard, solid, inert, purposeless matter can be quite useful in our everyday lives, it should not be confused or equated with "really real reality." Since the essential substance of the universe is as insubstantial as thought, it thus requires the presence of consciousness, a thinking agent, so that its potential can be transformed into matter.

BUT WHOSE MIND?

Our view of the world through the lens of classical science leads us to perceive the universe as a collection of separate, independent clumps of matter. The particular chunk we know as "mind" is thus conceived of as a physical organ (the brain) contained in a physical structure (the skull) that is, in turn, encased in a larger material package (the body). Furthermore, we have learned to regard our own lump of cerebral tissue as an entity of its own, existing separate and apart from each and every one of the six billion or so other humanoids with whom we cohabit the planet.

It is not surprising, given this perspective, that diehard classicists will experience enormous resistence to the "chaological" answer to the question: "Just whose mind is it anyway that can be held to account for transfiguring the quintessential haze of potential into the rock-solid world of everyday actuality?" As difficult as the implicit responsibility may be to grapple with, Chaos' claim that consciousness comprises the fundamental groundstate of the universe is well supported by the evidence, e.g., Einstein's own General Relativity. Newtonian thinkers are wont to reject the idea that there is but one consciousness—a single unity in which all manner of intelligent life, including but not limited to humankind, participates— as heretical to the extreme. In other words, the answer to "whose mind?" is the collective "ours"—your mind, my mind, in fact the collective consciousness— to whatever degree it has emerged, in each and every particle in the universe. For most advocates of the classical view, that is just too much responsibility to handle.

But there's an upside to consider: Remember that since the moment the capacity for self-reflexivity emerged among the human species, we have strived to make sense of the mind-boggling riddles of life and our existence. Today in the "new" science and its principle of consciousness, we have the key to unlocking the glorious mystery of the universe. As counterintuitive as it may seem, not only does the door to the orgmind, or for that matter the mind of the universe (the *unimind*?) lead inward, but it's locked from the inside as well. Indeed, no enterprise can be improved upon from the same orgmind that created it. More importantly, no organization can be changed in any essential or sustainable way (such change being required for survival in today's fiercely competitive and permanently turbulent marketplace) unless and until the orgmind is changed, and changed profoundly.

RIGHT THINKING, RIGHT RESULTS

According to Chaos' principle of consciousness, a physical object is a re-presentation of thought generated from the groundstate of consciousness. So too can the enterprise be regarded as the manifestation of thought in the orgmind: The whole system along with all its qualities, inefficiencies, virtues and vices, problems and accomplishments, effects and outcomes, is brought into being through the dynamical process of thinking—the thinking of all who participate in it.

It works something like this: Each and every moment of its existence, the orgmind selects one possibility from the vast sea of potential flowing in infinite waves through the universe. Instantaneously, all the rest "collapse" back into the groundstate of consciousness as the chosen is *real*-ized. The verity borne out by the evidence, although impossible to comprehend through our classical lenses, is that there is no pregiven world "out there" awaiting discovery. Rather, the entire universe exists "in here" as a wave of information (in *formation*) of boundless complexity each moment being brought into existence by an infinity of *mere* acts of consciousness. What enormous responsibility then we each have for the quality of our thinking!

Practitioners of the Buddhist tradition, an ideology that goes far in encompassing the principles of Chaos without ever using its lexicon, hold that *right* thinking leads to *right* action. (The term right is used in the sense of being ethical or mindful rather than factual.) In other words, *org-mindful* choice from the quantum wave leads to *org-mindful* enterprises that, as a matter of course, act in *right* ways to enact an orgmindful world. The inverse is also true: Thinking engaged in by orgminds that are flawed and inherently limited will ultimately result in *wrong-minded* action and subsequently, *wrong-minded* results.

The fundamental "cause" of the escalating financial, environmental, political, and psychosocial crises barraging modern enterprise is nothing less than incoherence in and partialness of the orgmind. It follows that the best chance a business has for averting the calamity of stagnancy and eventual collapse is to bring about a trans-formation of its mind—the orgmind.

Although easier said than done, the good news is that no matter how complex the system and regardless of how turbulent its environment, the enterprise is transformed the very instant it lets go of the prevailing thought structures—assumptions, beliefs, and values entrenched in its long favored classical view of reality, and dons the lenses of the "new" science called Chaos. All time and money spent on systemic analysis, detailed planning, business process re-engineering, and/or the detestable politicking that comes with the territory of classically-informed organizational change, are essentially squandered as long as the prevailing orgmind remains intact. However, by focusing resources directly upon the orgmind with the singular intent of revealing and correcting its incoherence and partialness, profound systemic change becomes truly a POC (change agent acronynimia for Piece Of Cake).

DEACTIVATING THE SELF-SEALING NATURE OF THE ORGMIND

The orgmind is a most remarkable medium for thought—some say it works around the clock, stopping only when it is confronted with evidence of defects in its content. All humans, especially those occupying positions of power and organizational status, tend to be peculiarly sensitive to any kind of information that contradicts or calls into question the fundamental assumptions they make about reality. Consequently, as long as we remain oblivious to our own thinking, we can go happily about our business without ever having to subject ourselves to the threat of embarrassment that typically arises from the possibility of errors in thought.

Due to the self-sealing nature of the orgmind, organizational members are prone to engage in "defensive routines"—largely sub-conscious patterns of behavior that serve to deflect attention away from flaws and inconsistencies in thinking. These protective patterns turn out to be the primary means by which we are able to sustain our operant world view, entrenched as it is in the incomplete and often erroneous assumptions fostered by classical science.

Although there is no reason to defend our assumptions (if they're right, they don't need defending, and if they're wrong, why would one want to defend them in any case), due to our tendency to experience our most deeply-held beliefs not as limited views but as universal truths, many people throughout history have been prepared to die for their beliefs. Patrick Henry's "Give me liberty or give me death!" attests to the strength of such an assumptive commitment. This very human proclivity poses a serious problem for people in organizations. When we defend our assumptions from our own questioning and/or the scrutiny of others, regardless of whether they are idiosyncratic or institutional in nature, our capacity for learning, growth, and change is effectively disabled.

Nevertheless, there seems to be nothing more disturbing to VIPs of Western enterprise than the "new" science's explicit assertion that there is no "enemy" lurking "out there" to blame for their business woes. Try as they might to claim an exemption from the "laws" of Chaos, immunity from the consequences of choices made "in here"—in the core of the orgmind—are not to be honored by the universe. Whether they are prepared to admit it or not, members of today's organizations desperately need the support and guidance of those who stand ready, willing, and able to challenge their collective mind's protective shield. By taking on the orgmind in a way that is both tenacious and considerate of the dignity of people facing hard choices, masterful change-agents can enable the whole system to attain and sustain a significantly higher level of personal "mindfulness," the indispensable prerequisite of system-wide org-mindfulness.

THE QUEST FOR HOW?

"How?" must be the most frequently asked question in the Western hemisphere. In recent years, news of the extraordinary discoveries of 20th century science, finding its way first to the general lay public and eventually into the corporate realm, has sparked a growing interest in the translation of theory and abstract concepts into practice. "Very interesting," some comment. "But how do you apply the 'new' science in the *real* world?" speaking as if quantum physics, the scientific foundation of chaos, were not a 'real' world science. "How does one *do* chaos?" Unfortunately, those who pose the "How?" question this way have more than likely spent their entire lifetimes being steeped in the reductionist determinism of classical science. Its root metaphor, the machine, and the assumptive commitments derived from it, have become so deeply ingrained in their psyches that they simply have no idea they ask the wrong question.

Ignorant of the fact that chaos is not something one *does* to an organization, but rather a powerful way of thinking, seeing, and being in the world of enterprise, the Newtonian-minded reveal their deep-seated belief in technique—their confidence in precise methods and orderly formulas that produce precise, orderly, and above all, predictable outcomes. Even though our historical quest for technological remedies has never produced the results desired, our faith in the "quick fix" has proven amazingly robust and resilient.

Peter Block (1993), management guru and author of the highly acclaimed *Stewardship* has opined that "How?" is frequently a "defense against action ... a leap past the question of purpose, past the question of intentions, and past the drama of responsibility." He goes on to say, "the question How? more than any other question, looks for the answers outside ourselves." I couldn't have said it better myself. If leaders of Western business and industry hope to survive, let alone thrive, in the world of the next millennium, they must relinquish their 500-year-old way of asking "How?" as if the answer was anywhere else but within where it is deeply embedded in the core of the orgmind.

Even as news of chaos' astonishing explanatory and change-catalyzing powers has begun to seep into corporate consciousness, it should not be a surprise to find managers reacting in the same old classically-informed ways. I've heard of a few who went so far as to charter a task force to "implement" Chaos, with the insinuation that it must be done quickly before the competition has a chance to beat them to the punch! Others more conservative are content to await "proof" the new science will work for them: Before making a single move, even something so simple as speed-reading one of the many fine books offering an intellectual explanation of Chaos theory, they demand stories of success, preferably from firms counted among the Fortune 100 or better.

At this point, some readers may be expecting to hear a "practical" answer to "How?" is not to be offered in this discussion. As the diehard Newtonian pragmatists may have suspected, all this Chaos-stuff is nothing but academic fluff, theoretical nonsense to be sure. Well, they would be terribly wrong. Chaos does indeed render an answer to "How?" and a very powerful one at that. However, before it can be fully grasped, new science skeptics must first disabuse themselves of their abiding belief in a magical elixir potent enough to cure all their business ills without requiring so much as a morsel of change on their part. Until they do, only others (perhaps their fiercest competitors) who possess a sufficiency of courage and the will to probe the depths of their individual minds, as well as the thinking core of their organizations, will succeed, raising their capacity for change and learning by an order of magnitude . . . or better. That said, perhaps now is an opportune time to introduce Chaos' answer to "How?"

TECHNOLOGIES OF THOUGHT

Although at first glance, grasping the subtle intricacies of human thought may seem to mandate a level of intellect and/or specialized competence well beyond that possessed by the average individual, there is no need for despair. A growing number of just-so-average working people disbursed throughout their organizations' hierarchies are learning how to gain access to the deepest reaches of the orgmind in which they participate. Realization of the essential role played by the mind (and/or the orgmind as the case may be) in generating our reality, has inspired the efforts of at least one consciousness pioneer to retrieve a highly generative "thought technology" from the dustbin of historical disuse: The scientist was the late but great quantum physicist, David Bohm, Professor emeritus of Theoretical Physics at the University of London. His re-discovery was the long forgotten mode of conversation known simply as **dialogue**.

A combination of the Greek terms *dia* meaning 'through' and *logos* which stands for 'meaning' gives us *dialogue* as the process of 'meaning through' or more precisely, 'meaning flowing through' a gathering consisting of two or more conversants. Compare this way of engaging with each other to the mode of interaction most commonly used in the realm of business. As Bohm liked to point out, *discussion* shares the same root as the words per*cussion* and con*cussion* each signifying some form of collision or hitting against. In fact, the term itself is derived from the Latin verb *discutere* which means 'to smash to pieces' which is quite literally what happens to the essential meaning in human communication based in discussion. From this distinguished physicist's point of view, discussion is very much like a game of ping pong "where people are batting the ideas back and forth and the object of the game is to win or to score points for oneself."

Among the several reasons why the seemingly benign form of conversation called dialogue has been so remarkably successful in penetrating the depths of the orgmind, is the fact that mind is not a "thing" occupying space and time. Rather it is an emergent quality of the "within" or the interior of a system. Interiors—an organization's collective mind, or for that matter the "within" of a single individual—can only be accessed dialogically. Surfaces, on the other hand, can be known monologically—that is, through the scrutiny of an "objective" observer. (Perhaps the greatest bone of contention between advocates of the Newtonian view and those who embrace the emerging frame of reference called Chaos, is the latter's outright dismissal of the cherished notion that humans in general, and scientists in particular, are privileged beings capable of standing back from the world about them and observing it objectively.)

To illustrate, imagine that I tell you that "I have a great idea!" You may make fairly reasonable inferences about the nature of my thought based on my vocal tone and inflection, my facial expression, the words spoken, and any number of other "surface" structures. You can hook me up to an EEG and run a tape of the electrical impulses running through my head. Or, if you were inclined to extremes (and managed to get me to hold still for it), you could perform open brain surgery and peer directly inside my skull where the Newtonian-inspired assume the "mind" is located. In fact, you can look "inside" me all you want, but all you will ever "know" about my thought is its external or surface correlates: You can never know my interior experience unless and until you venture within and share a lived experience of it. And the only way that can happen is by creating with me a shared interior space wherein meaning flows ... by definition—dialogue.

Bear in mind, dialogue's major purpose is not to make decisions, solve problems, or produce plans. Nor is it to facilitate consensus, resolve conflict, or gain agreement. Rather, its primary aim is to reveal the incoherence and partialness of thought. Bohm (personal communication, Monday, November 6, 1989) offers us a marvelous metaphor that explains the power and value of achieving mindful coherence via dialogue:

> *Ordinary light is called 'incoherent,' which means that it is going in all sorts of directions, and the light waves are not in phase with each other so they don't build up. But a laser produces a very intense beam which is coherent. The light waves build up strength because they are all going in the same direction. This beam can do all sorts of things that ordinary light cannot. Now, you could say that our ordinary thought in society is incoherent—it is going in all sorts of directions, with thoughts conflicting and canceling each other out.*

As individuals develop the ability to dialogue with each other in the shared relational context of their organization, they begin to create what Bohm called a "participatory consciousness—as indeed consciousness always is." By definition, the term itself is derived from the Latin word *consciere* which means "to know together." The key difference here between "normal" consciousness and the participatory variety is that in the latter, every conversant participates consciously, mindfully, or better, orgmindfully. And isn't that—penetrating the depths of the orgmind—precisely what this conversation has been about?

And so we return full circle to Einstein's profound admonition: that no problem can be solved from the same consciousness that created it. More to the point, no enterprise given the chaos, complexity, and discontinuity of the modern world, can be changed by the same orgmind that brought it into being.

CONCLUSIONS

In the first three decades of this century, an astonishing revolution took place in the experimental laboratories of modern science. Although the eyes of its leaders were on the physical universe, the frame-breaking impact of what was revealed about the nature of the quantum realm has only just recently begun to be felt in our ordinary world of enterprise. As the "new" science now known quite simply albeit provocatively as "chaos" continues to be expanded upon and refined; as more scientific laypeople are exposed to its power, an unprecedented and irreversible shift of the global mind to a wholly new way of understanding reality will inevitably ensue.

The intent of this essay, directed at people everywhere who care about the vitality and sustainability of their organizations, has been to make a watertight case for changing our systems by changing our own minds . . . the collective mind of the whole I have referred to as the *orgmind*. More importantly, I have attempted to convey the extreme urgency of doing so before the window of opportunity slams shut.

If the unchallenged prima among quantum revolutionaries is correct in his assessment, our chances of succeeding are appallingly slim. It was Einstein himself who warned that no problem can be solved by the same consciousness that created it. Regrettably, the collective mind of Western management that now struggles to cope with an increasingly turbulent and fiercely unpredictable global marketplace, an environment where chaos and not control reigns, is the very same consciousness that gave rise to the current reality.

As dismal as our plight may seem, there remains a small shred of hope. Where small pockets of leading edge consciousness—that is, cabals of those who have cast aside the centuries-old mindset of classical physics and subsequently donned the lenses of the 20th century science—have undertaken the perilous mission of unsettling the prevailing worldview, hints of the emergence of a remarkably powerful and profoundly encompassing worldview grow stronger with each passing day.

Finally, I have attempted to point to a newly rediscovered way of interacting, one that is most certainly the modus operandi of such higher consciousness alliances, as the master key that will unlock the tightly fastened door to the collective consciousness of the organization. If we are to survive, let alone survive in our uncertain world of chaos, complexity, and discontinuous change, there is little reason to doubt that *dialogue* must replace the dialectic as our primary means of engaging in the ongoing exploration and evolution of the orgmind.

REFERENCES

Argyris, C. (1993). *Knowledge for action: A guide to overcoming barriers to organizational change.* San Francisco: Jossey-Bass.

Block, P. (1993). *Stewardship: Choosing service over self-interest*, p. 234. San Francisco: Berett-Koehler Publishers.

Matsushita, K. (1988, Spring). From a speech delivered in 1987 to an international consortium of business executives. Quoted in the *American Society for Quality Control Newsletter, 2.*

Senge, P. M. (1990). *The fifth discipline: The art & practice of the learning organization.* New York: Doubleday Currency.

Wilber, Ken. (1993). *Sex, ecology and spirituality.* Boston: Shambhala.

Part Four

Special Clinical Issues and Chaos Theory

Part 4 of the book (Chapters 15 through17) focuses on several final issues that are of interest for clinicians, including the relationship of chaos and other cultures, a look at mathematical modeling using nonlinear theory, and the implications for the future of psychotherapy. It is our hope that these final chapters serve as a starting point for further exploration of chaos theory. We believe we are at the beginning of a new era in scientific understanding and that the human and natural sciences will be in the forefront of this new paradigm. Hopefully, the questions that end this book are of more interest than the conclusions reached. Our greatest wish is to inspire others to go further into unexplored territory and make new maps using this theory. May you enjoy your trip as much as we have enjoyed ours.

Chapter 15

Chaos Theory and
Cross-culturalism

Michael R. Bütz

Mental health practitioners are required time and again to boil down scientific, theoretical, and philosophical ideas to the point where they become useful in their daily clinical practice. For today's scientist-practitioner, these ideas emerge with ever greater frequency. As our communities become ever more complex and global, practitioners are increasingly required to consider cross-cultural issues as well.

Many distinctions have been made between different orientations to the world in the cross-cultural dialogue. Central to this dialogue have been the distinctions drawn between rational and so called irrational beliefs, as well as the differences between the individual and the community. Indeed, listing how often these issues are referenced exceeds the scope of this chapter.

A set of heuristic notions not commonly associated with this dialogue may be called on to not only clarify these issues, but enlarge the context. These heuristic notions include the scientific concepts described by chaos, complexity and the new physics. Still, what will be described here is a more philosophical approach to these notions, a look at the foundation of these constructs and how they have special relevance to issues in a multi-cultural dialogue.

Long before science enfolded chaos into its matrix, the term "chaos" had a mythological connotation that included chaos as a necessary process preceeding the emergence of new forms (Bütz, Duran, & Tong, 1995; Tong, 1992; Bütz, 1991; Briggs & Peat, 1989). This mythological chaos constitutes the under-belly of today's scientific chaos (Bütz, 1995a, 1997; Bütz, Duran, & Tong, 1995). Many cultures, if not most, already had a balanced mythology that included a dark side or what may be described in feeling terms as emotional chaos. In other writings (Butz, 1995a, 1997), it has been posited that chaos theory is so titled due to Yorke's (1975) attempt to describe Lorenz's (1963) work to a wider audience. Lorenz's thoughts regarding weather patterns strayed dramatically from classic modes of scientific thought (see Chapter 1). With the fortuitous use of the term "chaos" Yorke struck a cord that resonated with other scientists' experience of this phenomenon. While other scientists were slow to respond at first, many have come to embrace the concepts that now reside under the umbrella term chaos theory. Chaos theory examines the dark and frightening aspects of our science, bringing out of the shadows the complexities of real world experience. Scientists from a wide variety of fields have entertained this spectrum of new ideas and, it might be argued, so should social scientists.

Social scientists are charged with the duty of creating, integrating, and making use of notions that assist in understanding and transforming the human condition. Clinicians are requested on a day-to-day basis to make use of these new ideas in a way that will enhance the lives of their clients. As such, the implications of the cross-cultural issues of rationality and individual and communal dynamics warrant consideration here. One important aspect of what is being proposed is an integration, or perhaps a dialogue, between cultures that express different values, different thoughts, and different feelings about our relationship to reality and to each other. At the crux of the distinction between Euro-American values and those of a multitude of other cultures, lies chaos, not only as an ancient mythological concept, but as a pivotal scientific concept for the Euro-American culture.

Integrating a mythological concept of chaos and science's chaos theory into the scientist-practitioner dialogue obligates one to recognize four issues. First, that what mental health professionals use as the basis of their theory is pejoratively referred to as "good science," and parallels what is often described in physics as "classical physics." Second, that practitioners frequently deviate from theory which is supposed to direct practice. In part, this is due to the constraints of narrow and limiting theories that do not address the complexities encountered in clinical practice. Third, if clinicians are immersed in rational or logical theory, are they capable of handling the disturbing experiences of their clients without working them through within themselves? And fourth, when dealing with highly emotional, irrational material in therapy, is there a theory or a particularly relevant context for dealing with these experiences? Together, consideration of these four issues might engender a feeling that something has been wrong with the manner in which therapy has been practiced over the years.

The inability to shift out of a scientific mindset, and the inability to handle the emotional material clients present are two phenomena that point to the incongruence between what clinicians do as scientists, and what clinicians do as practitioners within the Euro-American culture. It is proposed that these differences become ever greater as rationalistic and individualistic perspectives are applied to other cultures in a Eurocentric manner. At the nexus of application lies the notion of rationality and the individual's relation to the community. Over the course of this chapter, the path will lead to these considerations. First, it focuses on a consideration of what constitutes the ethnocentrism witnessed in clinical practice today.

THE CURRENT NOTION OF SCIENCE IN SOCIAL SCIENCE

"Classical physics". What does this mean? Classical physics is predicated on the idea that the universe works like a clock, with lawful planetary orbits and the like (Hawking, 1988). In part, it owes its lineage to Aristotle, and its indoctrination to Newton. This is what most students were taught as the working model of the universe. It forms the basis of statistical theory in psychology. Statistical theory is often thought of as psychology's version of good science. There, behaviors supposedly come in nice, neat little data bundles which fit snugly into the normal distribution. But, as anyone who has actually done research knows, there is nothing nice and neat about a research project or the findings one typically derives. There's data that does not fit, and different statistics lend themsleves to different problems.

For instance, parametric and nonparametric tests lend themselves not only to different problems, but are based on two different assumptions about the population being measured. Kerlinger (1986) describes the properties of parametric tests: "The best known such assumption is that the population scores are normally distributed. A nonparametric test or distribution-free statistical test depends on no assumptions as to the form of the sample populations of the values of the populations parameters" (p. 266). This quotation makes nonparametric issues sound a bit like they have no laws or order. This conundrum is what classical physics encountered with issues like the three-body problem, turbulence, and quantum mechanics (Briggs & Peat, 1989). Suddenly, "classical assumptions," like the normally distributed population, no longer applied to everything in the universe. The universe was suddenly not so orderly or predictable as Newton described. Poincaré, a French mathematician, found that three planets in orbit near one another did not behave linearly. In fact, their behavior was nonlinear. Nick Herbert (1985) described the predicaments quantum physicists faced as, "1. There are too many of these quantum realities; 2. All of them without exception are preposterous" (p. 28). In short, classical physics worked for certain problems, but in practice there were always exceptions which Heisenberg dubbed "the uncertainty principle."

With regard to the research being done in psychology, many act as though there is no uncertainty to the findings that emerge. Some may need to be reminded of how messy actual research is, and that statistical theory is predicated on the probability of "being in the ballpark." As a science, psychology does have nonlinear tools available, but they are not utilized as much as they can be, nor is the basis for using them well understood. Far too many statistics courses are taught like high school algebra with the slogan "just do it," without any explanation of why one is doing it or what the outcome of the data actually means. This issue has been addressed elsewhere (Johnson & McCown, 1992; McCown & Johnson 1995; Bütz, 1997), but suffice it to say that clinicians often do not fully understand the scientific underpinnings of the "science" they are practicing. Consequently, all too often, clinicians treat a nonlinear, interpersonal dynamic as though it is a linear phenomenon, and subsequently are baffled by their clients' lack of progress.

DEVIATING FROM CLASSICAL THEORY, AND
UNDERSTANDING THE CONTEXT OF WORK

Why do clinicians deviate from theory when they engage in clinical practice? Simply put, they deviate from theory when the theory they are using does not work. The issues clinicians are called on to deal with in their practices continue to become more and more complex with the prevalence of blended families, sexual and physical abuse, and so on. Moreover, they are asked to deal with these issues more "efficiently," often without clinically-sound reasoning for the six to ten sessions provided by many managed care companies. How does one deal with more complex problems in less time?

First, clinicians need to stop agreeing to the limitations placed on them (Graham, 1995; Hannigan-Farley, 1996). Second, clinicians need to stop advocating linear approaches to nonlinear issues. Practitioners tend to chart linear change because that's what is comfortable and what makes managed care companies happy. But how many times can the reader recall the feeling that therapy has stalled for several sessions and then, suddenly, there is a lurch forward that could have never been predicted? Our ideas about the dynamics of change are what make this type of phenomenon so perplexing. Usually theory sounds very scientific, but does it address the dark and chaotic, nonlinear, emotional process that precipitates a client's entry into therapy? As Theodor Reik (1948) said, "the night reveals to the wanderer things that are hidden by day" (p. 147). Clinicians need to re-educate themselves about what change looks like and then share that knowledge with the agencies that request their services. Having advocated this elsewhere (Bütz, 1993a, 1997; Bütz, Chamberlain, & McCown, 1997), the reader is encouraged to educate his or her colleagues and clients about these processes as well.

THE INSTRUMENT OF CHANGE; KNOWING ITS
LIMITATIONS

As many psychotherapists are aware, before one is able to assist a client through an integration, the therapist, to some degree, must have been able to navigate the material the client is addressing. This has obvious implications for therapists entering a course of their own therapy, in their training, and thereafter when they encounter unusually challenging emotional hurdles. In essence, clinicians are called upon to maintain a balance interpersonally and professionally, despite personal struggles. Where does this balance come from, and what puts clinicians off balance? It appears that clinicians, like their clients, operate within a context, and whenever a context is unfamiliar, one tends to loose whatever balance had previously been achieved (Bütz, 1997; Bütz, Chamberlain, & McCown, 1997).

Clinicians operate within certain contexts, including historical–political contexts. Many cross-cultural theorists have argued that while the dynamics in other cultures are apparent, our own are difficult to see. The context, which is driven by historical–political forces, often seems to be invisible. When challenged on the unique dynamics involved, individuals retort "that's just how it is." Well is it? In the United States, individuals often identify themselves as "American." However, in examining the skin and eye color of the majority of these citizens, one cannot help but think—no, "European." While these individuals may have been born in the United States, their cultural history and political context originates from Europe. This context influences the manner in which these individuals think and feel about the world. From these contexts, each individual navigates the world via their unique perceptions. Clinicians cannot exclude themselves from being limited by the blinders that cultural and scientific contexts impose. Consequently, clinicians' awareness of their individual therapeutic issues is not enough. They need to be willing and able to consider their cultural issues as well, and to whatever extent possible, become aware of their cultural blinders.

GOOD SCIENCE AND CULTURAL CONTEXT; SEEING WHAT IS THERE

Good science is based on the empirically-derived scientific method which favors parsimony wherever it can be found. Chaoticians, however, often ask "how does good science account for nonlinearity?" The answer for at least a century has been to ignore or throw out nonlinear phenomena. The main focus in good science is on linear phenomena, not phenomena that are nonlinear. And, in the past, "good science" has steered clear of nonlinear data, as is indicated by a few chaoticians:

> "The discovery of chaos has created a new paradigm in scientific modeling. On one hand, it implies new fundamental limits on the ability to make predictions ... information gathered in the past—and shelved because it was assumed to be too complicated—can now be explained in terms of simple laws" (Crutchfield, Farmer, Packard, & Shaw, 1986, p. 46).

There was a cultural context that made it possible for a linearly biased science to gain the foothold it currently enjoys. There are the obvious gains people have enjoyed with linear science's modernization of the human condition. There are, however, consequences inherent in following a linear model, such as a hole in the ozone, deforestation, and pollution of the biosphere. Certainly, there are gains in the quality of life enjoyed through linear science and technology, and generally one does not find even the most ardent critic denying the affinity he has for his central air conditioning or CD player. But, those "things" that science affords us come at a cost, and so does the limiting context created through that model.

This cost has arisen out of the "good scientist's" arrogance, supported in part by the cluster of assumptions titled "logical positivism." The central, troublesome assumption in logical positivism is that scientists can "undo" or "fix" any of the side effects of their creations by sticking to the tenets of "good science." Eventually, "good science" will provide an answer. Just as it was once believed that "God will provide," the popular belief now is that "science will provide."

These contexts date back roughly 2,000 years with the Christian Cosmology that split the world into those aspects that were aligned with heavenly pursuits and those aspects aligned with hellish pursuits (Bütz, 1992a). Some would even push this split back to the time of Aristotle, where orderly phenomena were declared as heavenly (Lewin, 1931). In fact, it has been argued (Duran & Duran, 1995; Bütz, Duran, & Tong, 1995; Foucalt, 1965; Fanon, 1963), that this split was used as a ready tool to rationalize the colonization of the globe. So, one might ask—why not science too? And, indeed, science followed suit, as Galileo and others like Stephen Hawking (1988) found:

> "The Catholic Church had made a bad mistake with Galileo when it tried to lay down the law on a question of science ... Now, centuries later, it had decided to invite a number of experts to advise it on cosmology. At the end of the conference the participants were granted an audience with the pope. He told us ... we should not inquire into the big bang itself because that was the moment of Creation and therefore the work of God. I was glad then that he did not know the subject of the talk I had just given ... I had no desire to share the fate of Galileo" (p. 116).

Thus, even contemporary scientists avoid contradicting the proprietors of this cosmology, as the fate of Galileo remains ever-present in their minds. So it was that linearity became heavenly, and nonlinearity was decreed as hellish (which, by the way, is especially true when trying to work through a nonlinear equation).

No one would argue that nonlinear equations are difficult, or that integrating chaotic phenomena is anxiety provoking. As a matter of fact, solving this type of problem, described as the "three-body problem," nearly drove Poincaré, one of the founders of chaos theory, mad. Regardless of where one would trace the parallel lines that developed between good and evil, linear and nonlinear, this split has been around a very long time.

In the last several years, inroads have been made in a number of scientific disciplines, as well as psychology, in which nonlinearity has been entertained as an integral part of a holistic epistemology. Still, the context must continue to be widened so that the role of nonlinear and chaotic phenomena are expanded to include the issue of sufficient and tolerable therapeutic change.

TRANSLATING EMOTIONAL MATERIAL THROUGH SYMBOLS

Emotions have a special language that often is lost in the context of contemporary Euro-American culture. It is the language of the unconscious, which today is not only acknowledged by those with a psychodynamic orientation, but also by those from a cognitive-behavioral orientation (Bütz, 1992b, 1997; Azar, 1996; Freiberg, 1996a, 1996b; Mahoney, 1991). And, as clinicians have known for roughly a century, this language is not a linear one (Freud, 1900). Instead, it is a nonlinear language of idiosyncratic associations and derived meanings. On an ever-widening scale, these symbols are expressed in the individual, couple, family, community, and culture. Symbols at the cultural level are referred to as myths—our mythology (Bütz, 1995a). In order to grapple with the dark and forboding experiences our clients bring to therapy and to place science's chaos theory in proper context, practitioners would do well to consult mythologies or therapeutic approaches that address both scientific and mythological phenomena. Clinicians who attempt to understand the language of myth through the lens of rationality misunderstand their clients, and also miss the richness that this level of communication offers in the therapeutic exchange.

RUNNING COUNTER TO THE DOMINANT CULTURE; THE DOUBLE-BIND OF MANAGING NONLINEAR GROWTH

One hears the frustrations of colleagues expressed when an individual, couple, or family does not progress in a linear or predictable fashion in therapy. Chaoticians are quick to point out that nonlinear behavior occurs even in very simple systems. The more complex the system, the greater degree of variability one might find. Consequently, it seems that the therapeutic process almost constantly runs counter to the historical context where nonlinear is bad, and linear is good. Moreover, considering the ethnocentric perspective that many in the United States share, how does a therapist avoid the compulsion to colonize others who are from a different culture or race? Remembering the cultural predisposition to label that which we do not understand or that which is different as bad or evil (Bütz, 1995b), how do therapists move beyond this ethnocentrism to assist clients who differ culturally?

How does one handle the effects of nonlinearity, when it is so diametrically opposed to cultural beliefs and norms in the Western world? One well-established coping mechanism on which empirical science has relied for hundreds of years is to simply pretend it does not exist, or that "this thing that I don't understand is not worthy of serious study." Crutchfield and colleagues (1986) alluded to this in their discussion of the rising paradigm of chaos. Therapeutically, one could characterize this as a repressive approach which serves to minimize the effects of these dynamics on the whole of the clinician's experience and therefore the client's as well.

In deference to Descartes, this approach could be dubbed, "I think, therefore it does not exist." While it is not as mature or creative as other "solutions" to nonlinearity, it does hold the assurance of security one felt as a child when placing a blanket over one's head was a sure way to ward off monsters. Sadly, this sends a message to clients that therapists, like little children, are afraid of the unknown, and are unwilling to explore a world of possibilities that these clients have entertained. Equally disturbing is the proposition that therapists are sending their clients the message that they, too, need to be afraid of themselves and the interpersonal dynamics at work within them.

Another established method of coping with nonlinearity is to turn nonlinear situations into linear situations. This is the essence of calculus, where curves are chopped up and made into straight lines. Therapeutically, one might call this a nonlinear reaction-formation, where therapists are tempted to turn the dynamics that are observed in their clients into an opposite dynamic through a great deal of chopping and splicing. Unfortunately, as a therapeutic method this is not as effective as calculus, where successive approximations may provide some idea of what a curve looks like. The goal here is to allay anxiety. The distortion that follows not only confuses the clients, but may interfere with intrapsychic dynamics to such a degree that this particular organization is never seen again (Bütz, 1995b). As the therapist attempts to allay his or her own anxiety, and thereby doesn't address the client's needs, the client's therapeutic progress may be hampered; hampered to the point that the client's psychic system may never again be able to muster the energy, creativity, and flexibility he or she had at that period of time to adapt to the developmental milestone he or she faced (Bütz, 1997).

Another approach to avoiding chaos and nonlinearity might be termed the intellectualization approach. Its proponents describe dynamics by giving them fancy names. They pay very close attention to language, which they use to further obscure and make meaningless the descriptions shared with colleagues of the anxieties reported by their clients. Those anxieties are intellectualized away. So, by labeling these dynamics, their troublesome, anxiety-provoking nature has been dealt with. Just because something has been labelled, however, does not mean the label correctly describes the phenomenon, or that the etiology of the dynamics are well understood. Remember, "the map is not the territory" (Korzybski, 1948).

Consider the dynamics of diagnosing a client. One may have the diagnosis right or wrong, but even with the "correct" DSM-IV diagnosis (American Psychiatric Association, 1994), one may or may not have any understanding of the dynamic etiology. Making a diagnosis tells clinicians very little about the factors at work in the development or course of the problem. Therefore, clinicians may have no idea where this client or family is going. It is a little like flying a plane in the fog without instruments. One might be aware that he or she is in a plane, but have no understanding of aeronautics or knowledge of the plane's destination or why he or she is going there.

This culture has thrown labels on dynamics because that appeases our anxiety. It can be argued that labeling techniques have exceeded the ability to explain phenomena. Just because something sounds scientific and calms the anxiety of the clinician does not mean that it *is* scientific or addresses the issue. As a culture, are Euro-Americans really able to look at the answers to the questions they ask? Moreover, is chaos theory "the answer?" No, it is not. Chaos theory does, however, call on traditional science and its proponents to face up to some unpleasant aspects of being in the world.

THE INTEGRATION

Where does this discourse begin? It begins with each individual knowing his or her own mindset and culture, then honestly stating in those cases where one doesn't understand, to say "I don't know." The answer is not in mollifying the public, our clients, or colleagues with false assertions. It appears that there is a growing awareness of the need for honesty about the history of Euro-American culture. Acknowledging this history requires an integration of the successes and the failures, of the light and the shadow, of both science and culture.

How does chaos theory apply to this dilemma? For many who study this theory, there is a spiritual underpinning to chaos that is encapsulated in mythology. Chaos theory and its mythological roots are holistic thought forms with physical correlates in the real world. Chaos theory, by aligning the new with the old, is an integrationist approach to science.

Foucault (1965) made a penetrating commentary in his book *Madness and Civilization*, which focuses on a similar theme:

> "Unreason was once more present; but marked now by an imaginary stigma of disease, which added its powers to terror. Thus it is in the realm of the fantastic and not within the rigor of medical thought that unreason joins illness and draws closer to it. Long before the problem of discovering to what degree the unreasonable is pathological was formulated . . ." (p. 205).

Jung called this dark side "the shadow," commenting that it was common to all cultures (1966, p. 66). The shadow holds all those aspects of ourselves which we tend to consider "not us" or undesirable, or as in Foucault's words "unreason."

> ". . . lost memories, painful ideas that are repressed (i.e. forgotten on purpose), subliminal perceptions, by which are meant sense-perceptions that were not strong enough to reach consciousness, and finally, contents that are not yet ripe for consciousness. It corresponds to the figure of the shadow so frequently met with in dreams" (Jung, 1966, p. 66).

The imbalance or split (Bütz, 1995a), results in projection onto cultures in the "not us" or "not like us" category. This has been used as a rationalization to colonize. When Europeans encountered beliefs and customs different from their own which brought up uncomfortable reminders of their own shadow, instead of dealing with the anxiety, they projected it. Then, they sought to destroy these anxiety-provoking projections by decimating other cultures.

And, what of the therapist's choice of theory, and willingness to experience his or her shadow? Marie Louise Von Franz (1980) has commented that we are sucked into various situations through those blind-spots in our own unconscious. These blind spots are those aspects we have not dealt with or chosen to address. We must understand the symbols that constitute our own shadow both in our dreams and in the therapy we perform.

Knowing the issues that produce confusion and anxiety within us—our "chaos" (Bütz, 1992a)—is essential in order to see the "semi-truck" of an issue that is about to run over us emotionally. Otherwise, we are open to all sorts of defenses against the anxiety and the confusion we may feel—repression, reaction-formation and intellectualization—without the needed reintegration. This issue is addressed in our ethics (APA, 1992). We must know our limits and the limits of our culture and our science.

CONCLUSIONS

What are we able to do that will allow us to recognize the context from which we are working? First, honestly address the issue of cultural heritage. Second, know something about what science is doing now, not just the traditional, reified models that lose the essence of the field. Third, try to seek out the whole spectrum of statistics in our field, including an understanding of nonparametric and nonlinear statistical techniques. Fourth, read both theoretical and practical applications of chaos theory to the field of mental health, and what the arguments are for its use as a model. Fifth, be open with clients and colleagues about what we do and don't understand so we can explore the answers together. We do not have the type of medical training that necessitates giving each client a pill as they exit our office. If it's acceptable for us not to know, then it just might be acceptable for our clients to be confused as well. This encourages mutual exploration. Sixth, we must truly know ourselves and our culture. We are the instrument of change in therapy. If we think our clients need therapy and we don't, we are practicing the worst form of hypocrisy. And seventh, we must follow our clients' symbols to reveal the unique dynamics at work in their relationship to events in the world.

The journey described has not reached its destination. There are still dark roads to travel that engender anxiety and chaos. It is hoped, however, that the exploration of chaos is a journey that others will share as we search for ways to make therapy more meaningful to ourselves and our clients.

REFERENCES

American Psychiatric Association. (1994). *Diagnostic and statistical manual of mental disorders IV (4th ed.)*. Washington, DC: American Psychiatric Association.

American Psychological Association. (1992). Ethical principles of psychologists and code of conduct. *American Psychologist, 47*(12), 1597–1611.

Azar, B. (1996). Influence from the mind's inner layers. *APA Monitor, 27*(2), 1, 25.

Briggs, J., & Peat, F. D. (1989). *Turbulent mirror*. New York: Harper & Row.

Bütz, M. R. (1991). Older civilizations and chaos theory: Concern about horses, tigers and their relation to Heraclitus. *The Social Dynamicist, 2*(4).

Bütz, M. R. (1992a). Chaos, an omen of transcendence in the psychotherapy process. *Psychological Reports, 71*, 827–843.

Bütz, M. R. (1992b). The fractal nature of the development of the Self. *Psychological Reports, 71*, 1043–1063.

Bütz, M. R. (1992c). Looking for unification? Remember chaos theory? *The Social Dynamicist, 4*(1), 8–10.

Bütz, M. R. (1992d). The necessary chaos of development: Chaos theory, and a new symbolic developmental paradigm. *University Microfilms International, 52*(3).

Bütz, M. R. (1993a). Practical applications from chaos theory to the psychotherapeutic process, a basic consideration of dynamics. *Psychological Reports*, *73*, 543–554.

Bütz, M. R. (1993b). A model of developmental transformation: process, perspective and symobia—a view of symbols in chaos. *Studies in Psychoanalytic Theory*, *2*(2), 3–18.

Bütz, M. R. (1995a). Chaos theory, philosophically old, scientifically new. *Counseling and Values*, *39*(2), 84–98.

Bütz, M. R. (1995b). Hegemonic therapy, not recognizing the symbol: A case study of a Russian family's attempt to self-organize. *Journal of Family Psychotherapy*, *6*(2), in press.

Bütz, M. R. (1997). *Chaos and complexity: Implications for psychological theory and practice.* Washington, DC: Taylor & Francis.

Bütz, M. R., Chamberlain, L. L., & McCown, W. G. (1996). *Strange attractors: Chaos, complexity and the art of family therapy.* New York: John Wiley & Sons.

Bütz, M. R., Duran, E., & Tong, B. R. (1995). Cross-cultural chaos. In R. Robertson, & A. Combs (Eds.), *Chaos theory in psychology and the life sciences.* Hillsdale, NJ: Lawrence Erlbaum Associates.

Crutchfield, J. P., Farmer, J. D., Packard, N. H., & Shaw, R. S. (1986, December). Chaos. *Scientific American*, 46–57.

Duran, E., & Duran, B. (1995). *Native American postcolonial psychology.* Albany, NY: University of New York Press.

Fanon, F. (1963). *The wretched of the earth.* New York: Grove Weidenfeld.

Foucault, M. (1965). *Madness and civilization, a history of insanity in the age of reason.* New York: Vintage.

Freiberg, P. (1996). New insights on the eye of the beholder. *APA Monitor*, *27*(2), 26.

Freud, S. (1900). *The interpretation of dreams.* New York: Modern Library.

Graham, S. R. (1995). Divided we fall. *Psychotherapy Bulletin*, *30*(3), 4–5.

Hannigan-Farley (1996). Change management and psychotherapy. *Psychotherapy Bulletin*, *31*(1), 4.

Hawking, S. W. (1988). *A brief history of time, from the big bang to black holes.* New York: Bantam Books.

Herbert, N. (1985). *Quantum reality: Beyond the new physics.* New York: Anchor Press.

Johnson, J., & McCown, W. G. (1992, August). Chaos theory and family therapy: A new and unifying paradigm? In W. G. McCown (Chair), *Chaos theory and family therapy: A new unifying paradigm?* American Psychological Association National Convention. Washington, DC.

Jung, C. G. (1966). *Two essays on analytical psychology.* (Hull, R. F. C., Trans.). (2nd ed.). Princeton, NJ: Princeton University Press.

Kerlinger, F. (1986). *Foundations of behavioral research.* New York: Holt, Rinehart and Winston.

Korzybski, A. (1948). On structure. In A. Korzybski (Ed.), *Science and sanity.* Lakeville, CT: International Non-Aristotelian Library Publishing Company.

Lewin, K. (1931). The conflict between Aristotelian and Galileian modes of thought in contemporary psychology. *Journal of General Psychology*, *5*, 141–177.

Lorenz, E. N. (1963). Deterministic nonperiodic flow. *Journal of Atmospheric Sciences*, *20*, 130–141.

Mahoney, M. J. (1991). *Human change processes, the scientific foundations of psychotherapy.* New York: Basic Books.

McCown, W. G., & Johnson, J. (1995, August). Discussants. In W. McCown (Chair), *Chaos, complexity, spirituality, and self-organization—contemporary implications for family therapy.* American Psychological Association National Convention, New York, NY.

Reik, T. (1948). *Listening with the third ear.* New York: Grove Press.

Vandervert, L. (1990). Opening remarks. In L. Vandervert (Chair), *A chaotic/fractal dynamical unification model for psychology.* Symposium given at the American Psychological Association National Convention, Boston, MA.

Von Franz, M. L. (1980). *Projection and re-collection in Jungian Psychology.* La Salle, IL: Open Court.

Yorke, J. (1975). Period three implies chaos. *American Mathematical Monthly*, *82*, 985–992.

Chapter 16

Feedback, Chaos, and Family Conflict Regulation

Stephen Proskauer and Michael R. Bütz

A few years ago, the senior author was involved in conducting a long-term evaluation of a family-skills training program with families of children at high risk for delinquency and substance abuse. Most of the families surveyed were still using the skills they had learned in this brief training long afterwards, and reported substantial positive gains in family functioning lasting for years after completing twelve weekly group sessions or less. It was confusing how such a short-term didactic intervention could have a sustained positive impact on highly dysfunctional families. Linear causality did not offer any satisfactory mechanism, and the search for another approach led first to a familiar principle, the self-reinforcing circular causality described in family systems theory, and then into the wilder terrain of chaos theory (Proskauer, 1996a, 1996b). The purpose of this chapter is to present a mathematical model of family conflict-regulation based upon chaos theory, and to explore its implications for understanding and intervening with dysfunctional families.

Others have pointed the way down this path. Kristjanson (1992) stressed the need for a research methodology consistent with the paradigm of family systems theory, and Ward (1995) identified chaos theory as capable of filling this need. But up to now, nonlinear dynamics has not fulfilled its full potential in family studies. As Bütz, Chamberlain, and McCown (1997) point out in their recent book on chaos, complexity, and family therapy, investigators who have applied chaos theory to the family field tend either to use it only metaphorically to clarify the complexities of human interaction or to present mathematical constructs that are largely incomprehensible to clinicians.

With the exception of the dynamic modeling of marital interaction by Gottman and his associates (Gottman, 1991, 1993a, 1993b; Cook et al., 1995) and the family therapy studies of Elkaïm and his colleagues (Elkaïm, 1981, 1990; Elkaïm, Goldbeter, & Goldbeter-Merinfeld, 1987), there seems to be scant middle ground where mathematical models are invoked to generate clinically-relevant hypotheses and conclusions in family studies. Our model is presented in the spirit of seeking this middle ground. The model is intended both as a metaphor linking chaos theory with clinical reality and also as a mathematical construct capable of suggesting variables and testable hypotheses for future study. It was developed in collaboration with an interdisciplinary study group on the application of mathematical models in family research.

POSITIVE AND NEGATIVE FEEDBACK IN FAMILY SYSTEMS

Family systems theory views the complex and ever-changing flow of family process as arising continuously through the interplay of intermeshing positive and negative feedback loops (Whitchurch & Constantine, 1993). The notion of feedback, which essentially is communication in family systems, dates back to some of the early progenitors of this field (Bateson, Jackson, Haley, & Weakland, 1956). Feedback has been associated with cybernetic theory (Wiener, 1961) and the applications of this theory to families both early in the development of the field (Haley, 1959) and later (Selvini-Palazzoli, Boscolo, Cecchin, & Prata, 1978). The use of feedback and feedback loops in family therapy lies at the very foundation of the discipline. It was one of the fundamental scientific concepts in family therapy. The concept of feedback puts the "systems" in family systems theory. Without feedback there is no growth and, therefore, no adaptation to changes in the environment or within the system itself.

To avoid confusion, it needs to be emphasized at the outset that the use of the terms 'positive feedback' and 'negative feedback' has nothing to do with whether feedback has favorable or unfavorable consequences, but rather with whether the feedback promotes change (positive feedback) or inhibits change (negative feedback). Thus, runaway positive feedback can, and often does, have unfortunate consequences in a family, and negative feedback can be very beneficial, helping to maintain balance in the family by damping deviations from stable conditions. The traditional emphasis on homeostasis in cybernetic theory reflects a bias of attention in favor of negative feedback mechanisms (DeAngelis, Post, & Travis, 1986; Maruyama, 1963), and this is where the "systems" aspect arises in contemporary family therapy. Among other noteworthy and paradigm-breaking concepts introduced by von Bertalanffy's general systems theory (1968), the notion of a steady state was advanced. Von Bertalanffy's steady state differed greatly from the notion of homeostasis, in that it connoted an evolutionary process. A steady state was merely a period of stability in a biological system's ongoing development, whereas homeostasis described a particular preference for one state, such as a setting of sixty-five degrees on a thermostat. Periods of stability amid the ceaseless process of development constitute the recognizable stages of the unique activity that biological organisms, like families, use to transform through feedback. Therefore, if all feedback were negative, a family system would stagnate in its steady state condition and would be unable to evolve or adapt to new situations because the focus would be on limiting or constraining the dynamics of the system. Positive feedback, on the other hand, promotes change and creates the possibility of adaptation and evolution.

Modern dynamical systems theory directs attention to the positive feedback loops that are normally kept in check by negative feedback. Under certain conditions, positive feedback can cause the system to destabilize and can thereby bring about transitions from one steady state to another (Goerner, 1994; Vallacher & Nowak, 1994). When unopposed, positive feedback loops can produce accelerating change by exponential amplification of any deviation from equilibrium. Therefore, positive feedback cannot operate unconstrained for long without generating overload, resulting in system dissolution or in self-organization (Jantsch, 1980; Prigogine, 1980)—the spontaneous transformation to a new functional pattern with different characteristics from the original system.

Positive and negative feedback loops thus imbue the family with opposite and complementary characteristics. Both are needed: Positive feedback makes change and adaptation possible while negative feedback preserves system coherence and stability. Positive feedback can greatly amplify the impact of small disturbances on system behavior, but this effect is highly dependent on the relative strength of the negative feedback elements that maintain the stability of the family system. More precisely, the deviation-amplifying effect of positive feedback creates an accelerating change process whenever a critical variable (or combination of variables) deviates beyond a threshold defined by the limits of the system's capacity to maintain its steady state. Once positive feedback becomes relatively strong, the stability of a system is fragile. After a critical threshold is crossed, the accelerating change process can quickly proliferate throughout the system, drastically altering its usual characteristics, until the system self-destructs or a new steady state has been established. In the literature of chaos theory, this is generally referred to as a period-doubling route to chaos (Gleick, 1987). This new state may not resemble the previous one at all, and the system may now have very different thresholds and zones of fragility.

Besides producing escalating change, positive feedback can generate complex patterns of behavior in systems: threshold effects, fragility of stable states, rapid change of adaptation in response to new conditions, catastrophic reactions to crisis, and the capacity to undergo spontaneous reorganization and system-wide transformation (DeAngelis et al., 1986). These properties have been observed empirically in many dynamical systems and are predicted by nonlinear mathematical models (Goerner, 1994; Vallacher & Nowak, 1994).

A MATHEMATICAL MODEL FROM POPULATION DYNAMICS

Studying the mathematics of feedback processes can help us more fully appreciate the dynamics of these phenomena and the circumstances under which they can arise. In general, linear feedback leads to exponential change: Exponential deviation increases with positive feedback and exponential damping of deviation occurs with negative feedback. In thermodynamics, linear feedback applies to near-equilibrium conditions under which phenomena are regular and predictable. With far-from-equilibrium conditions (Prigogine & Stengers, 1984), however, feedback becomes nonlinear and steady states in this regime can become chaotic and unpredictable (Çambel, 1993).

One classic example of the transition from regular to complex and chaotic behavior is the discrete form of the logistic equation, well-known in the study of population dynamics (May, 1974), and more recently in chaos theory (Gleick, 1987). This equation expresses the universal tendency of a breeding species population to seek its maximum carrying capacity, the highest population density that the environment is capable of supporting:

(1) $x_{n+1} = rx_n(1 - x_n)$ or, for our purposes,
(2) $x_{n+1} = rx_n - rx_n^2$

where r is a rate constant, or control parameter, representing the fertility of the species, and x is normalized such that $0 < x < 1$. Equation (1) states that the population of the next generation is the product of three quantities: the fertility constant, r; the present population, xn; and the difference between the maximum carrying capacity and the present population, $(1 - xn)$.

This type of mathematical expression is called a difference equation, an algorithm for an iterative feedback process, in this case a formula for computing a new value of a single variable, $xn + 1$, from the immediately preceding value, xn. In Equation (2), each new value of x is related positively to the first power of its previous value and negatively to the square of its previous value, creating, in effect, a mathematical model of competition between linear positive feedback and nonlinear negative feedback.

As simple as this equation may appear to be, the sequence of x-values follows a regular pattern only at certain values of the control parameter, r (Çambel, 1993). When r is less than 1, x decays asymptotically toward zero with progressive iterations. When r is between 1 and 3, x fluctuates around, and eventually reaches a limiting value. This limiting value increases with increasing r according to the expression $x = (r-1)/r$ (i.e., x increases from 0 to .66 as r increases from 1 to 3; and the higher r is, the fewer iterations of x are needed to reach its limiting value). When r is larger than 3, a variety of behaviors can occur—from simple to complex oscillations when r is between 3 and 3.57, to apparently random fluctuations at higher values of r, a zone of deterministic chaos.

When chaos reigns, the iterations of x are so sensitive to the initial x value that it becomes impossible to predict the behavior of the system for more than a brief period in the future. Baker and Gollub (1990) give a precise description of this phenomenon:

"The unique character of chaotic dynamics may be seen most clearly by imagining the system to be started twice, but from slightly different initial conditions. We can think of this small initial difference as resulting from measurement error, for example. For nonchaotic systems this uncertainty leads only to an error in prediction that grows linearly with time. For chaotic systems, on the other hand, the error grows exponentially in time, so that the state of the system is essentially unknown after a very short time. This phenomenon, which occurs only when the governing equations are nonlinear, is known as sensitivity to initial conditions . . ." (pp. 1–2).

This quotation goes on to indicate that chaotic systems may appear to be very similar to stochastic or random systems. In this case, however, the system only appears to be random, and irregularity is part of the innate dynamics of the system.

Furthermore, within the wide bands of chaos, narrower bands of complex oscillatory, but nonchaotic, behavior recur at intervals in an intriguing, self-similar fractal pattern that has been extensively studied. It is a mysterious and remarkable fact that a simple mathematical expression like the discrete logistic equation can give rise to such richness and diversity of pattern which fits a general description offered by many authors in this field.

APPLICATIONS TO FAMILY CONFLICT REGULATION

How does this intriguing iterative algorithm relate to family dynamics? As Ward (1995) notes, "a family is always emergent, because it has a new history that includes at each moment the last interaction" (p. 632); in other words, the family is an iterative system. Ward goes on to say, "According to chaos theory, any system can operate in a variety of states ranging from frozen to chaotic, and it may shift among them as one or more important system parameters are modified" (p. 635). The discrete logistic equation contains just such a system parameter, r, and the equation can give rise to a variety of states according to its value. Finally, the logistic equation expresses mathematically a complex competition between positive and negative feedback processes, an important feature of family systems theory (Whitchurch & Constantine, 1993). For these reasons, the discrete logistic equation would seem to qualify as a promising starting point to explore the mathematical modeling of family regulatory patterns. Of course, other mathematical expressions could be chosen for this purpose, but the logistic equation is one of the simplest and most parsimonious.

Let x represent the level of overt family conflict. The control parameter r then is indicative of the propagation rate of family conflict. The family conflict pattern will depend on the value of r, and thus we can distinguish four modes of regulation for different ranges of r. Each of these four regulatory patterns has an adaptive aspect as well as a characteristic downside if the family remains stuck in that one pattern for a prolonged period (see Table 1).

When r is less than 1, a constraining regulatory pattern prevails. Some disturbed families control and ritualize their patterns of communication to a greater degree than normal families as a means of avoiding conflict. For example, conflict is damped out in rigidly-controlled or enmeshed families. Such a family pattern

Table 1

r Value	Dynamic Regulatory Pattern	Adaptive Aspects of Each Pattern	Risks of Remaining Stuck in Each Pattern
Less Than 1	Constraining	Security Survival	Depression Inhibition
1 To 3	Stabilizing	Steadiness	Boredom Conventionality
Between 3 And 3.57	Oscillating	Stimulation Tension Release	Delinquency Addiction
Greater Than 3.57	Chaotic	Transformation Creativity	Disorientation Despair

is usually dysfunctional and has been associated with depression and inhibition of individual autonomy (Barber, 1996; Barber, Olsen, & Shagle, 1994). Under critical circumstances, however, survival may depend on tight control within the family.

When r falls between 1 and 3, a stabilizing pattern occurs. The family is interacting under near-equilibrium conditions and even large variations in the initial value of x do not alter the tendency of the system to return to a stable state. This is the range of adaptive functioning for most stable families, wherein life events may create a temporary change in the family conflict level, but the family resolves the problem within a short period and returns to a certain steady state level of conflict that is normal for that family. The most familiar landmark for many family therapists may be the graphic illustration of an adaptive range in the Circumplex Model (Olson, Sprenkle, & Russell, 1979). While the Circumplex Model is both qualitatively and quantitatively different, it provides a ready heuristic that therapists not familiar with the notion of adaptation in chaos, complexity, and the new physics may be able to grasp metaphorically in this discussion.

In regard to the value of r and family functioning, the adaptive side is that this mode of regulation provides a safe environment of steadiness and security. On the other hand, life can get boring and the family may not respond well to challenges that cannot be met simply by maintaining the familiar status quo. Witness, for instance, the dysfunctionally negative response of some conventional families to involvement of their adolescent children in counterculture groups and activities. While the particular child in question may imbue novel dynamics into the family system, these dynamics are unwelcome and unnerving. Family members, typically the parents, may quickly move to limit the destablizing effects this positive feedback is having on the system by limiting the adolescent's activities. And, as many family therapists have witnessed, an oscillation begins between dampening (negative feedback) on the parents behalf and amplification (positive feedback) on the part of their adolescent child, though it is not typically referred to with such calming or scientific phrases.

As r increases above 3, regular fluctuations in family conflict of increasing complexity develop and create the oscillating regulatory pattern. A period-doubling phenomenon occurs at each bifurcation, leading to progressively longer and more elaborate cycles of repetitive behavior as r increases. This pattern is adaptive in that it gives an element of drama and excitement to family life and allows for release of pent-up tensions through periodic blow-ups. On the dysfunctional side, oscillating patterns of conflict are frequently found in chronically troubled families in the form of episodic quarrels or violence separated by temporary periods of calm, but with no lasting resolution. This kind of pattern is commonly seen clinically in delinquent and addictive families (Bütz et al., 1996).

At r values above about 3.57, the periods double to infinity and the family's steady state does not show any regularly repeating pattern at all. This is the chaotic regime in which there is such sensitivity to perturbations that a very small event may lead to unpredictable outbursts of conflict. Chaotic patterns of this sort are seen with families in crisis and in extremely disorganized dysfunctional families, wherein there may be high risk of disorientation and despair. Antonovsky (1993, p. 972) gives a vivid description of this pattern: "Rules, rituals and responsibilities disintegrate. Structure disappears. Life is suffused with arbitrary, unpredictable, meaningless violence." On the other hand, chaos can disrupt rigidly entrenched dysfunctional patterns and open the way to a transformation of the family system that may be highly adaptive under rapidly changing conditions. Kauffman (1995) describes natural systems as evolving best in the complex region on the edge of chaos where responsiveness to new information reaches the highest peak that is consistent with system coherence and survival.

IMPLICATIONS OF THE MODEL

Context appears to be the key determinant of whether a particular regulatory pattern is adaptive or disabling. Each pattern has drawbacks as an invariant mode of functioning, and yet has advantages under specific circumstances. Thus it is important to distinguish a chronic pattern from a transitory one.

A family that is stuck in the constraining pattern will not ordinarily adapt well to change, but there are circumstances, such as surviving in hiding during the Nazi occupation, when being capable of adopting a constraining style of regulation could be life-saving. Even the stabilizing pattern, seemingly the most adaptive, can lead to shallow conventionality and poor tolerance for novelty if it is fixed and unvarying, admitting of no adjustment nor potential for transformation. Çambel (1993) gives an interesting example:

> "The urbanologist Jane Jacobs describes how during the industrial revolution, Manchester, England, deteriorated because it was orderly, indeed regimented, with its large ponderous factories, and did not have the flexibility to be competitive or the ability to adjust to a changing economic environment. In contrast, Birmingham, England, was quite disorganized with many diverse businesses. Birmingham was '... a muddle of

oddments,' according to Ms. Jacobs. Thus it was able to adjust to changing circumstances. It continues to thrive to this day, and the quality of life is high (p. 15)."

Like cities, most families go through periods of instability or chaos at one time or another, whether in response to traumatic internal changes, like death or divorce, or intense external stresses, such as economic upheavals or natural catastrophes.

At one extreme, "normative transitions in a chaotic system are likely to be similar to traumatic events in a regulated system" (Gottman, 1991, p. 262). On the other hand, a family that is fixated on constraining or stabilizing dynamic patterns is less likely to cope well with major change than a more flexible family that, in response to upheaval, can move from a stable state through instability and chaos, self-organize, and then reach a new state of balance (Bütz et al., 1996). Such flexible families might be described as having higher chaos tolerance than either more rigid family types that are confined to tightly controlled dynamic patterns or unstable families stuck in a chaotic regime.

Thus chaos tolerance needs to be distinguished from the chronic chaos of disorganized families that have no adaptive resources with which to reorganize. A way to represent these relationships quantitatively might be to define chaos tolerance, T, as r divided by the level of family symptoms, s: $T = r/s$. By this definition, we would expect to find the lowest levels of chaos tolerance in the rigidly controlled or enmeshed family, where symptom level may be quite high while r is low, and in the highly disorganized chronically chaotic families with high r and even higher symptom levels. The highest chaos tolerance levels would be found in flexible families that have relatively low symptoms when r is high. Such families are likely to possess strong underlying coherence and cohesiveness (Bütz, 1997), like a deeply-rooted and flexible tree that can bend and sway wildly in a high wind without breaking.

An interesting line of research using this model might be to examine the nature of family conflict propagation and to identify specific factors that lead to different patterns of conflict regulation. The propagation of conflict is likely to be a function of an interplay between family reactivity to stress and the effectiveness of available conflict-reduction resources. Therefore, both the factors triggering family conflict, and the dynamics of intrafamilial mechanisms to cope with conflict, need to be considered.

A variety of interesting questions arise. What makes a family highly labile and highly reactive to stress, either suppressing conflict entirely (constraining pattern) or erupting with rapidly propagating strife (oscillating or chaotic patterns)? What are the key mechanisms that enable cohesive and flexible families to respond constructively to conflict? The model is useful in addressing these questions in that it links qualitative patterns of conflict regulation to a mathematical relationship between positive and negative feedback processes.

In the discrete logistic equation, the different roles of x and r can be related to the concepts of first and second order change in systems theory. Perturbations in x constitute first order change in that different values of x, while representing temporary variations in family functioning, do not in and of themselves affect the pattern of family regulation. Changes in r value, however, can transform the family process to a new pattern, producing second order change.

The fractal nature of the complex and chaotic phenomena when r is greater than 3 suggest the possibility of self-similarity in the oscillating and chaotic patterns of family regulation. That is to say, there could be similar family regulatory patterns observable from minute to minute in a family interview as there are from week to week, month to month, or year to year in the life of the family. Longitudinal research would be needed to test this hypothesis.

The discrete logistic equation demonstrates how small changes in the balance between positive and negative feedback can have dramatic consequences for family regulation. In the language of modern thermodynamics, a relatively high ratio of positive to negative feedback is characteristic of far-from-equilibrium conditions (Prigogine & Stengers, 1984). If positive and negative feedback were reversed in the equation so that the positive feedback term were squared and the negative term were linear, $x_{n+1} = ax_n^2 - bx_n$, the result would be a catastrophe model in which iterations of x would increase exponentially without limit for starting values of x above a threshold $= b/a$, where a and b are constants (DeAngelis et al., 1986, p. 13). Such a model might be usefully applied to explosive family violence.

FEEDBACK AND FAMILY STRESS

The relative strength of positive and negative feedback becomes especially important when family systems are under stress. In a highly stressed family where key variables are close to critical thresholds, a very small amount of additional stress, like the proverbial straw that breaks the camel's back, would be capable of raising r and throwing the family system into instability or chaos, a downward spiral into family dysfunction, or a sudden crisis. Thus, under chaotic or catastrophic conditions, small amounts of reciprocal negative reinforcement between members of a family could escalate to an extent that is way out of proportion to the perturbation that sets off the change. For example, when a parent is overstressed, a mildly misbehaving child can provoke a stronger-than-usual negative response from the parent. The parental overreaction can then trigger more child misbehavior and so forth, in a vicious cycle. This process is exemplified by the deterioration of parent–child relations described in Patterson's coercive family process model for families of children with conduct disorders (Patterson, DeBaryshe, & Ramsay, 1989), a pattern aptly described as "escalating cycles of reciprocated aggression" (Baden & Howe, 1992).

Conversely, in well-functioning families it has been found that unusual challenges can produce enhanced family functioning, an adaptive rather than a disabling response to stress. Families that are high in cohesiveness and expressiveness, for example, may be drawn even closer when faced with caring for a chronically ill member (Patterson & Garwick, 1994). Ward (1995) explains why such adaptive responses are more likely to occur in the middle zone of complexity at the edge of chaos than at very low or high chaos levels:

> "Systems are most likely to remain poised for change if they exist at the border of ordered and chaotic regimes. The former can be considered 'frozen' because little information is accepted from the environment or shared among parts. At the other extreme are systems in a chaotic phase. While these are very responsive to environmental change, their behavior is too disordered to provide stability. At the border between frozen and chaotic states, many bifurcations occur. In this band, there is both the communication necessary for change and sufficient structure to ensure a degree of continuity and stability" (p. 634).

RELEVANCE TO FAMILY INTERVENTION

Crisis intervention is based upon the principal that families thrown into chaos by overwhelming stress are temporarily open to fundamental change in system organization and functioning. Because chaotic systems are so sensitive to input, a relatively small intervention at the proper moment can have enormous impact on the direction and magnitude of the family's self-organizing process, and therefore, on the future adaptation of the family. The scientific study of chaotic processes in families should have special relevance to interventions with highly disorganized families (Bütz et al., 1996; Bütz, 1997). If intervention efforts are focused on a key family subsystem or interactive process, then system reorganization can occur with attainment of a new stable state instead of an escalating crisis. A relatively brief and economical intervention effort, when strategically timed and placed, has the potential of producing a profound and far-reaching impact.

In the logistic equation model, transient fluctuations in family conflict are represented by x, whereas overall shifts in the pattern of conflict regulation are related to changes in r. Therefore, an effective intervention not only should temporarily reduce the level of family conflict, x, but should also lower the value of r from the chaotic zone to more stable ranges. The model predicts that it is the intervention-induced change in the pattern of conflict regulation, rather than the reduction in family conflict alone, that best accounts for lasting improvements in family functioning. It would follow, then, that the family and contextual factors influencing the value of r should be crucial to the success of family interventions.

The evaluation of family skills training programs with families of youth at high risk for delinquency found that lasting effectiveness in imparting positive relationship skills and improving family functioning depended not only upon the curriculum, but also upon group support among the participating families and especially upon the warmth and nurturance given to the families by the group leaders (Harrison & Proskauer, 1996). From these findings it could be surmised that a lasting increase in r was achieved through the boost in family relationship skills, social support, and interpersonal warmth resulting from the family skills training experience.

As a closing example, strategic family therapy specializes in interventions that rely on induction of positive feedback to intentionally destabilize a rigidly dysfunctional family system, as a means of achieving a more adaptive balance (Hoffman, 1971). The paradoxical intervention of "prescribing the symptom," for instance, can be viewed as a means of switching the feedback loop in which the symptomatic behavior is imbedded from negative to positive, and thereby overloading the system so that it is open to transformation. While caution should be taken with such interventions (Bütz et al., 1996) strategic therapy introduces a bit of creative chaos into pathologically fixated families. In Thomas's words (1993):

> "Chaos is often thought to be the state of the house after a wild party or the aftermath of a hurricane. It may also be seen as a state in which new sensitive influences may play a formative role in contrast to a stifling order prohibiting the emergence of anything new (pp. 23–24)."

REFERENCES

Antonovsky, A. (1993). Complexity, conflict, chaos, coherence, coercion and civility. *Social Science and Medicine, 37*(8), 969–981.

Baden, A. D., & Howe, G. W. (1992). Mothers' attributions and expectancies regarding their conduct-disordered children. *Journal of Abnormal Child Psychology, 20*(5), 467–485.

Baker, G. L., & Gollub, J. P. (1990). *Chaotic dynamics: An introduction.* New York: Cambridge University Press.

Barber, B. K. (1996). Parental psychological control: Revisiting a neglected construct. *Child Development,* in press.

Barber, B. K., Olsen, J. E., & Shagle, S. C. (1994). Associations between parental psychological and behavioral control and youth internalized and externalized behaviors. *Child Development, 65,* 1120–1136.

Bateson, G., Jackson, D. D., Haley, J., & Weakland, J. H. (1956). Toward a theory of schiziphrenia. *Behavioral Science, 1*(4), 251–264.

Bütz, M. R. (1997). *Chaos and complexity, implications for psychological theory and practice.* Washington, DC: Taylor & Francis.

Bütz, M. R., Chamberlain, L. L., & McCown, W. G. (1996). *Strange Attractors: Chaos, complexity and the art of family therapy.* New York: John Wiley & Sons.

Çambel, A. B. (1993). *Applied chaos theory.* New York: Academic Press.

Cook, J., Tyson, R., White, J., Rushe, R., Gottman, J., & Murray, J. (1995). Mathematics of marital conflict: Qualitative dynamic mathematical modeling of marital interaction. *Journal of Family Psychology, 9*(2), 110–130.

DeAngelis, D. L., Post, W. M., & Travis, C. C. (1986). *Positive feedback in natural systems.* New York: Springer-Verlag.

Elkaïm, M. (1981). Non-equilibrium, chance and change in family therapy. *Journal of Marital and Family Therapy, 7,* 291–297.

Elkaïm, M. (1990). *If you love me, don't love me: Constructions of reality and change in family therapy.* New York: Basic Books.

Elkaïm, M., Goldbeter, A., & Goldbeter-Merinfeld, E. (1987). Analysis of the dynamics of a family system in terms of bifurcations. *Journal of Social and Biological Structures, 10,* 21–36.

Gleick, J. (1987). *Chaos: Making a new science.* New York: Viking-Penguin.

Goerner, S. (1994). *Chaos and the evolving universe.* Langhorne, PA: Gordon & Breach Science Publishers.

Gottman, J. M. (1991). Chaos and regulated change in families: A metaphor for the study of transitions. In P. A. Cowan & M. Hetherington (Eds.), *Family transitions* (pp. 247–272). Hillsdale, NJ: Lawrence Erlbaum Associates.

Gottman, J. M. (1993a). The roles of conflict engagement, escalation, and avoidance in marital interaction: A longitudinal view of five types of couples. *Journal of Consulting and Clinical Psychology, 61,* 6–15.

Gottman, J. M. (1993b). A theory of marital dissolution and stability. *Journal of Family Psychology, 7,* 57–75.

Haley, J. (1959). The family of the schizophrenic: A model system. *Journal of Neuroses and Mental Diseases, 129,* 357–374.

Harrison, R. S., & Proskauer, S. (1996). *The impact of family skills training on children at risk for substance abuse and their families: A five-year evaluation.* Paper in preparation.

Hoffman, L. (1971). Deviation-amplifying processes in natural groups. Chapter 22 in J. Haley (Ed.), *Changing Families.* New York: Grune & Stratton.

Jantsch, E. (1980). *The self-organizing universe, scientific and human implications of the emerging paradigm of evolution.* New York: Pergamon Press.

Kauffman, S. (1995). *At home in the universe.* New York: Oxford University Press.

Kristjanson, L. J. (1992). Conceptual issues related to measurement in family research. *Canadian Journal of Nursing Research, 24*(3), 37–52.

Maruyama, M. (1963). The second cybernetics: Deviaton-amplifying mutual causal processes. *American Scientist, 51,* 164–179.

May, R. M. (1974). Biological populations with non-overlapping generations: Stable points, stable cycles, and chaos. *Science, 186,* 645–647.

Olson, D. H., Sprenkle, D. H., & Russell, C. S. (1979). Circumplex model of marital and family system: Cohesion and adaptability dimensions, family types, and clinical applications. *Family Process, 18,* 2–28.

Patterson, G. R., DeBaryshe, B. D., & Ramsey, E. (1989). A developmental perspective on antisocial behavior. *American Psychologist, 44,* 329–335.

Patterson, J. M., & Garwick, A. W. (1994). The impact of chronic illness on families: A family systems perspective. *Annals of Behavioral Medicine, 16*(2), 131–142.

Prigogine, I. (1980). *From being to becoming—time and complexity in the physical sciences.* San Francisco: W. H. Freeman & Sons.

Prigogine, I., & Stengers, I. (1984). *Order out of chaos.* New York: Bantam.

Proskauer, S. (1996a, June, July). *Dynamic modeling: A new paradigm in couple and family research.* Paper presented at the Annual Meeting of the Society for Chaos Theory in Psychology and Life Sciences, June 1996, University of California, Berkeley, CA, and at the Fourth International Social Sciences Methodology Conference, July 1996, University of Essex, Colchester, England.

Proskauer, S. (1996b, June, July). *Shannon's entropy as a measure of chaos and constraint in couple and family communication.* Paper presented at Annual Meeting of the Society for Chaos Theory in Psychology and Life Sciences, June 1996, University of California, Berkeley, CA, and at the Fourth International Social Sciences Methodology Conference in July 1996, University of Essex, Colchester, England.

Selvini-Palazzoli, M., Boscolo, L., Cecchin, G., & Prata, G. (1978). *Paradox and counterparadox, a new model in the therapy of the family in schizophrenic transaction.* Northvale, NJ: Jason Aronson.

Thomas, N. (1993). Chaos theory and projective geometry. In W. Forward & A. Wolpert (Eds.), *Chaos, rhythm and flow in nature.* Edinburgh, Scotland: Floris Books.

Vallacher, R. R., & Nowak, A. (1994). *Dynamical systems in social psychology.* San Diego, CA: Academic Press, Inc.

von Bertalanffy, L. (1968). *General system theory, foundations, development, applications*. New York: Braziller.

Ward, M. (1995). Butterflies and bifurcations: Can chaos theory contribute to our understanding of family systems? *Journal of Marriage and the Family, 57,* 629–638.

Watzlawick, P., Beavin, J., & Jackson, D. D. (1967). *Pragmatics of human communication*. New York: W. W. Norton & Co.

Whitchurch, G. G., & Constantine, L. L. (1993). Systems theory. Chapter 14 in P. G. Boss et al. (Eds.), *Sourcebook of family theories and methods: A contextual approach*. New York: Plenum Press.

Wiener, N. (1961). *Cybernetics, or control and communication in the animal and the machine*. (2nd ed.). New York: John Wiley & Sons.

Chapter 17

Chaos Theory and the Future of Psychotherapy: Conclusions and Questions

Michael R. Bütz & Linda L. Chamberlain

By design, the journey to this point has encompassed diverse opinions about the meaning of chaos, complexity, and the new physics for the clinician. While many theoretical orientations and therapeutic modalities have been presented and some hypotheses put forward, there are always others to explore. No doubt some will disagree with the theoretical arguments offered here, and these differences of opinion should be encouraged as they broaden and enrich a dialogue that has been a long time in the making. The more clinicians engage in a dialogue on this topic, the more facile their debate on this new set of theories will become. Ultimately, this will lead to new ideas, new propositions that have not emerged in the dialogue before. In so doing, clinicians may, as a product of their debates, create the type of cross-fertilization that Kuhn described (1970/1962, p. 7) where new ideas emerge that did not exist as part of the original paradigm. This is one type of exchange we hope to generate through the material presented in this book. Still, there are other considerations besides a lively debate that may contribute to the evolution of this set of ideas. The other type of exchange may be more personal and political.

In Chapter 2, mention was made of the clinician's commitment to becoming not only a practitioner, but a scientist–practitioner. By definition, a scientist–practitioner has one foot in each realm, and is able to use these domains of knowledge to both assist his or her clients in treatment, and advance the field in which he or she practices. As the focus of this book may suggest, the success of this model has been limited, or it may be more appropriate to say—artificially restricted.

There are a few pieces of clinical folklore that have been part of this debate for years, and this seems an appropriate place to bring them forth. The two that it seems important to address here are that (1) clinicians do not read research, and (2) the only good research is the research published within the last five years.

There was a study conducted several years ago which indicated that there was a disparity in the amount of research clinicians studied (Strupp, 1989). The finding was not that clinicians don't read research, the finding was that they do not read irrelevant research! In examining the research literature, one will quickly find that it is not, so to speak, user-friendly. Further, much of the current research provides little in the way of answering the "so what" questions. Typically, research answers common-sense questions in an obscure fashion. It is no wonder that the general public does not understand mental health research very well when even clinicians are alienated by the vague nature of what is reported. In the future, research must be more accessible, and answer the basic questions of "so what?"

The second point of folklore that "the only good research has been published in the past five years," is absolutely absurd. As we have noted throughout this text, studies have been conducted in the past that are much more rigorous and answer relevant questions more directly than much of the research being conducted today. Poincaré anticipated the revolution science has gone through in the past two decades (Gleick, 1987), over a hundred years ago. Freud and Jung constructed a separate field when they could not find answers through strictly scientific research models. They closely approximated some aspects of the models we have discussed in this book. Approximately fifteen years ago, family therapists ventured into chaos theory. Nevertheless, researchers continue, for all intents and purposes, to re-invent the wheel. This is perhaps why psychology, and other social sciences, continues to re-invent notions that have been around for decades, such as cognitive-behavioral theorists' "ground-breaking" finding that there is indeed an unconscious (Bütz, 1997; Azar, 1996).

THE "SO WHATS?" OF CLINICAL PRACTICE

So far, this chapter has dealt with two "so what?" questions. "So what" that studying current models about nonlinear dynamics inform the clinician about how systems are thought to develop and how they evolve—the process that unfolds through the course of therapy? The other "so what?" involves the perspective a clinician takes during the therapeutic process, where, metaphorically, technicians differ greatly from scientists in their ability to appreciate the larger process as it unfolds. These two questions, lead to a third "so what?"—how do these theories change a clinician's understanding of what they do in therapy? Inherently, this query also begs the question of how human beings are different from this theoretical perspective. The reader may begin to reflect on some of the concepts reviewed in Chapter 1, where certain aspects of these theories were described. This set of theories is differentiated from others that examine human development in the therapeutic process.

Certainly, empirical techniques have improved with each passing year. But our question is this: Are these techniques attempts to rescue a dying paradigm? In Kuhn's (1970/1962, pp. 79–80) well known (and often over-referenced) text, he describes how desperate attempts are made to save the existing paradigm—in this case empiricism. Is it possible that these bits of folklore are also efforts to exclude clinicians from the research paradigm of empiricism, to stop them from asking relevant questions?

We have seen these exclusionary dynamics at work even in the field of non-linear dynamics. For years, chaoticians commonly stated that one needed to gather one thousand points of data to find out if he or she actually had "chaos" in his or her data set. However, in real world mental-health repeated-measures studies, how does one go about getting a thousand pieces of data, or even a hundred? Simply put, this was not a reality except in very limited areas of study (Rapp et al., 1989; Kelso & Fogel, 1987), and only tentatively applied to clinical practice (Reidbord & Redington, 1992). When clinicians attempted to describe their observations of clients using metaphors to decipher whether or not this pattern actually existed, they were admonished. Yet, years later it became clear how difficult (Rapp, 1993), if not impossible it was to measure dynamic systems such as individuals in therapy (Burlingame & Hope, 1996; Burlingame & Bloch, 1996). The field harkened back to the idea that chaos theory was a science of pattern (Abraham, Abraham, & Shaw, 1990; Garfinkel, 1983).

It appeared that in all of these studies, scientists, and scientist–practitioners, lost track of the basis for their studies—the scientific method. Before application and measurement, one is instructed to thoroughly work through the philosophical problems with their ideas and theories (Bütz, Chamberlain, & McCown, 1997; Bütz, 1996, 1997). All too often, before these ideas have been worked through, the object of study is subjected to the scrutiny of measurement, and suddenly, magically—it is scientific. A step is missed, and poorly conceptualized research findings are the result. It has indeed turned into a fast-food approach to research, where a side of fries has replaced a full, well-balanced meal. The step that is missing? Well, obviously that is the step developed through philosophical discussion and metaphorical description. These dialogues are the foundation upon which substantive and relevant research is based. Premature measurement, modeling, or the like, only gives us a side of fries and leaves us undernourished and hungry for more.

Addressing these and other problematic issues makes science and research relevant to the clinician, and thereby strengthens the commitment scientists have to practitioners, and practitioners have to science. Without thoughtful dialogue, neither is able to enhance or assist the other's work. Clinicians are not free from blame in this arena either. Why is it that managed care came into existence? If companies and clients were getting what they wanted and needed from clinicians, would managed care companies be in existence?

Brief psychotherapy was designed to address a certain domain of psychological problems (Cummings & VandenBos, 1981), but it was not a cure-all by any means. Instead of making arguments that addressed the issues (Hannigan-Farley, 1996; Graham, 1995), practitioners were content to accept the scraps that insurance companies offered them. In turn, psychotherapy has also become dominated by not only restrictive management, but has increasingly been replaced by drug therapies despite controversy (Sanua, 1994; Kramer, 1993; DeLeon, 1993; De Nelsky, 1992; Fox, Schwelitz, & Barclay, 1992). It is not that psychotherapy is not as effective as these treatments (Antonuccio, Danton, & DeNelsky, 1995; Breggin, 1991), but practitioners have not had the wherewithal to challenge the scientific premises of these notions. The premises of these arguments are as basic and straightforward as any set of ideas leveled in this text. For instance, psychopharmacology is a "fix it" type of process that assumes that there is something wrong with a client. Sounds awfully mechanistic doesn't it? How about managed care? The assumption there is that a quick tune-up is all that is required—mechanistic. Still, even oil filter companies know that quick tune-ups don't always work. As the old ad goes, "You can pay me now or pay me later."

Clinicians must take off their blinders and understand the science that they are practicing. Then the question becomes, "are we technicians or scientists?"

THE SCIENTIST VS. THE TECHNICIAN

In some areas of scientific endeavor, one doesn't really need a thorough knowledge of the underlying theory or concepts. People who assembled the triggers for atomic weapons probably had very little understanding of the dynamics explored by nuclear physicists which made the bomb a reality. The assemblers were technicians, not scientists. They functioned under the directives of scientists, trusting that those who directed them understood what they were doing.

As clinical trainers and supervisors, we have sometimes felt like the physicists who are supposed to offer some clear directives about how to do psychotherapy, without any need to challenge our students and trainees regarding the nature of what they engage in as therapists. Increasingly, clinicians seem to pursue learning techniques over understanding dynamics. In fact, some of the methodologies like Touch/Field Therapy and EMD-R (Eye Movement Desensitization and Reprocessing) are strictly atheoretical. The attendance at these types of training seminars attests to the popularity of a technique-based approach to therapy. Certainly, some advocates of brief therapy (including insurers) are becoming increasingly enamoured of quick fixes and easy-to-learn, technical methods of psychotherapeutic treatment. We view this change in our profession with some alarm. Delving into chaos theory and understanding the implications for psychotherapy that are embedded in this paradigm have reawakened questions about the dynamics and basic nature of what clinicians do. Chaos and complexity theories provide credence for some paradigms in psychotherapy and challenge others. Therapy becomes more of a process than an event.

It is the authors' hope that this book will have challenged some readers to reacquaint themselves with the foundation of the profession and the ideas that guide our work. Certainly, chaos theory raises more questions than it answers. How exciting, though, that the questions are arising once again. "It makes me so happy. To be at the beginning again, knowing almost nothing" (Stoppard, 1993, p. 47).

REFERENCES

Abraham, F. D., Abraham, R. H., & Shaw, C. D. (1990). *A visual introduction to dynamical systems theory for psychology.* Santa Cruz, CA: Aerial.

Antonuccio, D. O., Danton, W. G., & DeNelsky, G. Y. (1995). Psychotherapy versus medication depression: Challenging the conventional wisdom with data. *Professional Psychology: Research and Practice, 26*(6), 574–585.

Azar, B. (1996). Influence from the mind's inner layers. *APA Monitor, 27*(2), 1, 25.

Breggin, P. (1991). *Toxic psychiatry: Why therapy, empathy, and love must replace the drugs, electroshock, and biochemical theories of the "new psychiatry."* New York: St. Martin.

Burlingame, G. M., & Bloch, G. J. (1996). Complexity theory: A new direction for psychoneuroimmunology. *ADVANCES: The Journal of Mind-Body Health, 12*(1), 16–20.

Burlingame, G., & Hope, C. (1996). Dynamical systems theory and social psychology: The promise and pitfalls. *Psychological Inquiry,* in press.

Bütz, M. R. (1996, June 26). Chaos and complexity's gestation in the unconscious, and the energy of an emerging integrative myth. In R. Robertson (Chair), *A sense of wonder: Philosophical issues of chaos/complexity in the study of mind.* Symposium given at the Annual Meeting of the Society for Chaos Theory in Psychology and Life Sciences, Berkeley, CA.

Bütz, M. R. (1997). *Chaos and complexity, implications for psychological theory and therapy.* Washington, DC: Taylor & Francis.

Bütz, M. R., Chamberlain, L., & McCown, W. G. (1997). *Strange attractors, chaos, complexity and the art of family therapy.* New York: John Wiley & Sons.

Cummings, N. A., & VandenBos, G. R. (1981). The twenty years Kaiser-Permanente experience with psychotherapy and medical utilization: Implications for national health policy and national health insurance. *Health Policy Quarterly, 1*(2), 159–175.

De Leon, P. (1993). Prescription privileges—a qualitative difference. *The Psychotherapy Bulletin, 28*(3), 10–13.

De Nelsky, G. Y. (1992). The case against prescription privileges for psychologists. *Psychotherapy in Private Practice, 11*(1), 15–24.

Fox, R. E., Schwelitz, F. D., & Barclay, A. G. (1992). A proposed curriculum for psychopharmacology training for professional psychologists. *Professional Psychology: Research and Practice, 23*(3), 216–219.

Garfinkel, A. (1983). A mathematics for physiology. *American Journal of Physiology, 245,* 455–466.

Graham, S. R. (1995). Divided we fall. *Psychotherapy Bulletin, 30*(3), 4–5.

Gleick, J. (1987). *Chaos: Making a new science.* New York: Viking Press.

Hannigan-Farley (1996). Change management and psychotherapy. *Psychotherapy Bulletin, 31*(1), 4.

Kelso, J. A., & Fogel, A. (1987). Self-organizing systems and infant motor development. *Developmental Review, 7*(1), 39–65.

Kramer, P. D. (1993). *Listening to prozac.* New York: Penguin.

Kuhn, T. S. (1970/1962). *The structure of scientific revolutions.* (2nd ed.). Chicago: University of Chicago Press.

Rapp, P. E. (1993). Chaos in the neurosciences, cautionary tales from the frontier. *Biologist, 40*(2), 89–94.

Rapp, P. E., Bashore, T. R., Martinerie, J. M., Albano, A. M., Zimmerman, I. D., & Mees, A. I. (1989). Dynamics of brain electrical activity. *Brain Topography, 21*(1/2), 99–118.

Reidbord, S. P., & Redington, D. J. (1992). Psychophysiological processes during insight-oriented therapy, further investigations into nonlinear psychodynamics. *The Journal of Nervous and Mental Disease, 180,* 649–657.

Sanua, V. D. (1994, March). *Prescription privileges versus psychologist's authority; psychologists do better without drugs*. Paper presented at Annual Mid-Winter Convention of the American Psychological Association, Scottsdale, AZ.

Stoppard, T. (1993). *Arcadia*. Boston: Faber & Faber.

Strupp, H. H. (1989, April). Psychotherapy: Can the practitioner learn from the researcher? *American Psychologist, 44*(4), 717–724.

Biographies of Authors

Michael R. Bütz, Ph.D. is Director of Child, Adolescent and Substance Abuse Services at Cornerstone Behavioral Health in Evanston, Wyoming. Dr. Bütz has presented nationally and internationally and published numerous articles on chaos theory. He is co-author of *Strange Attractors: Chaos, Complexity and the Art of Family Therapy,* and recently published *Chaos and Complexity: Implications for Psychological Theory* with Taylor and Francis. His particular area of interest is in chaos and complexity theory's integration into psychological theory and practice.

Linda L. Chamberlain, Psy.D. is a psychologist in private practice in Denver, Colorado. She also serves on the adjunct faculties of the University of Denver, the University of Colorado at Denver and Regis University. She is co-author with Michael R. Bütz and William McCown of *Strange Attractors: Chaos, Complexity and the Art of Family Therapy* and has published numerous articles on chaos theory, family therapy and compulsive gambling. Her clinical and research interests include family therapy with substance dependence, assessment and treatment of compulsive gambling, and child custody evaluation.

Laurie A. Fitzgerald, Ph.D. is a Senior Consultant for The Consultancy, Inc., a Colorado-based specialist in the field of organizational design and transformation. For the past decade, she has anchored her practice with such clients as Motorola, Kodak, Digital Equipment, Keebler and the FBI in the principles and tenets of quantum physics and the "new" science of Chaos. In addition to her consulting activities, Dr. Fitzgerald serves on the adjunct faculty for Cornell University's Center for Executive Education.

Stephen E. Francis, M.A. is a Clinical Instructor in the Department of Diagnostic Sciences and is the attending behavioral medicine specialist at the Pacific Center for Orofacial Pain at the University of the Pacific School of Dentistry in San Francisco, California. He is a former editor for California Biofeedback and has served as the President of the Biofeedback Society of California.

Catherine A. Hawkins, Ph.D. is an assistant professor of Social Work at Southwest Texas State University. Her research interests have included family systems interventions for chemical dependency, particularly adult children of alcoholics.

Raymond C. Hawkins II, Ph.D. is a clinical psychologist at Austin Regional Clinic, where for several years he was coordinator of the Family Recovery Program, an outpatient chemical dependency treatment program. Formerly an assistant professor of Psychology at the University of Texas at Austin, he currently is an adjunct lecturer in the Graduate School of Social Work.

Barbara Hudgens, Ph.D. is a psychologist who teaches school psychology and educational psychology at National-Louis University in Evanston, Illinois. She also works part-time with Family Service Agency of North Lake County where her counseling load includes individuals and families, many of whom are adult survivors of childhood sexual abuse.

Ross Keiser, Ph.D. is a Professor of Psychology at Northeast Louisiana University and a Fellow in the Society for Personality Assessment. Dr. Keiser's research is in the area of personality assessment and he has a large, independent practice devoted to assessment.

William G. McCown, Ph.D. is an Associate Professor of Psychology at Northeast Louisiana University. He is author/co-author of numerous professional articles and books including *Strange Attractors: Chaos, Complexity and the Art of Family Therapy, Therapy with Treatment Resistant Families*, and *Family Therapy of Neurobehavioral Disorders*.

Michael G. Moran, M.D. is an Associate Professor of Psychiatry at the University of Colorado. He is also the Director of Adult Psychosocial Medicine at the National Jewish Medical and Research Center in Denver, Colorado.

Stephen Proskauer, M.D. was originally trained in child psychiatry and has published a number of clinical and research papers in that field. Now a Zen Buddhist monk, he supports his life as a research consultant to the Social Research Institute at the University of Utah Graduate School of Social Work, where he has led the effort to apply nonlinear dynamics to family studies.

Graywolf Fred Swinney, M.A. is internationally recognized as a shaman by scientific authorities and many tribal shamans. He is a member of the AHP, ITAA, Transpersonal Psychology Association, and founding member of the Society for Chaos Theory in Psychology. He is also the founder of Asklepia Foundation for Consciousness Science and founder and director of the Institute of Applied Consciousness Sciences. Graywolf is a contributing editor for the Dream Network Journal and has published many articles in a variety of books and journals.

Ray Quakenbush, M.A. is a doctoral candidate in clinical psychology at the California Institute of Integral Studies. He has a Master's degree in Family Therapy from the University of Houston at Clear Lake and in Psychology from the California Institute of Integral Studies. For the last ten years he has worked primarily with child abuse. He conducts dependency investigations for Children's Protective Services, Oakland, California, where he is frequently called upon as an expert witness in child abuse cases. He also consults with social service agencies nationally and conducts treatment of families and individuals with a history of sexual molestation at the Giarretto Institute, San Jose, California.

Author Index

Subject Index